The BIBLIOPHILE'S *Devotional*

365 DAYS OF LITERARY CLASSICS

HALLIE EPHRON, PhD

Aadamsmedia
Avon, Massachusetts

Published by
Adams Media, a division of F+W Media, Inc.
57 Littlefield Street, Avon, MA 02322. U.S.A.
www.adamsmedia.com

ISBN 10: 1-60550-105-0
ISBN 13: 978-1-60550-105-5

Printed in the United States of America.

J I H G F E D C B A

Library of Congress Cataloging-in-Publication Data
is available from the publisher.

This publication is designed to provide accurate and authoritative information with regard to the subject matter covered. It is sold with the understanding that the publisher is not engaged in rendering legal, accounting, or other
professional advice. If legal advice or other expert assistance is required, the
services of a competent professional person should be sought.
—From a *Declaration of Principles* jointly adopted by a Committee of the
American Bar Association and a Committee of Publishers and Associations

Many of the designations used by manufacturers and sellers to distinguish
their product are claimed as trademarks. Where those designations appear in
this book and Adams Media was aware of a trademark claim, the designations have been printed with initial capital letters.

This book is available at quantity discounts for bulk purchases.
For information, please call 1-800-289-0963.

Contents

Introduction

The Library in the Garret
by Elizabeth Barrett Browning

Books, books, books!
I had found the secret of a garret-room
Piled high with cases in my father's name;
Piled high, packed large,—where, creeping in and out
Among the giant fossils of my past,
Like some small nimble mouse between the ribs
Of a mastodon, I nibbled here and there
At this or that box, pulling through the gap,
In heats of terror, haste, victorious joy,
The first book first. And how I felt it beat
Under my pillow, in the morning's dark,
An hour before the sun would let me read!
My books! . . .

MOST OF US do not have the great good fortune of growing up, like Elizabeth Barrett Browning, in a house with a garret-room overflowing with book-filled boxes. Nevertheless, many of us are unabashed bibliophiles who, if we could, would line our walls with books and read as many as our busy lives permit. We savor the heft of a book in our hands. Thrill at reading a book's opening paragraphs and slow down to delay reaching The End despite a bedside table stacked high with books beckoning to be read.

The Bibliophile's Devotional contains the merest preview of 365 books, one a day, each handpicked to nourish the book lover in each of us. Some are classics that have stood the test of time; others look as if they will. Think of this as a tasting menu. It is my dearest hope that each taste will send you scurrying to your bookseller or library so you can read (or reread) that book, cover to cover. Some you will want to savor slowly, others you will find yourself compelled to devour in a single sitting, while others will need to be chewed and digested.

January

WHITE TEETH

BY ZADIE SMITH

At 06.27 hours on 1 January 1975, Alfred Archibald Jones was dressed in corduroy and sat in a fume-filled Cavalier Musketeer Estate face down on the steering wheel, hoping the judgement would not be too heavy upon him.

THIS DAZZLING NOVEL tells the modern Dickensian saga of interconnected families, one from Jamaica and the other from Bangladesh. It begins New Year's Day, 1975. Hapless, coin-flipping, forty-seven-year-old Archibald Jones, bereft over his divorce from the mad Ophelia, tries to gas himself. But "the thinnest covering of luck was on him like fresh dew" and an irate butcher rousts him from his illegally parked car. On New Year's Eve, 1992, the story ends with Archie's accidental (pre-ordained?) release of a mutant mouse programmed to do away with the randomness of creation.

With satirical bite and an ironic take on race and religion, the novel tells of an improbable friendship between working-class Jones and Bengali Muslim Salmad Iqbal, forged during World War II in a stifling five-man tank. Salmad is torn between his deep Muslim faith and his growing attraction to Poppy Burt-Jones, his twin sons' lovely music teacher. As an act of contrition and to keep the boy pure, Salmad has one of the twins kidnapped and sent to Bangladesh. His plan goes awry. Just as improbably, Archie falls for beautiful seventeen-year-old Clara, "black as ebony and crushed sable," who lost her front teeth courtesy of a motor scooter accident.

White Teeth won the Whitbread and Guardian prizes for first novel in 2000.

"Some fearless outside referee had to barge in and try to adjudicate the culture wars, so let us rejoice that it's Zadie Smith. She brings almost everything you want to the task: humor, brains, objectivity, equanimity, empathy, a pitch-perfect ear for smugness and cant, and then still more humor."

—FRANK RICH, *NEW YORK TIMES*

MIDDLEMARCH

BY GEORGE ELIOT

Miss Brooke had that kind of beauty which seems to be thrown into relief by poor dress.

GEORGE ELIOT TAKES on Victorian marriage and mores in this novel set in the provincial English town of Middlemarch.

Dorothea Brooke is stuck in a lifeless marriage with Mr. Casaubon, an aging academic. Miss Brooke seethes with ideas and yearns to be useful, but upper-class society offers her no outlets. Casaubon is blind to her intelligence as well as to her passion. She, on the other hand, "was able enough to estimate him—she who waited on his glances with trembling, and shut her best soul in prison, paying it only hidden visits, that she might be petty enough to please him. In such a crisis as this, some women begin to hate." Fortuitously, Casaubon dies, but his will specifically forbids Dorothea's marriage to the man she loves.

Also unwisely wed is Dorothea's friend, the young, poor, ambitious physician Tertius Lydgate. He's tethered to the frivolous Rosamond Vincy ("the flower of Mrs. Lemon's school, the chief school in the county, where the teaching included all that was demanded in the accomplished female—even to extras, such as the getting in and out of a carriage") whose pursuit of wealth and status brings them both to the brink of ruin.

Eliot doesn't satirize so much as sharply observe, and even her most odious characters are sympathetic and believable. The novel is considered a masterpiece, and Dorothea Brooke is one of English literature's first intellectually aspiring women. Readers were ready for her—in 1871, its first year in print, the novel sold an amazing 20,000 copies.

"*[George Eliot's] power is at its highest in the mature* Middlemarch, *the magnificent book which with all its imperfections is one of the few English novels written for grown-up people.*"

—VIRGINIA WOOLF, *THE COMMON READER*

THE DEATH OF IVAN ILYICH

BY LEO TOLSTOY

Isn't it obvious to everyone but me that I am dying . . . ?

THIS NOVELLA, FIRST published in 1886, takes the meaning of life as its subject. It begins in Saint Petersburg as friends and colleagues of high-court judge Ivan Ilyich learn of his death ("'Well, isn't that something—he's dead, but I'm not,' was what each of them thought or felt."). Then, Tolstoy takes the reader to the preceding months of Ilyich's illness and his struggle to take the measure of his own life.

As Ilyich looks back, "the nearer he came to the present the more worthless and doubtful were the joys." Death approaches, and Ilyich sees his successful life as a sham. His only source of solace is the simple caring acts of "a clean, fresh peasant lad," Gerasim. Unlike the others, Gerasim actually pities him.

By the end, the novella comes full circle to a moment when Ilyich emerges from self-pity, accepts death, and pities those he leaves behind: "And suddenly it became clear to him that what had been oppressing him and would not leave him suddenly was vanishing all at once—from two sides, ten sides, all sides. He felt sorry for them, he had to do something to keep from hurting them. To deliver them and himself from this suffering. 'How good and how simple!' he thought."

Translated from the original Russian, this slender work was judged "that greatest of great short stories" by Vladimir Nabokov.

"The Tolstoyan formula is: Ivan lived a bad life and since a bad life is nothing but the death of the soul, then Ivan lived a living death; and since beyond death is God's living light, then Ivan died into a new Life—Life with a capital L."

—VLADIMIR NABOKOV,
LECTURES ON RUSSIAN LITERATURE

THE NAKED AND THE DEAD

BY NORMAN MAILER

Nobody could sleep.

SATURATED IN BITTERNESS and disillusionment, this novel presents a realistic, compassionate depiction of war. It tells the story of a fourteen-man infantry platoon of raw, inexperienced soldiers fighting in World War II. The story opens onboard a ship as they prepare to invade the fictional island of Anopopei, embarking on a campaign to drive out the Japanese.

Mailer based the novel on his own experiences. He doesn't flinch at depicting the raw terror of battle with its gore and violence, or the numbing boredom of the endless wait that inevitably preceded it.

The stories of these average men are revealed in flashbacks. There are no heroes here, no last-minute bestowal of mercy or noble sacrifice. They are less the victims of an enemy than of the hubris of senior officers and the horrifying ineptitude of Army command.

Very much under the influence of Tolstoy's *Anna Karenina* and using flashbacks in the kaleidoscopic style perfected by John Dos Passos, Mailer wrote this novel when he was only twenty-three and completed it in fifteen months. Published in 1948, critics heralded it as one of the finest war novels ever written. In the introduction to the fiftieth anniversary edition of this book, Mailer admits to seeing considerable flaws in the writing, but the novel remains a landmark antiwar book.

"My first reaction to The Naked and the Dead *was: it's a fake. A talented, admirably executed fake. I have not changed my opinion of the book since...."*

—GORE VIDAL, WHOSE WAR NOVEL *THE CITY AND THE PILLAR* WAS PUBLISHED THE SAME YEAR

JANE EYRE

BY CHARLOTTE BRONTË

There was no possibility of taking a walk that day.

IN THIS CLASSIC gothic romance a plain, plucky orphan is raised like Cinderella by callous, hateful relatives who pack her off to the aptly named Lowood boarding school. There, Jane becomes a teacher, but she yearns for a life beyond the school's cloistered walls. Barely eighteen, she posts an advertisement: "A young woman accustomed to tuition is desirous of meeting with a situation in a private family. . . ."

Off she goes to Thornfield Manor to take care of the delightful, frivolous, French-speaking Miss Adele, the young ward of Edward Fairfax Rochester. When at last Jane meets the mysterious Mr. R., twenty years her senior, they fall passionately in love. But he and the house harbor a secret that stands in the way of their happiness. (This is the book that added "the mad-woman in the attic" to the gothic vocabulary.)

As a child, Brontë and her sisters were sent off to an institution much like Lowood following their mother's death. The two oldest sisters died there. Charlotte, along with her surviving sisters Anne and Emily, all became published authors. Charlotte first published this book under the androgynous pseudonym Currer Bell.

No one had seen anything like it when *Jane Eyre* was first published in 1847. It was a bestseller but its passion and frank sexuality, tame by today's standards, generated considerable controversy—particularly once it became known that the author was a woman.

"One isn't ever quite prepared for the rich, assured, unfailingly intelligent prose of Charlotte Brontë or for the remarkable integrity of her heroine, who speaks in a forthright manner of such unfeminine subjects as despair, envy, physical hunger and failure."

—JOYCE CAROL OATES, *NEW YORK TIMES*

WIDE SARGASSO SEA

BY JEAN RHYS

They say when trouble comes close ranks, and so the white people did.

MR. ROCHESTER'S MAD first wife in Charlotte Brontë's *Jane Eyre* is the protagonist of this 1939 novel. When Jane first glimpses the Creole Bertha Mason, imprisoned in the garret, she cannot tell whether it is "beast or human." Bertha's presence prevents Jane's marriage to Rochester.

British novelist Jean Rhys's version of Brontë's Bertha Mason, reincarnated as Antoinette Cosway, narrates *Wide Sargasso Sea*. Because Brontë told her readers nothing about Bertha, Rhys is free to create a wholly original character, a white Creole heiress who grew up in Jamaica in the early nineteenth century. Beautiful, pathetic, and doomed, she marries a nameless Englishman who is after her dowry. He betrays her and drives her mad. The chapters are hallucinatory and dreamlike, and the story ends at Thornfield Hall as Antoinette, whom Rochester insists on calling "Bertha," prepares to set the fire that will release and destroy her.

Comparing this with *Jane Eyre,* Joyce Carol Oates notes, "Rhys's prose is oblique and sparing, yet poetic, and as disturbing in its cadences as Brontë's prose is reassuring."

Rhys grew up on the West Indies island of Dominica and wrote about what she knew, both from experience and from reading history. She was encouraged to write by Ford Madox Ford. Her books were critically acclaimed, but only this one brought her a wide readership.

"*[Jean Rhys has] a terrifying instinct and a terrific—an almost lurid!— passion for stating the case of the underdog. . . .*"

—FORD MADOX FORD, IN THE PREFACE TO RHYS'S NOVEL *THE LEFT BANK*

GULLIVER'S TRAVELS

BY JONATHAN SWIFT

I attempted to rise, but was not able to stir: for as I happened to lie on my back, I found my arms and legs were strongly fastened on each side to the ground; and my hair, which was long and thick, tied down in the same manner.

AN ALLEGORICAL WORK rich with political satire, this four-part traveler's tale tells of the voyages of Lemuel Gulliver ("first a surgeon, then a captain of several ships"). In print since 1726, it could have been subtitled "A Journey into Misanthropy."

In the first part, most familiar to modern readers, Gulliver is held hostage by the Lilliputians, a race of six-inch-tall people at war with their neighbors, the Blefuscudians. Swift uses their conflict over (among other things) whether to break eggs at the large or small end to satirize conflict between the English and French, and between Catholics and Protestants. On the second voyage, Gulliver is captured by a seventy-two-foot-tall farmer and sold to the queen of Brobdingnag. In vain, he tries to explain English mores, politics, and history to the king. Next time out, Gulliver is captured by pirates and abandoned on a desert island. The island of Laputa floats by and Gulliver hitches a ride. With this society's all-consuming reverence of science and mathematics, Swift gets in his digs at London's Royal Society. On the final voyage, he's abandoned on Houyhnhnms. Its race of intelligent horses rule over detestable creatures known as Yahoos. Turns out Yahoos are human. When Gulliver returns home, his family and friends remind him all too much of Yahoos.

"The author of these Travels, Mr. Lemuel Gulliver, is my ancient and intimate friend; there is likewise some relation between us on the mother's side."

—SWIFT, IN HIS TONGUE-IN-CHEEK INTRODUCTORY NOTE
WHICH HE SIGNED "RICHARD SYMPSON"

To Kill a Mockingbird

BY HARPER LEE

When he was nearly thirteen, my brother Jem got his arm badly broken at the elbow.

THIS BELOVED NOVEL, set in the small, sleepy Alabama town of Maycomb in the depths of the Depression, is steeped in violence and racial hatred. Two stories intertwine to show how sympathy and understanding can humanize our demons.

Six-year-old Scout Finch, her brother Jem, and their friend Dill (an effeminate schemer based on Lee's friend since childhood, Truman Capote) become obsessed, as only children can, with a run-down house and the reclusive Boo Radley who lives there with his brother Nathan. Scout and Jem's fascination deepens when they find gifts in the knothole of the Radley's tree, apparently left for them.

Later, they trespass on the Radley property and Nathan Radley shoots at them. In the skirmish, Jem loses his pants. He returns to find them hanging over the fence, mended. This and other acts of kindness convince Scout that Boo is far from the bogeyman he's assumed to be.

In a second "adult" plot, Scout's father, attorney Atticus Finch, defends a black man imprisoned and brought to trial on trumped-up charges of raping a white girl. The drama of the trial and its aftermath still has heart-wrenching power, even when you know the ending.

The book was published in 1960. In its forty-first week on the bestseller list, it was awarded the Pulitzer Prize. It has become one of the best-loved and most frequently banned novels of our time.

"It's interesting that all the folks that are buying it don't know they're reading a child's book."

—FLANNERY O'CONNOR, COMMENTING ON
TO KILL A MOCKINGBIRD

CANDIDE

BY VOLTAIRE

Pangloss was professor of metaphysico-theologico-cosmolo-nigology. He proved admirably that there is no effect without a cause, and that, in this best of all possible worlds, the Baron's castle was the most magnificent of castles, and his lady the best of all possible Baronesses.

CONSIDERED A COMIC masterpiece, this 1759 novel relates the misadventures of Candide, a hapless and, today we would say clueless, youth. The opening chapter relates "how Candide was brought up in a Magnificent Castle, and how he was expelled thence," and it's downhill from there.

Despite misfortune atop misfortune (Candide is beaten, banished, separated from the woman he loves...), Candide continues to declare this "the best of all possible worlds" in which "things cannot be otherwise, for, everything being made for an end everything is necessarily for the best end."

The novel is a scathing satire of the hypocrisy of the church, popular philosophy, and other established institutions—so potent, in fact, that Voltaire published the work using the pseudonym Monsieur le docteur Ralph. Some ideas Voltaire holds up to ridicule remain controversial today—the existence of design in the universe, for example, which Dr. Pangloss "proves" by saying that noses were made to carry spectacles, and so we have spectacles.

Voltaire is said to have written this, his only novel, in a frenzied three days. Generations later, it still makes us laugh at ourselves.

"[Voltaire's] whole intelligence was an implement of war, a weapon. And what makes me cherish him is the disgust I feel for his followers, the Voltaireans, those people who laugh at great things. Did he laugh, himself? He ground his teeth."

—GUSTAVE FLAUBERT

THE BROTHERS KARAMAZOV

BY FYODOR DOSTOEVSKY

*Alexey Fyodorovitch Karamazov was the third son of Fyodor Pav-
lovitch Karamazov, a landowner well known in our district in his
own day, and still remembered among us owing to his gloomy
and tragic death, which happened thirteen years ago, and which
I shall describe in its proper place.*

AUTHOR FYODOR DOSTOEVSKY'S father was a miserly,
greedy, and corrupt petty tyrant who was assassinated by his
own servants. Like him, Fyodor Karamazov, the fictional father
in *The Brother's Karamazov*, is a cruel philandering buffoon.
He has four sons by four women, three of whom he married.
The intellectual Ivan questions faith and religion. Dimitri is a
headstrong soldier. Saintly Alyosha is a follower of the teach-
ings of Father Zossima. Smerdyakov is Fyodor's illegitimate son
and servant.

These four vastly different young men agree on only one
thing: that their father is a villainous creature. Dmitri argues
that he deserves to die. When Fyodor is killed, one of them must
stand trial.

At its simplest, this is a murder mystery in which four sons
are complicit in the murder of their father. At its most complex,
the novel explores the suffering of humanity and the injustice
of the world. It asks whether man is better off with complete
freedom or with church-directed happiness and security.

Dostoevsky's last novel, this was published in 1880 a few
month's before the author's death. Alyosha, the novel's hero, is
named after Dostoevsky's three-year-old son who died while
Dostoevsky was writing this book.

*"Rosewater said an interesting thing to Billy [Pilgrim] one time about
a book that wasn't science fiction. He said that everything there was to
know about life was in* The Brothers Karamazov, *by Feodor
Dostoevsky."*

—FROM *SLAUGHTERHOUSE-FIVE* BY KURT VONNEGUT

THE LEOPARD

BY GIUSEPPE TOMASI DI LAMPEDUSA

If we want things to stay as they are, things will have to change.

THIS NOVEL SETS the decline of a family of Italian aristocrats against a backdrop of the birth of a new Italian republic. Evoking a lost world, it opens with the landing of armed forces in the 1860s, intent on unifying Italy, in the Kingdom of the Two Sicilies. It ends there, a half-century later, in a completely altered political landscape.

Don Fabrizio, Prince of Salina, is a melancholy realist. He's the last scion of a feudal family. Resigned to the inevitable, he watches as the social order he knows crumbles. Standing in contrast, the prince's favorite nephew is an opportunist who supports the unification. Realizing that the new world requires money for success, he marries a wealthy woman who is beneath him in class and works his way into a position of power.

But the order of this world reverses itself. At the end, Don Fabrizio refuses to become a senator in the new Italian republic. He recommends, instead, the peasant father of his nephew's wife.

Lampedusa's only novel, this was not accepted for publication until after his death. It went on to become one of the bestselling Italian novels of the twentieth century. Critic Edward Said compared Don Fabrizio, the last Lampedusa, to "a Sicilian Ivan Ilyich." Critics compare Lampedusa's writing to the work of Flaubert and Stendhal.

"Reading and rereading [The Leopard] has made me realize how many ways there are of being alive, how many doors there are, close to one, which someone else's touch may open."

—E. M. FORSTER, INTRODUCTION TO
LAMPEDUSA'S *TWO STORIES AND A MEMORY*

OF MICE AND MEN

BY JOHN STEINBECK

A few miles south of Soledad, the Salinas River drops in close to the hillside bank and runs deep and green.

THIS GREAT NOVELLA of the Great Depression, first published in 1937, tells of two migrant workers in California's Salinas Valley. George Milton is "small and quick, dark of face, with restless and sharp, strong features." Lennie Small is mentally unstable, "a huge man, shapeless of face, with large, pale eyes, with wide sloping shoulders; and he walked heavily, dragging his feet a little, the way a bear drags his paws." The drifters follow a path along a riverbank, dreaming of a better life—of getting together enough money to buy a farm where they can make a living and where Lennie can raise rabbits. Lennie's passion for touching soft things has gotten him into serious trouble. For touching a woman's dress he was accused of rape, fired from his last job, and run out of town.

They find work harvesting grain, and just when it looks as if they're going to catch a break (one of their coworkers agrees to invest in their dream), things fall apart. The ending is at once shocking and heartbreaking; only the reader can say if it is inevitable.

The Salinas Valley, where Steinbeck grew up and worked as a farm hand, is known today as "Steinbeck country."

"But, Mousie, thou art no thy lane / In proving foresight may be vain: / The best laid schemes o' mice an' men / Gang aft agley, / An' lea'e us nought but grief an' pain / For promis'd joy."

—ROBERT BURNS'S POEM, "TO A MOUSE"

(Burns is expressing his regret for inadvertently destroying the home of a mouse while plowing a field.)

WATERSHIP DOWN

BY RICHARD ADAMS

The primroses were over.

THIS ALLEGORICAL NOVEL opens with an excerpt from Aeschylus's *Agamemnon*, a dialogue between Cassandra, who foresees a terrifying future ("The house reeks of death and dripping blood. . . . The stench is like a breath from the tomb"), and a disbelieving Chorus.

Twenty pages later, like Cassandra, Fiver the rabbit foresees grave danger: "Oh, Hazel, look! The field! It's covered with blood!" Like the Greek Chorus, at first Hazel responds in disbelief: "Don't be silly, it's only the light of the sunset."

Fiver convinces his warren-mates to abandon their den just before bulldozers annihilate it. The intrepid rabbits, led by Hazel, search for a safe new home. At last they reach Watership Down, but their search for mates brings them to Efrafa, a warren of docile rabbits where they must take a courageous stand against dictatorial General Woundwort.

Following in a tradition that goes back to Aesop, we're not really talking bunny survival here; we're talking totalitarianism and ecological disaster. The *New York Times* called this widely acclaimed 1974 book "the rabbits' *Iliad* and *Odyssey*."

Adams laced his story with fascinating facts about rabbits—how yearlings migrate, the effects of overcrowded warrens, the buck rabbit's capacity to fight stoats, and more—which he found in R. M. Lockley's *The Private Life of the Rabbit*.

The novel was a huge bestseller and made into an animated movie; there was even a *Watership Down* float in the 1977 Macy's Thanksgiving Day parade.

"[R]abbits, it turns out, are just as interesting as lions, alligators, or seagulls—and not at all the nervous blobs of fur we generally take them to be."

—CHRISTOPHER LEHMANN-HAUPT, *NEW YORK TIMES*

THE FORTUNES AND MISFORTUNES OF THE FAMOUS MOLL FLANDERS

BY DANIEL DEFOE

Who was Born in Newgate, and during a Life of continu'd Variety for Threescore Years, besides her Childhood, was Twelve Year a Whore, five times a Wife (whereof once to her own Brother), Twelve Year a Thief, Eight Year a Transported Felon in Virginia, at last grew Rich, liv'd Honest, and dies a Penitent.

POOR MOLL. In this racy, cautionary morality tale published in 1722 by the author of *Robinson Crusoe*, a baby girl, born to a convict in Newgate Prison, is abandoned and raised by a foster mother. She sets off, determined to make something of herself. Her weapons: artful thievery, conniving, sex, and marriage. Utterly on her own, she commits all manner of crime, including adultery, prostitution, child neglect, and incest in order to survive and to get what she wants. Cavorting with the wealthy upper classes, Moll exposes their vanity and shallowness. The tale is narrated with wit and élan by a heroine who refuses to give her real name. In the end, it's only through confession and God that Moll finds peace and redemption.

In its day, a novel was expected to tell a true story and to preach a sound moral. Defoe takes great pains to say that Moll's adventures are based on facts, and that his intention is not to titillate the reader but to warn the innocent. He spent eighteen months researching his subject, visiting Newgate and talking with prisoners on whom he based his characters.

Virginia Woolf credited Defoe with having "shaped the novel and launched it on its way."

"Courage, said Moll Flanders, was what women needed, and the power to 'stand their ground'; and at once gave practical demonstration of the benefits that would result."

—VIRGINIA WOOLF, *THE COMMON READER*

PARTING THE WATERS: AMERICA IN THE KING YEARS 1954–63

BY TAYLOR BRANCH

Nearly seven hundred Negro communicants, some wearing white robes, marched together in the exodus of 1867.

THIS DEFINITIVE ACCOUNT of the American civil rights movement reveals how Dr. Martin Luther King's "dream" was born. It chronicles King's youth and brings the Montgomery bus boycott, Freedom rides, voter registration campaigns, the bombing of the Sixteenth Street Baptist Church, and the murder of Medgar Evers vividly to the page. The turning point—what Branch calls "the children's miracle," when teenagers in Birmingham, Alabama, faced down police with dogs and fire-hoses—is electrifying.

The narrative ties together such disparate figures as old Mother Pollard, who marched in the Montgomery bus boycott ("My feets is tired, but my soul is rested"), Presidents Eisenhower and Kennedy, and Dr. King's rivals within the black community. It sets the civil rights movement in the context of national politics and shows how the Kennedys knuckled under to blackmail and FBI chief J. Edgar Hoover's obsessive hatred of King. Branch's meticulous research gives an insider's perspective, revealing King as an activist and an intellectual, a pragmatist and idealist.

This first volume of a trilogy took the 1989 Pulitzer Prize and the National Book Award.

"Jail is what you make it. It determines what you think when you get out. Dr. King thought that America had ears of stone, but going to jail changed him and the Government. I think the lesson in the movement is that it's up to you. When the Martin Luther King holiday comes around, you can think about challenging the system, too."

—TAYLOR BRANCH,
SPEAKING TO RIKERS ISLAND INMATES

CROSSING TO SAFETY

BY WALLACE STEGNER

*Floating upward through a confusion of dreams and memory,
curving like a trout through the rings of previous risings, I surface.*

THIS RUMINATION ON friendship and marital love revolves around a pair of English professors and their wives. Larry Morgan and Sally, who is crippled with polio, are reunited with old friends, Sid Lang and the vivacious and controlling Charity, who is dying of cancer.

Just as she has managed to call the shots in her life, Charity prepares to orchestrate her death while Larry reminisces about the past. He remembers how the couples became friends during the Depression when both men were academics. Morgan and his wife, transplanted westerners, were poor and struggling; the Langs, well-heeled, old-money New Englanders, took them under their wing.

Larry ponders the paths their lives have taken. Their yearning to "leave a mark on the world" remains unfulfilled: "Instead, the world has left marks on us. We got older. Life chastened us so that now we lie waiting to die."

This is a moving story of ordinary lives braided together by love and friendship, and of the compromises we make in order to find happiness and fulfillment. The extraordinary writing is that of a modern master. This was the Pulitzer-winning author's final novel and his only one set in academia. Admittedly autobiographical, it was published in 1987 when Stegner was seventy-eight, fifty years and twenty-three books after his first novel, *Remembering Laughter*.

"The book is about a kind of hunger for order in the world that I think afflicts Westerners more than Easterners. There's a way between absolute liberty, which equals chaos, and absolute order, which equals petrifaction."

—WALLACE STEGNER, *NEW YORK TIMES* INTERVIEW

SHOW BOAT

BY EDNA FERBER

Bizarre as was the name she bore, Kim Ravenal always said she was thankful it had been no worse.

NO SCREEN OR stage adaptation has captured this sprawling, colorful, heartbreaking 1916 novel of riverboat life or its courageous handling of the stigma of miscegenation. A gripping, romantic tale, it spans four decades and chronicles three generations of the Hawks family on the riverboat *The Cotton Blossom*.

The novel traces the fortunes and misfortunes of Captain Andy Hawks and his wife, Parthy, who own the riverboat; of their daughter Magnolia "Noli" and her ne'er-do-well gambling husband, Gaylord Ravenal; and of their daughter Kim, who grows up to become an internationally known performer. Riverboat star Julie Dozier is forced to leave the riverboat when it's revealed that she's mulatto and her husband, Steve Baker, is white. In defiance, he draws blood from her finger and sucks it so that he "becomes black" according to the "one-drop" rule.

Ferber, who grew up in Michigan, Illinois, Iowa, and Wisconsin knew nothing of colorful riverboat life or the shows that traveled on them until she was well into her career. In 1925 she spent several weeks on the James Adams Floating Palace Theater in Bath, North Carolina, researching what would become *Show Boat*.

"I had been slumped, a disconsolate heap, on a cushion on the floor. Now I sat up and up like a cobra uncoiling. . . . Here was news of a romantic and dramatic aspect of America of which I'd never heard or dreamed."

—EDNA FERBER,
RECALLING FIRST LEARNING ABOUT RIVERBOAT SHOWS,
FROM HER AUTOBIOGRAPHY *A PECULIAR TREASURE*

FOUCAULT'S PENDULUM

BY UMBERTO ECO

That was when I saw the pendulum.

THE ITALIAN PUBLICATION of this book provoked nearly as much frenzied media speculation as the publication of the seventh Harry Potter book. Weighing in at 640-plus pages, it tells of a coded document that reveals the secret of harnessing the earth's magnetic currents. The Knights Templar have placed the document under a pendulum invented by nineteenth-century physicist Jean Bernard Léon Foucault. There it awaits discovery.

Three editors at a Milan publishing house are given the document by a retired colonel who promptly disappears. The three strive to discover the meaning hidden in the code. They concoct an elaborate imaginary computerized plot (their computer is named Abulafia) to take over the world—only to discover that their plan comes true.

Before publishing fiction, Eco was a little-known Italian scholar and semiotics (the study of signs and symbols) professor. Virtually overnight, he became a pop icon with the overwhelming response to his first literary thriller, *The Name of the Rose*. With this second effort, he went one better.

Eco's novels are for readers who didn't get enough Knights Templar in *The Da Vinci Code* and are up for a much more challenging read.

"I was obliged to read [The Da Vinci Code] because everybody was asking me about it. My answer is that Dan Brown is one of the characters in my novel, Foucault's Pendulum, *which is about people who start believing in occult stuff."*

—UMBERTO ECO, *NEW YORK TIMES* INTERVIEW

BASTARD OUT OF CAROLINA

BY DOROTHY ALLISON

I've been called Bone all my life, but my name's Ruth Anne.

RUTH ANNE "BONE" Boatwright, the child narrator of this 1992 novel, is one of the most original and unforgettable characters in literature. With *illegitimate* stamped on her birth certificate in red letters, she grows up in a desolate world of poverty, violence, and sexual abuse.

Set in rural South Carolina, *Bastard* is a sharply drawn portrait of a poor, rural white family in which an innocent life is ravaged by brutality and incest. Allison's semiautobiographical tale of the Boatwright clan is the story of how an extended family struggles to survive its own tragedies and find dignity and love in their lives. Strong stuff, the book gives "stand by your man" a whole new level of tragic meaning.

A *New York Times* book review in 1992 declared this debut novel "as close to flawless as any reader could ask for," and "simply stunning." Critics compare Allison's writing to that of William Faulkner, Flannery O'Connor, and Harper Lee, and praise her ability to capture the lives and language of poor whites in the Deep South. It went on to win the National Book Award and its controversial story remains a book group favorite.

"I believe that storytelling can be a strategy to help you make sense out of your life. . . . Bastard out of Carolina used a lot of the stories that my grandmother told me and some real things that happened in my life. But I . . . made it a different thing. I made a heroic story about a young girl who faces down a monster."

—DOROTHY ALLISON, *NEW YORK TIMES* INTERVIEW

John Adams

BY DAVID MCCULLOUGH

In the cold, nearly colorless light of a New England winter, two men on horseback traveled the coast road below Boston, heading north.

CELEBRATE INAUGURATION DAY with McCullough's masterful, Pulitzer Prize–winning portrait of the second president of the United States. Published in 2002, it tells us of the great Yankee patriot—a lawyer and farmer, a graduate of Harvard, husband of Abigail Smith Adams, father of four children—who was above all a revolutionary.

Overshadowed by the presidents who bracketed him, Adams was a great if somewhat reluctant leader. McCullough credits him as the tireless statesman who drafted the Constitution of the Commonwealth of Massachusetts, which became the model for the federal constitution. He was the one primarily responsible for making the Declaration of Independence "happen when it did."

Later, Adams negotiated a treaty with Britain that enabled the newly formed nation to survive. During his one term as president, Adams's courageous decision not to go to war with France was wise but politically unpopular. Adams vied bitterly with Jefferson, with whom he later became friends. They died on the same day, July 4, on the fiftieth anniversary of the Declaration of Independence.

McCullough is a meticulous historian and a fluent storyteller who reveals Adams as an engaging, ambitious, and vain statesman, a towering intellect who nevertheless was devoted to his family and enjoyed the simple chores of farm life. Above all, he was a politician who always spoke his mind.

"I desire no other inscription over my gravestone than: Here lies John Adams, who took upon himself the responsibility of peace with France in the year 1800."

—JOHN ADAMS, IN A LETTER TO A FRIEND

THE FOUNDLING

BY GEORGETTE HEYER

The Most Noble Adolphus Gillespie Vernon Ware, Duke of Sale and Marquis of Ormesby; Earl of Sale; Baron Ware of Thame; Baron Ware of Stoven; and Baron Ware of Rufford—is a mild-mannered, young man with not-so-good looks.

HIS GRACE, LADEN with all those titles laid out in the novel's opening line (above), has been coddled and cared for all his life. Wan and sickly at twenty-four, can Ware get along without his butler, valet, steward, footmen, grooms, gameskeepers, and well-meaning guardian? One morning he resolves to "discover whether I am a man, or only a duke."

Off he goes, disguised as a humble Everyman, to Hertford-shire to help a young relative who has professed his love (in writing) to an unsuitable young lady who now threatens to sue him for breach of promise. Instead, Ware finds himself coming to the aid of a beautiful but oblivious foundling named Belinda, rescuing her from greedy malefactors so he can reunite her, safe and untouched, with her handsome farmer.

Heyer, a reclusive British author whose work became literally synonymous with "Regency romance," wrote more than fifty books. Most were like this one, a lighthearted historical novel that doesn't take itself too seriously. Her books can be read without fear of finding characters who lose life, limb, or even temper. This one was published in 1948 at the peak of her career.

"Georgette Heyer remains as witty as any writer of the past century, as accomplished as P. G. Wodehouse in working out complex plots, and as accurate as a professional historian in getting her background details right."

—MICHAEL DIRDA, *CLASSICS FOR PLEASURE*

The Book of Evidence

BY JOHN BANVILLE

My lord, when you ask me to tell the court in my own words, this is what I shall say. I am kept locked up here like some exotic animal, last survivor of a species they had thought extinct.

IN THIS CHILLING novel, the Irish writer's seventh, Freddie Montgomery is an arrogant but oddly likeable cad who lives in exile on a Mediterranean island. His wife and child are kidnapped when a debt he owes comes due, and Montgomery returns to Ireland to get the money to pay it off. While stealing a painting from an old friend, he brutally murders the household maid with a hammer—not because he has to, but because he can: "He had scores to settle with the world, and she, at that moment, was world enough for him."

Freddie blunders into murder like Mersault in Albert Camus's *The Stranger*, blinded by sunlight. And like Mersault, he notes the indifference of nature to human suffering: "Nothing cared."

Told in the guise of Montgomery's confession as he awaits trial in jail, the evidence he gives is of his life, not his crime. What emerges is a portrait of a charming psychopath.

The story is based loosely on a notorious true crime. Dubliner Malcolm MacArthur murdered a twenty-seven-year-old nurse with a hammer in order to steal her car, and drove off with her as she was dying. He was arrested in the home of a friend, Patrick Connelly, the Irish government's chief adviser on legal matters, with whom he was reputedly having a homosexual relationship. The incident gave rise to the Irish slang expression *GUBU* (Grotesque. Unbelievable. Bizarre. Unprecedented.).

"Here is an astonishing, disturbing little novel that might have been coughed up from hell."

—ERICA ABEEL, *NEW YORK TIMES*

INTERPRETER OF MALADIES

BY JHUMPA LAHIRI

The notice informed them that it was a temporary matter: for five days their electricity would be cut off for one hour, beginning at eight P.M.

LAHIRI SEDUCES HER reader with unhappy marriages in this wondrous collection of nine short stories about Indians living in America or India. All are laced with the intricacies of Indian domesticity and the details of displacement; endings are bittersweet, with disappointment often tinged with hope. Characters are often well-educated and living comfortably, but their lives are imbued with the dissonance of displacement as couples face exhaustion, infidelity, and mismatched passions and habits.

The first story, "A Temporary Matter," is set in Boston and tells of a young couple dealing with the death of their first-born child. Dining by candlelight (their electricity has been cut off), they try to find their way past grief to each other.

In "This Blessed House," lonely, ambitious businessman Sanjeev is married to Twinkle. He craves order; she thrives in chaos. About all they share is an appreciation for Wodehouse novels and an aversion to sitar music. They nearly come to blows over religious tchotchkes left in their apartment by previous tenants.

This collection, the author's first published book, won the Pulitzer Prize in 2000. The title story was selected for the O. Henry Award.

"Lahiri's Indian-Americans struggle for dignity out of their element, like ornate shells left behind by the tide—still lacquered and colored with the wealth of the sea, incongruous on a beach of democratic sand where the only decorations are patterns of drift."

—CALEB CRAIN, *NEW YORK TIMES*

MOBY DICK

BY HERMAN MELVILLE

Call me Ishmael.

THE NARRATOR OF this 1851 novel, Ishmael, is a seafaring wanderer who signs on to crew the whaling vessel *Pequod*. Its tyrannical and increasingly erratic Captain Ahab is not looking for just any whale—he's looking for *the* whale: "the white-headed whale with a wrinkled brow and a crooked jaw." It's the whale that took Captain Ahab's leg, and the voyage is Ahab's doomed attempt to wreak vengeance.

Large sections describe the whaling business in fascinating detail, and the novel is full of symbolism and metaphor. It addresses the very nature of good and evil, an individual man's place in the great scheme of things, and the existence of God. The epilogue famously begins with a quote from Job: "And I only am escaped alone to tell thee."

The book was inspired by two historical events. First was the sinking of the Nantucket whaling ship *Essex*, which was rammed and sunk by a huge sperm whale in 1820. First mate Owen Chase survived and told the tale in a book. Second, the stories of an albino sperm whale, Mocha Dick, who was riddled with harpoons, souvenirs from his numerous battles, and who often attacked ships with what seemed to whalers like premeditated ferocity.

Considered one of the greatest books in American literature, initially it received mixed reviews and never sold through its initial 3,000-copy printing in Melville's lifetime. He dedicated it to his friend Nathaniel Hawthorne.

"[Moby Dick] is, to me, the kind of rare, titanic achievement in artistic language—without equal in American literature—that possesses the power to comment shrewdly on virtually every complex aspect of the human condition."

—ARNOLD RAMPERSAD, *WASHINGTON POST*

ANNA KARENINA

BY LEO TOLSTOY

Happy families are all alike; every unhappy family is unhappy in its own way.

CONSIDERED BY MANY to be one of the best novels of all time, this tragic story of passionate love and disastrous infidelity takes place in imperial Russia. It opens with Anna's brother, Stepan Oblonsky, having a thoughtless fling with his children's former tutor. Afterward, he begs Anna to help him reconcile with his wife. Anna has her own temptations. She's married to Karenin, a much older, stodgy Saint Petersburg government official. At Oblonsky's house, she meets the attractive, charismatic young Count Vronsky, whom her sister-in-law, Kitty, adores. Kitty's suitor, Levin, abandons all hope of winning Kitty's heart. But Vronsky has eyes only for Anna. Despite Anna's good sense and virtuousness, she succumbs.

She confesses to her husband. He offers to forgive her and take her back, but Anna defies convention and leaves him to be with Vronsky. But there are harsh consequences. Anna is shunned by polite society and her uncontrollable jealousy increasingly alienates Vronsky. She desperately misses her only son; Vronsky desperately misses his military career. Crazed, she stands in the path of an oncoming train and begs God to forgive her. The counterpoint to their doomed misery is Kitty, who returns to Levin, won over by his integrity and strength; through marriage, family, and hard work they find fulfillment. When the novel was first published in the 1870s, critics dismissed it as a trifling romance ("Show me one page that contains an idea," said *The Odessa Courier*) But over time, its estimation has soared.

"Tolstoy is a great writer—maybe he is our greatest novelist—because no other can match his sense of human proportion. We feel awe supported by compassion when we read Tolstoy."

—NORMAN MAILER, *THE SPOOKY ART: SOME THOUGHTS ON WRITING*

BEOWULF

So lived the clansmen in cheer and revel
a winsome life, till one began
to fashion evils, that field of hell.
Grendel this monster grim was called . . .

THIS LONG (3,183 LINES) epic fantasy poem, written in Old English sometime between A.D. 800 and 1000 and set in Scandinavia, tells a story of that most traditional hero's quest—a long journey during which a warrior is repeatedly tested and must prove his mettle against overwhelming odds and supernatural beings.

The hero of the tale is young Beowulf. The monsters he battles are formidable—Grendel, an angry outcast from society who has been attacking the mead hall and devouring Hrothgar's soldiers, and Grendel's mother, who seeks vengeance after Beowulf mortally wounds Grendel. When Beowulf tracks Grendel's mother to her cavern beneath a lake, his weapons turn out to be useless. He prevails only by stealing one of her swords, which the poet tells us no other man could heft. Beowulf returns to his home of Geatland and becomes king. His final tragic battle is with a fearsome dragon who guards a hoard of gold.

No one knows who wrote this poem that has become one of the most important works of Anglo-Saxon literature.

"[Beowulf] is an heroic-elegiac poem; and in a sense all its first 3,136 lines are the prelude to a dirge: him þa gegiredan Geata leode ad ofer eorðan unwaclicne: *one of the most moving ever written. . . . If the funeral of Beowulf moved once like the echo of an ancient dirge, far-off and hopeless, it is to us as a memory brought over the hills, an echo of an echo. There is not much poetry in the world like this."*

—J. R. R. TOLKIEN,
BEOWULF: THE MONSTERS AND THE CRITICS

THE HOBBIT

BY J. R. R. TOLKIEN

In a hole in the ground there lived a hobbit.

BILBO BAGGINS IS a small, furry-footed hobbit who wants nothing more than to be left alone to sit contentedly by the fire, smoke his pipe, and sip a good beer. With great reluctance, he agrees to Gandalf the Grey's invitation to partake of a "great adventure." In the company of dwarves, he sets off on a perilous journey, a hero's quest to the Lonely Mountain to reclaim a stolen fortune from the dragon Smaug.

This fantasy, subtitled "There and Back Again," is set "between the dawn of Færie and the Dominion of Men." It unfolds in episodes as Bilbo ventures from his cozy burrow into increasingly dark and dangerous realms, encountering many strange creatures. The climactic Battle of Five Armies (Men, Elves, Dwarves, Goblins, and Eagles of the Mountain) is deadly and destructive.

Of course, this was only the first book about hobbits and Middle Earth, to be followed by the *Lord of the Rings* trilogy. *The Hobbit* was widely acclaimed when first published in 1937 and has since sold an estimated 100 million copies.

Tolkien, a twentieth-century Homer, was also a pre-eminent scholar. As a youth, he worked on the *Oxford English Dictionary*. Later he was a professor of Anglo-Saxon. To fans of *The Hobbit* and its sequels, he admitted, "I am in fact a Hobbit (in all but size). I like gardens, trees and unmechanized farmlands; I smoke a pipe, and like good plain food. . . ."

"Seventeen years ago there appeared, without any fanfare, a book called The Hobbit *which, in my opinion, is one of the best children's stories of this century."*

—W. H. AUDEN, "A REVIEW OF THE ALTERNATE"

THE HOUND OF THE BASKERVILLES

BY ARTHUR CONAN DOYLE

A hound it was, an enormous coal-black hound, but not such a hound as mortal eyes have ever seen. Fire burst from its open mouth, its eyes glowed with a smouldering glare, its muzzle and hackles and dewlap were outlined in flickering flame.

DOYLE BASED THIS gothic tale, one of four novel-length Sherlock Holmes works he wrote, on local legends of black dogs and ghosts haunting foggy, desolate Dartmoor. Was the wealthy Sir Charles Baskerville killed by the infamous Hound of the Baskervilles, a demonic dog that had tormented his family for generations? Footprints show that the elderly man was running from the house when he suffered a fatal heart attack. Gigantic paw prints near Sir Charles's dead body suggest his death was no accident. Holmes and Watson are brought in by Dr. Mortimer in order to protect Charles's heir. Watson ends up baffled after investigating suspicious neighbors, an escaped mass murderer, and a mysterious stranger. The brilliant Holmes steps in. Though he doesn't believe in the curse, he is intrigued. Through the power of observation, reason, and cunning (of course), he thwarts an apparently supernatural adversary. Readers snapped up the book—the first bestseller of the twentieth century—hoping that Holmes had somehow survived his plunge at the Reichenbach Falls in Doyle's earlier story, "The Final Problem." They were disappointed, because this novel deals with events that predate Holmes's deadly encounter with Moriarty.

"Peek up Conan Doyle's literary sleeve and you will at first be disappointed: no fine turns of phrase, no clever adjectives that leap off the page, no arresting psychological insights. Instead, what you are looking at is a kind of narrative perfection: a perfect interplay between dialogue and description, perfect characterization and perfect timing."

—JOHN LE CARRÉ, INTRODUCTION TO
THE ANNOTATED SHERLOCK HOLMES

CATCH-22

BY JOSEPH HELLER

It was love at first sight. The first time Yossarian saw the chaplain he fell madly in love with him.

SET NEAR THE end of World War II, this novel takes a darkly satirical look at the absurdities of the military and the insanity of war. Yossarian is the hapless Everyman, the soldier whose one goal is staying alive while everyone else seems intent on getting him killed. He believes, with good reason, that his senior officers are more dangerous than the Germans. He tries in vain to get himself thrown out of the war.

Elliptical reasoning abounds: "There was only one catch and that was Catch-22, which specified that a concern for one's safety in the face of dangers that were real and immediate was the process of a rational mind. Orr was crazy and could be grounded. All he had to do was ask; and as soon as he did, he would no longer be crazy and would have to fly more missions."

Heller based the work on his experiences as a bombardier with the Twelfth Air Force in the Mediterranean during World War II. First published in 1961, this novel quickly captured the imagination of the reading public. Anti-Vietnam War bumper stickers of the time read *Yossarian Lives*. The title has become a metaphor for the insanity of not only war but of life itself.

"When Catch-22 *came out, people were saying, 'Well, World War II wasn't like this.' But when we got tangled up in Vietnam, it became a sort of text for the consciousness of that time."*

—E. L. DOCTOROW, ASSOCIATED PRESS INTERVIEW
QUOTED IN HELLER'S *NEW YORK TIMES* OBITUARY

WINTER'S TALE

BY MARK HELPRIN

There was a white horse, on a quiet winter morning when snow covered the streets gently and was not deep, and the sky was swept with vibrant stars, except in the east, where dawn was beginning in a light blue flood.

IN PROSE THAT reads like the lushest Dickensian fairy tale, this unique novel opens with an escaped milk-cart horse trotting to freedom across a newly built Brooklyn Bridge ("The horse could not do without Manhattan"). The horse, which turns out to have magical powers, rescues Peter Lake from a villainous gang of armed thugs with "strange bent faces, clifflike brows, tiny chins, noses and ears that looked sewn-back-on, and hairlines that descended preposterously far (no glacier had ever ventured farther south)."

Like a latter-day Moses in the bulrushes, as a babe Peter is launched ashore in Bayonne by parents who are refused entry to the United States. He's raised by a band of renegades and pirates who subsist on the Hudson's clams and oysters, fish and waterfowl. As a boy, he's sent to Manhattan, where he becomes a master burglar and falls in love with the daughter of the owner of a New York mansion that he attempts to rob. The narrative meanders and leaps from the late nineteenth century through the end of the twentieth, and encompasses time travel, romance, killing blizzards, and a bizarre mayoral race.

Published in 1983, reviewers praised the novel's wild eccentricities, elaborate construction, and "breathtaking verbal pyrotechnics." When the *New York Times* asked its readers to nominate "the new New York classics," this was the book most often mentioned.

> "[T]he heart of this book resides unquestionably in its moral energy, in the thousand original gestures, ruminations, Woola Woola writing feats that summon its audience beyond the narrow limits of conventional vision, commanding us to see our time and place afresh."
>
> —BENJAMIN DEMOTT, *NEW YORK TIMES*

THE RIGHT STUFF

BY TOM WOLFE

Within five minutes, or ten minutes, no more than that, three of the others had called her on the telephone to ask her if she had heard that something had happened out there.

WHAT DID IT take to become one of America's first astronauts? This book reveals how the Original Seven selected for the NASA space program were a special breed, true heroes dedicated to accomplishing what no other person had done: fly to the moon. Wolfe tells the individual stories of the first Project Mercury astronauts and contrasts them with test pilot Chuck Yeager, considered the best pilot of all time but never selected as an astronaut.

This nonfiction reads like a novel, turning real people into characters in the exhilarating, epic tale of America's manned space program, and shows that they had the mental and physical wherewithal for flight into the unknown. It asks: "What is it . . . that makes a man willing to sit up on top of an enormous Roman candle, such as a Redstone, Atlas, or Saturn rocket, and wait for someone to light the fuse?"

It took Wolfe nearly six years of research to find the answers. Along the way he interviewed the men and their families and friends and coworkers. He read every book he could find on space and fighter pilots and even computers. The results push our understanding of that special fraternity of astronauts and space travel far beyond clichéd images. "The right stuff," Wolfe said, was "the uncritical willingness to face danger." The Original Seven exemplified it.

In 1980, this book won the National Book Critics Circle and the American Book awards.

"[Tom Wolfe] probably put his finger on what the public psychology was, why all this big thing about us."

—DONALD "DEKE" SLAYTON,
ONE OF THE ORIGINAL SEVEN

February

UP FROM SLAVERY: AN AUTOBIOGRAPHY

BY BOOKER T. WASHINGTON

I was born a slave on a plantation in Franklin County, Virginia.

IN THIS MOVING autobiography, the celebrated nineteenth-century educator, activist, and businessman tells the story of his life. His mother was a black slave, his biological father a white slave owner. He experienced only hard labor, his dreams of going to school denied. His account of the powerlessness and sheer exhaustion of slave life is chilling.

After emancipation, his mother moved him to West Virginia where, like his stepfather, he worked in a salt furnace and later a coal mine. He learned to read and went on to study to become a teacher at Hampton Institute under the tutelage of General Samuel C. Armstrong.

The core of this autobiography concerns Washington's singular achievement: the founding of the Tuskegee Institute in Alabama, with its curriculum designed to instill values of cleanliness, honest labor, and self-help. He modeled his thirty-five-year presidency of Tuskegee after Armstrong's.

The story builds to Washington's lauded and later much criticized 1895 Atlanta Compromise speech in which he famously urged self-reliance, arguing that black and white southerners should help one another ("You can't hold a man down without staying down with him") but seemed willing to postpone indefinitely a demand for full civil equality.

"So from an old clay cabin in Virginia's hills, Booker T. Washington rose up to be one of the nation's great leaders. He lit a torch in Alabama; then darkness fled."

—MARTIN LUTHER KING JR.

THE WIND IN THE WILLOWS

BY KENNETH GRAHAME

Toad sat straight down in the middle of the dusty road, his legs stretched out before him, and stared fixedly in the direction of the disappearing motor-car. He breathed short, his face wore a placid satisfied expression, and at intervals he faintly murmured "Poop-poop!"

NO GROUNDHOGS IN the book—just Ratty (a water vole), Mole, Badger, the irrepressible Toad, and a host of other creatures who dwell along the river in the English countryside.

This children's novel tells a timeless tale of friendship. Wealthy, spoiled Toad is besotted with cars. His friends, concerned that his obsession will get him into serious trouble, place him under house arrest. But wily Toad escapes. No sooner has the hapless Toad stolen a car than the "brutal minions of the law" fall upon him, load him with chains, and throw him into a "dank and noisome dungeon."

Toad worms his way into the good graces of the jailor's daughter. With her help, and disguised as a washerwoman, he manages to escape. Escapades and the inevitable disaster ensue. When all seems lost and Toad has pushed his friends beyond their limit, they band together to save him.

First published in 1908, this was based on bedtime stories Grahame told his son. A. A. Milne (creator of Winnie the Pooh) saved the book from obscurity when he adapted it into a successful play, *Toad of Toad Hall*, in 1929.

"The book is a test of character. We can't criticise it, because it is criticising us. . . . But I must give you one word of warning. When you sit down to it, don't be so ridiculous as to suppose that you are sitting in judgement on my taste, or on the art of Kenneth Grahame. You are merely sitting in judgement on yourself."

—A. A. MILNE

FIFTH BUSINESS

BY ROBERTSON DAVIES

*My lifelong involvement with Mrs. Dempster began at
5:58 o'clock P.M. on 27 December 1908, at which time
I was ten years and seven months old.*

DUNSTABLE RAMSAY IS a fusty history professor, retiring
after a forty-five-year teaching career at a Canadian boys'
school. Disgusted by the newspaper report that portrays him
as a doddering schoolmaster with a fondness for hagiology (the
study of saints), he writes a lengthy autobiographical letter to
set the record straight.

His life may seem pedestrian—he grew up under his mother's thumb, lost a leg in World War I and was nursed back to
health by a lovely young woman, and spent forty-five years
teaching and writing about saints—but inside he has been a
"collaborator with Destiny." He reveals the secret of a hero's
birth, a doomed heroine, and his role as the "fifth business," or
that character (in an opera) who is the "odd man out" and
tangentially responsible for events. The first event, he recalls, is
an argument over a sled and a badly aimed snowball, which
resulted in the premature birth of Paul Dempster, who would
grow up to be the world's greatest magician.

Myth and mysticism, good and evil, materialism and spiri-
tualism, and Jungian archetypes are just some of themes Davies
explores. One part satire, one part romance, much of the story
is autobiographical. Davies's father, like Dunstable Ramsay's,
published a village newspaper. The first of the Deptford trilogy,
this was Davies's fourth novel. Published in 1970, it has been
called the Canadian *Citizen Kane*.

*"It is autobiographical, but not as young men would do it; it will be
rather as Dickens wrote* David Copperfield—*a fictional reworking of
some things experienced and much rearranged—a spiritual autobiography in fact, and not a sweating account of the first time I backed a
girl into a corner."*

—ROBERTSON DAVIES

BABBITT

BY SINCLAIR LEWIS

The towers of Zenith aspired above the morning mist;
austere towers of steel and cement and limestone, sturdy
as cliffs and delicate as silver rods.

THROUGH THE EYES of average, middle-aged real-estate agent George F. Babbitt, Sinclair Lewis takes a scathing look at the empty provincialism of middle-class American life. Babbitt, the original "ugly American," lives with his family somewhere in the well-heeled neighborhood of Floral Heights in midwestern Zenith, where conformity and "boosterism" prevail. Like his neighbors, he's focused on the petty drama of his own life and ignorant of the greater world. But Babbitt is also an unfulfilled dreamer, unhappy and dissatisfied.

His best friend Paul Riesling rebels and has an affair with tragic consequences. Rather than being chastened, Babbitt begins an affair of his own with a young widow, whom he's convinced is the "fairy girl." Through her and her bohemian friends, Babbitt grows increasingly sympathetic to the plight of local workers. He advocates for their strike, shocking and alienating old friends who accuse him of becoming, horror of horrors, a "liberal."

But Babbitt discovers that it's not so easy to change in midlife. The reader is left to wonder if, perhaps, it is simply too late.

Lewis dedicated the novel, published in 1922, to Edith Wharton. It was an immediate bestseller and by 1936 had sold over a million copies.

"To follow Babbitt one day is to get a hideously true view of the worst in American ways and thoughts and speech at this particular moment of history, to feel its vulgarity and noise and glare, its aimless rush, its motor-and-movie-madness, its spiritual emptiness."

—R. M. GAY, *ATLANTIC'S BOOKSHELF*

RAGTIME

BY E. L. DOCTOROW

*In 1902 Father built a house at the crest of the Broadview
Avenue hill in New Rochelle, New York.*

DOCTOROW INTERTWINES THE stories of three families in
New Rochelle and New York City at the dawn of the twentieth
century. One is white, American, and upper middle class;
another is lower-class, struggling, Jewish, and immigrant; third
is the family of Coalhouse Walker Jr., an African American
ragtime musician whose fine new car, a Model T Ford, is van-
dalized by the members of a firehouse company. In wreaking
revenge he ignites a deadly armed rebellion that costs his fiancée's life and finally his own.

Ragtime unfolds in a montage of episodes. Most controversial, at the time of its 1975 publication, were Doctorow's
highly entertaining scenes with real historical figures. Jung and
Freud take a boat together through a Tunnel of Love at Coney
Island. J. P. Morgan and Henry Ford have a tête-à-tête in a
mansion on New York's West Thirty-Sixth Street, discuss reincarnation, and "found the most secret and exclusive club in
America, The Pyramid, of which they were the only members."
Booker T. Washington talks the fictional Coalhouse Walker out
of blowing up the J. P. Morgan Library.

Fiction, in turn, fed truth. As a result of the novel, the director of the J. P. Morgan Library convinced the trustees to upgrade
the library's security system.

Doctorow set some of this novel in the rambling New
Rochelle house where he wrote it.

*"I was staring at the wall, and had arranged my desk so that the only
way out was through the sentences. I began to write about the wall,
and I realized that this house was the first house on the hill built at that
time. And then I imagined what things looked like from the bottom of
the hill. From one image to another, I was off the wall and in a book."*

—E. L. DOCTOROW, *NEW YORK MAGAZINE* INTERVIEW

HOTEL DU LAC

BY ANITA BROOKNER

From the window all that could be seen was a receding area of grey.

EDITH HOPE IS a "serious woman." She's a middle-aged, slender, birdlike creature who resembles Virginia Woolf. She's also "a writer of romantic fiction under a rather more thrusting name," Vanessa Wilde. With the "wedding fiasco" her life takes a sharp turn that resembles the plot of one of her novels. Edith's scandalized, buttoned-down friends banish her to the Hotel du Lac in Switzerland, hoping she'll get a grip.

Edith finds herself riveted by other guests who seem to all have been, in one way or another, injured in love. This cast of comic side characters is worthy of Jane Austen. There's the pair of blowsy blonds, indefatigable shopper Mrs. Pusey and her devoted daughter who may or may not stand for everything Edith has missed in life, and Monica, who is supposedly recuperating from an eating disorder. Edith writes letters about her new friends and their foibles to David, her married lover.

Unexpectedly, Edith draws the attentions of the worldly, enigmatic Mr. Neville. Surprised by his marriage proposal (he argues that their marriage would be eminently sensible), she must decide what it is in life that really matters to her.

Brookner is an English novelist. In this, her fourth novel, which won the Booker Prize in 1984, she asks: Does a woman really need a man in her life?

". . . *in its own way* Hotel du Lac *itself is a 'Tortoise and the Hare' story, and the tortoise does win—in her own way. . . . We tortoise readers can close the novel feeling well-satisfied—not least by Miss Brookner's intimation that it's sort of silly even to run the race, let alone to win it."*

—ANNE TYLER, *NEW YORK TIMES*

THE INFORMATION

BY MARTIN AMIS

Cities at night, I feel, contain men who cry in their sleep and then say Nothing. It's nothing. Just sad dreams. Or something like that. . . . Swing low in your weep ship, with your tear scans and your sob probes, and you would mark them.

WRITER RICHARD TULL—A forty-year-old book reviewer, vanity press publisher, and failed novelist—is obsessed with immortality. If only his writing can reach a vast audience and garner rave reviews, he will find redemption. He seethes as his former college roommate, Gwyn Barry, churns out books and reaps the success Tull craves. It's Barry's lousy writing that leaves him most indignant and outraged.

When Gwyn's novel hits the bestseller list, Tull strikes his son in impotent rage and schemes to get "even." The comeuppances he contrives are, at first, relatively innocent. Then, in a darkly comic plot twist, he hires a thug to rub out Gwyn, only to have the hit man get confused over whom to kill.

This book made waves when it received what was at the time an unheard of £50,000 advance. There was much speculation that Amis modeled Gwyn on the author Julian Barnes, a close friend since college with whom he'd recently had a rift. But Amis insists that both Gwyn and Tull are based on himself.

Martin Amis's father, Kingsley Amis, was the first Angry Young Man on Britain's literary scene; Martin became its enfant terrible.

"[Martin Amis is] the crown prince of literary hipness, the stud Beau Brummell of the blasé."

—CHRISTOPHER BUCKLEY

THE COLOR PURPLE

BY ALICE WALKER

You better not tell nobody but God. It'd kill your mammy.

THE HEARTBREAKING, LIFE-AFFIRMING story of Celie, a poor, barely literate black woman in rural Georgia, is told in diary entries and letters. In her isolation, at first Celie addresses her letters to God. She tells of being sexually abused by a man she thought was her father. Of the two babies who were taken from her "to be with God." Of being forced to marry Albert, a violent widower. Instead of surrendering to degradation and violence, she grew stronger.

Her story, stretching from the early 1900s to the mid-1940s, is the ultimate tale of survival. Support from other women sustains her, including, ironically, Albert's mistress and true love, Shug, who protects Celie and leads her into her first tender, loving relationship.

There is hope in this exploration of the toxic relationships between black men and women as, in the end, the entire family, Albert included, are reconciled and transformed by Celie's triumph over adversity.

This is a novel about the power of female friendship, and, as one critic put it, Walker's "strong dedication to unveiling the *soul* of the Black woman." Walker lived what she wrote about; she was single-handedly responsible for bringing back to public attention the writing of Zora Neale Hurston.

Alice Walker had previously published ten books, but this one drew her national attention. It won both the National Book Award and the Pulitzer Prize for Literature in 1983.

"I've noticed that the readers of Alice Walker's work tend to speak of her as a friend: someone who has rescued them from passivity or anger; someone who has taught them sensuality or self-respect, humor or redemption."

—GLORIA STEINEM, FROM "DO YOU KNOW THIS WOMAN? SHE KNOWS YOU" IN *OUTRAGEOUS ACTS AND EVERYDAY REBELLIONS*

THEIR EYES WERE WATCHING GOD

BY ZORA NEALE HURSTON

Ships at a distance have every man's wish on board.

THIS 1937 HARLEM Renaissance novel, a deeply moving story steeped in the African American folklore tradition, opens at dusk in rural South Florida. "The sun was gone, but he had left his footprints in the sky." The townspeople sit on their porches "in judgment" watching Janie Crawford return from burying her husband, Tea Cake.

In an extended flashback, Janie tells of the pain and unhappiness of her marriages. Her grandmother, in an attempt to keep Janie from being sexually exploited, forced Janie into her first marriage to a much older man, a good provider who would give her security and protection. But Janie yearned for more and left him for a fast-talking, ambitious man, hoping to find love and excitement. He placed her on a "pedestal," like her first husband, and treated her as property, undermining her desire to blossom "like a pear tree in spring."

When he died and she left town with the free-spirited young Tea Cake, she finally found a soul mate who loved and respected her for herself.

Though Hurston was a prolific writer and journalist, she died impoverished in 1960 and was buried in an unmarked grave. Alice Walker's 1975 *Ms.* magazine article, "In Search of Zora Neale Hurston," revived interest in Hurston's writing and brought this book back into print.

"*Reading* Their Eyes *for perhaps the eleventh time, I am still amazed . . . that it speaks to me as no novel, past or present, has ever done; and that the language of the characters, that 'comical nigger dialect' that has been laughed at, denied, ignored, or 'improved' so that white folks and educated black folks can understand it, is simply beautiful.*"

—ALICE WALKER

THE CORRECTIONS

BY JONATHAN FRANZEN

The madness of an autumn prairie cold front coming through.

PAST FAILURES AND tortured relationships are grist for this realistic saga of the Lambert family. Patriarch Alfred is losing his grip on reality courtesy of drugs he takes for Parkinson's. Enid, with her frazzled niceness, wants "one last Christmas" family gathering. Oldest son Gary is an unhappy married banker. Middle sister Denise is a chef, rebounding badly from prior relationships. And youngest son Chip, a failed teacher and writer, is floundering in Lithuania where he's been hired to produce a profit-making website for a failed nation.

Franzen paints an intimate and tragic family portrait. "Corrections"—therapy and drugs and vacation cruises—do little to stop the decay.

The author's riffs on contemporary life have been compared to the writing of Don DeLillo and William Gaddis (the title echoes Gaddis's novel *The Recognitions*). But this character-driven fiction is even more reminiscent of the earlier works of Sinclair Lewis (*Babbitt*) or Booth Tarkington (*The Magnificent Ambersons*).

Since Franzen expressed ambivalance about his book being selected by Oprah's Book Club, he did not appear on the show when it was discussed.

"[T]he novel leaves the reader with both a devastating family portrait and a harrowing portrait of America in the late 1990s—an America deep in the grip of that decade's money madness and sick with envy, resentment, greed, acquisitiveness, and self-delusion, an America committed to the quick-fix solution and determined to try to medicate its problems away."

—MICHIKO KAKUTANI, *NEW YORK TIMES*

THE BELL JAR

BY SYLVIA PLATH

It was a queer, sultry summer, the summer they electrocuted the Rosenbergs.

IN THIS AUTOBIOGRAPHICAL novel set in the 1950s, Esther Greenwood arrives in Manhattan full of aspiration and prodigious talent. She takes a job at a magazine, but depression keeps her from realizing her dream. "I just bump from my hotel to work and to parties and from parties to my hotel and back to work like a numb trolleybus." When she reads about the execution of the Rosenbergs, she wonders what it must be like "being burned alive all along your nerves."

In one psychiatric facility Esther receives poor treatment. "Wherever I sat . . . I would be sitting under the same glass bell jar, stewing in my sour air. . . . To the person in the bell jar, blank and stopped as a dead baby, the world itself is the bad dream." In another hospital, electroshock brings her back to life, as electricity sent the Rosenbergs to their deaths.

This sad, scathingly honest look at depression and mental breakdown comes from a writer who knew both intimately. Written between suicide attempts, this was the great poet's only novel. It was first published in London in 1963 under the pseudonym Victoria Lucas, just a month before Plath gassed herself to death at the age of thirty. An American edition, blocked for years by Plath's mother, was published in 1971 under Plath's name. It became an immediate bestseller.

"Practically every character in The Bell Jar *represents someone—often in caricature—whom Sylvia loved; each person had given freely of time, thought, affection . . . during those agonizing six months of breakdown in 1953. . . . [A]s this book stands by itself, it represents the basest ingratitude."*

—AURELIA PLATH (SYLVIA PLATH'S MOTHER)

THE MARCH

BY E. L. DOCTOROW

*At five in the morning someone banging on the door and shout-
ing, her husband, John, leaping out of bed, grabbing his rifle,
and Roscoe at the same time roused from the backhouse, his
bare feet pounding. . . .*

THE MAIN CHARACTER of this 2005 novel is a true historical event—General William Tecumseh Sherman's infamous
"March to the Sea" that took 62,000 Union soldiers from
Atlanta through Georgia and then the Carolinas at the end of
the Civil War. Early in the novel, slaves in Georgia see a brown
tint in the sky, "as if the world was turned upside down." It
takes on a reddish cast, then advances, "thin as a hatchet blade
in front and then widening like the furrow from the plow."
Advancing from the horizon are Sherman's troops.

As the march moves inexorably onward, it picks up a cast
of fictional characters. Among them: a pair of imprisoned Confederate soldiers who have fought for and been imprisoned by
both sides; two southern women, Mattie Jameson and Emily
Thompson, whose homes have been invaded and who find
work with the army surgeon; Emily's house maid, Wilma Jones;
and the pale-skinned Pearl who is the daughter of Mattie's
husband and a female slave.

Doctorow intertwines their stories against the backdrop of
a relentless and epic battle. He has a historian's eye for rendering the military logistics and tactics of this war and a poet's
voice so eloquent that the reader can smell the march of tens
and thousands of unbathed men.

The story continues up to the Southern surrender and the
sudden horror of Lincoln's assassination.

"[The March] *celebrates its epic war with the stirring music of a brass
marching band heard from afar, then loud and up close, and finally
receding over the horizon.*"

—JOHN UPDIKE

45

PORTNOY'S COMPLAINT

BY PHILIP ROTH

She was so deeply imbedded in my consciousness that for the first year of school I seem to have believed that each of my teachers was my mother in disguise.

FORGET CHICKEN SOUP and chopped liver: Nothing is so quintessentially Jewish-American as guilt. In this extended monologue, one long therapy session delivered from his analyst's couch, poor Alexander Portnoy bares all: "Doctor Spielvogel, this is my life, my only life, and I'm living it in the middle of a Jewish joke!"

Portnoy, a worldly, single, thirty-three-year-old Assistant Commissioner of Human Opportunity for the City of New York, confesses to being "torn by desires that are repugnant to my conscience, and a conscience repugnant to my desires." Having suffered a mother ("the patron saint of self-sacrifice") who eroticized his ears, he argues that he comes by his sexual perversity and obsession with masturbation honestly. Neurotic? You should only know.

What finally drives him to the psychiatrist's couch? Impotence in the State of Israel.

This autobiographical novel with its tour-de-force supine comedy was a sensation, and 275,000 copies were sold within two days of its 1969 publication. Roth became instantly infamous. To an interviewer he recalled Jacqueline Susann's remark to Johnny Carson that she wouldn't mind meeting the author of *Portnoy*, but she'd rather not shake his hand.

"Twenty-five years later, in the chaste pages of the Library of America, Portnoy's Complaint still goes off like a car bomb. It's irreverent; brash and angry at times, full of feeling and affection at others; and in those censorious times, it surely contained more masturbation scenes than any book not sold from under the counter."

—CHARLES McGRATH, *NEW YORK TIMES*

Stranger in a Strange Land

BY ROBERT A. HEINLEIN

Once upon a time there was a Martian named Valentine Michael Smith.

THE "STRANGER" OF this classic 1961 science fiction novel is Valentine Michael Smith, a young man born during the first manned mission to Mars. The rest of the crew dies, leaving him orphaned and alone. A quarter century later, a second mission to Mars returns him to the "strange land"—Earth.

Educated by an advanced race of wise Martians, Smith is a true innocent. Government officials frantically try to keep him under wraps because, through a legal fluke, he owns Mars. A sympathetic nurse spirits him off to the estate of the wealthy, free-thinking writer, Jubal Harshaw (think: a middle-aged Orson Welles).

As much as Smith must adjust to earth's environment, rich atmosphere, and gravity, he struggles to "grok" terrestrials with their obsessions with sex and religion, their social prejudices, and that odd thing they call politics. Like a 1960s Gulliver, Smith's picaresque adventures show him what it means to be human—and the answer isn't always pretty.

Heinlein was once an aviation engineer, and he brought both a vivid imagination and technical expertise to this work. He wrote over forty novels in his lifetime. *Stranger* won the Hugo Award for science fiction. It was also the American Bookseller Association's "Book of the Year," breaking through genre boundaries to a wide audience.

"I was not giving answers. . . . [Stranger in a Strange Land] is an invitation to think—not to believe."

—ROBERT HEINLEIN

THE HISTORY OF LOVE

BY NICOLE KRAUSS

When they write my obituary. Tomorrow. Or the next day. It will say LEO GURSKY IS SURVIVED BY AN APARTMENT FULL OF SHIT.

LEO GURSKY, A retired locksmith living in Brooklyn, spends his days terrified that no one will notice when he dies. The Polish war refugee and Holocaust survivor came to America in search of Alma, the woman he loved and lost. From afar he watches his and Alma's son, whom he cannot acknowledge, and mourns his lost novel.

In a parallel story, Alma Singer is a precocious fourteen-year-old, an obsessive list-maker who writes in a notebook entitled "How to survive in the wild." Her father recently died of cancer, and she tries to comfort her emotionally distant, widowed mother, Charlotte, a literary translator who buries her sorrow in nonstop work.

Alma becomes convinced that the only way to help her mother is to unravel the provenance of a manuscript, "The History of Love," which Charlotte translated, and to track down the characters in it. Alma is named after one of them.

Meanwhile, Alma's brother "Bird" records apocalyptic fantasies in a diary as he, too, aches for the father he's lost.

Published in 2005, this is a poignant, intricately constructed novel in which Leo and Alma, a most unlikely pair, make an astonishing connection.

"The novel's achievement is precisely, and not negligibly, this: to have made a new fiction—alternately delightful and hilarious and deeply affecting—out of what has come before."

—CLAIRE MESSUD, *LA WEEKLY*

MISS LONELYHEARTS

BY NATHANAEL WEST

Miss Lonelyhearts of the New York Post-Dispatch *(Are you in trouble?—Do-you-need-advice?—Write-to-Miss-Lonelyhearts-and-she-will-help-you) sat at his desk and stared at a piece of white cardboard.*

MISS LONELYHEARTS IS a journalist who casually takes on the job of writing an advice column for a New York City paper during the Depression. "She" is a he, and at first feels confident that the column will be a goof. But letters he reads from desperate New Yorkers with "their inarticulate expressions of genuine suffering" depress him deeply.

Soon he learns that his correspondents take him seriously—very seriously—and as he responds to their pleas for help, he is forced to confront his own, up to now unquestioned, values.

West was inspired to write this novel when he met a woman who wrote a lovelorn column for the *Brooklyn Eagle*.

Very dark, often surreal and funny, West called his novella a "moral satire." How close did he get to the "truth"? After the book's publication, several women threatened to sue West for using "their" letters—letters he had never seen.

When West died in 1940 at the age of thirty-seven, his slender output of four novels, some short stories, essays, and two plays were in relative obscurity but his fans included F. Scott Fitzgerald, Ezra Pound, and William Faulkner. Today his work speaks powerfully to modern audiences.

"[West] tried out for baseball, but was the sort of boy who, in fielding a fly, would be struck by the ball on the forehead and fall to the ground, which did, in fact, once happen to him."

—ROBERT EMMET LONG, WEST'S BIOGRAPHER

THE SHIPPING NEWS

BY ANNIE PROULX

Here is an account of a few years in the life of Quoyle, born in Brooklyn and raised in a shuffle of dreary upstate towns.

HEARTBREAK AND HUMOR coexist in an unforgettably bleak landscape in this bestselling novel. The book's hero, Quoyle, the Brooklyn-born newspaper reporter with a "great damp loaf of a body," is the ultimate self-deprecating loser. In quick succession, he loses his parents, his best friend, and his job. His faithless wife leaves him, sells their two daughters (Bunny and Sunshine) to a pornographer, and then perishes in a car accident on her way to Florida.

Quoyle rescues his children and, on the advice of his rediscovered Aunt Agnis, moves to his ancestral home in Killick-Claw, a harbor village in a desolate corner of Newfoundland. There, "brimming with grief and thwarted love," he finds work writing about car wrecks and covering the "shipping news" for *The Gammy Bird*, a small newspaper "famous for its birdhouse plans and good recipes."

On the way to reclaiming his life, Quoyle discovers cod fishing, sailor's knots, and seal flipper pie. By the end, Quoyle is still the same bumbler but he's transformed his life.

Proulx's writing style has been called elliptical and fractured, and she revels in the regional dialect of rural Newfoundland. Each chapter begins with an excerpt from the 1944 book *The Ashley Book of Knots*, which Proulx says she discovered at a yard sale. It defines "quoyle," for instance, as "a coil of rope."

Proulx's second novel, this won both the 1994 Pulitzer and National Book Award.

"To read The Shipping News *is to yearn to be sitting in the Flying Squid Lunchstop, eating Seal Fin curry, watching icebergs clink together in the bay."*

—*TIMES* (LONDON)

Tobacco Road

BY ERSKINE CALDWELL

Lov Bensey trudged homeward through the deep white sand of the gully-washed tobacco road with a sack of winter turnips on his back.

IN THE OPENING episode of this satirical Southern gothic from 1932, Lov Bensey visits his twelve-year-old wife Pearl's family of beaten-down sharecroppers. Pearl's father, Jeeter Lester, sold Pearl to Bensey for $7, some cylinder oil, and a few quilts. Bensey has a complaint: After a year of marriage, Pearl still won't have anything to do with him.

Bensey arrives at the Lesters's decaying hovel with a sack of turnips on his back—he's just walked seven and a half miles to buy them for fifty cents, half of what he makes in a day. He torments the starving Lesters by eating one. Lester's other daughter, the voluptuous Ellie May, her face disfigured by an unfortunate harelip, entices the sex-starved Bensey. When he begins to fondle her, Jeeter makes off with his turnips.

It's just the first appalling thing that these dirt-poor, uneducated sharecroppers do to one another in this dark, searing portrait of the downtrodden during the Great Depression. What readers may take as gruesome, lurid humor, Caldwell considered realism.

Not an easy book, but as a reviewer for *Slate* wrote, "few novels have as much stripped-down force and inspire as much terror and pity."

"[Jeeter and Ty Ty are] based on a po' white family that Erskine Caldwell's minister father tried and failed to take under his wing, and I can't help thinking that the author is getting back at them for being too much for his daddy."

—ROY BLOUNT JR.,
FOREWORD TO CALDWELL'S *GEORGIA BOY*

I Know Why the Caged Bird Sings

BY MAYA ANGELOU

When I was three and Bailey four, we arrived in the musty little town, wearing name tags on our wrists which instructed—"To Whom It May Concern"—that we were Marguerite and Bailey Johnson Jr., from Long Beach, California, en route to Stamps, Arkansas, c/o Mrs. Annie Henderson.

POET AND AUTHOR Angelou grew up in Stamps, Arkansas. Though life there with her paternal grandmother and uncle was sheltered and stable, steeped in Gospel, Ms. Angelou was not entirely satisfied: "How maddening it was to have been born in a cotton field with aspirations of grandeur."

Her glamorous mother reclaimed her and moved her to Saint Louis. There, she faced a very different, brutal world. She met deep-seated racism and lynch mobs. After her mother's boyfriend raped her, she stopped speaking.

When she returned to Stamps, Mrs. Bertha Flowers threw her a "life line" and Angelou found the courage to write. Once again she moved, this time to California, living alternately with her mother and father. The book ends with her giving birth to a son at the age of sixteen.

This first of a five-volume autobiography was published in 1970 (the same year that Toni Morrison and Alice Walker published their first novels), when Angelou was forty-two years old. As with her poetry, her story inspires with her quest for self-acceptance.

"You never get over the fear of writing. The fear never goes away. I go off to a room to write, and I take legal pads, a dictionary, a bottle of sherry, a solitaire deck, and a lot of prayers. Then I give myself permission."

—MAYA ANGELOU, *CONVERSATIONS WITH MAYA ANGELOU*

THE CENTAUR

BY JOHN UPDIKE

Caldwell turned and as he turned his ankle he received the arrow.

A MYTHOLOGICAL CENTAUR is part beast, part man. This autobiographical novel, published in 1963 when Updike was thirty-two years old, is an amalgam of myth and fiction. It recasts the myth of Prometheus and Chiron as a 1940s father-son story and sets it during three ice-bound days in a small Pennsylvania town.

Each character has a mythological analogue (the book provides a mythological index to guide the reader). The father, George Caldwell, is Chiron, the noblest of centaurs. A kind, shambling high school teacher, he's lost any zest he had for teaching and may have cancer. In the novel's opening, an unruly student shoots George in the leg with an arrow. George's other tormentor is the school principal, Zimmerman (Zeus). Peter Caldwell (Prometheus), George's son, is the schoolboy hero. A sensitive, troubled fifteen-year-old who yearns to become an artist, he grows up to become a second-rate painter. Much of the novel is narrated from his adult viewpoint.

Updike blends mythical figures and their stories into his story, dissolving and shifting between the two. In the myth, Zeus grants Chiron death as atonement for Prometheus stealing fire from the gods. In return, Prometheus is released from the rock. In the "real" narrative, George sacrifices for his son by choosing to return to the job he hates.

This book won the National Book Award.

"*I don't mind admitting that George Caldwell was assembled from certain vivid gestures and plights characteristic of [my father]; once, upon returning to Plowville after* The Centaur *came out, I was upbraided by a Sunday-school pupil of my father's for my outrageous portrait, and my father, in typical sanctity, interceded, saying, 'No, it's the truth. The kid got me right.'*"

—JOHN UPDIKE, *CONVERSATIONS WITH JOHN UPDIKE*

PORTRAIT OF THE ARTIST AS A YOUNG MAN

BY JAMES JOYCE

Once upon a time and a very good time it was there was a moo-cow coming down along the road and this moocow that was down along the road met a nicens little boy named baby tuckoo. . . .

AS THE TITLE suggests, this autobiographical novel portrays a young man, Stephen Dedalus, growing into an artist. It opens with Dedalus as a young child in London, continues through the torment of Jesuit boarding school, and on into adolescence.

Along the way, Dedalus has dreamy romantic fantasies and raw encounters with prostitutes. He struggles to come to grips with the competing claims of religion and art, ultimately rejecting his Catholicism and Irish roots. As he matures, he looks back at his former self with doubts and misgivings.

The name Joyce chose for his hero-self is a symbolic amalgam. Stephen, for the first Christian martyr, and Dedalus, evoking Daedalus of mythology, the father who crafts wings of wax so he and his son Icarus can fly. The wax melts when Icarus flies too close to the sun and he dies. But Daedalus survives to create a labyrinth to imprison the Minotaur.

Joyce worked on this, his first novel, for twelve years. It was published as a book in 1916.

The writing is highly impressionistic, some would say at times incomprehensible. W. H. Auden praised Joyce as the inheritor of Flaubertian realism. Today Joyce is considered the most influential writer of the twentieth century; this is his most widely read novel.

"Dear Joyce, I'm not supposed to know much about prose but I think your novel is damn fine stuff."

—EZRA POUND, IN A 1913 LETTER

FOUNDING BROTHERS: THE REVOLUTIONARY GENERATION

BY JOSEPH J. ELLIS

No event in American history which was so improbable at the time has seemed so inevitable in retrospect as the American Revolution.

JUST HOW IMPROBABLE was the success of the American Revolution? American soldiers were vastly overmatched by British army and naval forces. The thirteen colonies comprised a huge land mass to protect. There was no historical precedent. Success required improvisation and enormous amounts of sheer good luck. After armed combat ended, conflict raged between federal and state sovereignty, between agrarian and commercial interests, and among regional interests. Consensus on a national Constitution was elusive.

In a brisk 288 pages, Ellis looks at the political crises that erupted in the 1790s, the decade following the Constitutional Convention. He tells how a "band of brothers"—John Adams, Thomas Jefferson, George Washington, James Madison, Alexander Hamilton, and Aaron Burr—came together to found a nation. With Federalists (Adams and Washington) on one side and Republicans (led by Jefferson and Madison) on the other, it seemed hopeless since "neither side possessed the verbal or mental capacity to regard the other as anything but treasonable." Fractious, competitive, often with dramatically different visions, these leaders are examined by the Pulitzer-winning historian through six crucial events in their shared lives.

What emerges is a lively, illuminating portrait of men and an era and of a new nation.

"In this volume are friendship and betrayal, loyalty and philosophy, conspiracy and collaboration, high ideals and petty rivalries—in short, the entire human condition."

—DAVID SHRIBMAN, *BOSTON GLOBE*

THE GREAT GATSBY

BY F. SCOTT FITZGERALD

In my younger and more vulnerable years my father gave me some advice that I've been turning over in my mind ever since. "Whenever you feel like criticizing any one," he told me, "just remember that all the people in this world haven't had the advantages that you've had."

IT'S THE JAZZ AGE, that giddy time in the run-up to the great stock market crash. Narrator Nick Carraway, one of many midwesterners who moved to New York to seek their fortunes, tells the story of millionaire Jay Gatsby.

Though wealthy and powerful, Gatsby has no friends, only business associates and sycophants who throng to his mansion for extravagant Saturday night soirees. Ostensibly he has everything anyone could want, but still he yearns for Daisy Buchanan (the character is partially based on Fitzgerald's wife Zelda), the girl who spurned his advances years earlier because he wasn't rich enough. Now he is, but she's married.

Nick arranges for Gatsby and Daisy to meet. Nothing good comes of it.

This is not a book to ignite one's faith in humanity. Its characters go to any lengths to get what they want.

Though initially the novel received tepid reviews and sales were sluggish, it has endured to become what is arguably *the* most influential novel of the twentieth century.

Fitzgerald lived the kind of life he wrote about.

"The Great Gatsby *was my* Tom Sawyer *when I was twelve.*"
—BUDDY GLASS, THE CHARACTER IN J. D. SALINGER'S
STORY "RAISE HIGH THE ROOF BEAM, CARPENTERS"
WHO IS CONSIDERED SALINGER'S ALTER EGO

THE COUNT OF MONTE CRISTO

BY ALEXANDRE DUMAS

On February 24, 1815, the lookout at Notre-Dame de la Garde signalled the arrival of the three-master Pharaon, *coming from Smyrna, Trieste and Naples.*

EDMOND DANTÈS IS a young man with too much good fortune. A jealous trio—magistrate Villefort, croupier Danglars, and fisherman Fernand—hatch a plot to frame him for treason. On the day of his wedding to his beloved, the beautiful Mercédès, he's arrested, summarily charged, and thrown into a dungeon in the island prison Château d'If.

During fourteen years of captivity, he gets to know fellow prisoner, the Abbé Faria. Written off by his jailers as insane, Faria shares with Dantès the location of a secret treasure. Dantès escapes, journeys to a grotto hidden on the island of Monte Cristo and recovers the treasure. With his freedom and vast newfound wealth, Dantès remakes himself as a count and sets out to reward those who have done him kindnesses and to wreak vengeance on those who have done him ill.

First published in 1845, this completely satisfying revenge fantasy remains one of the most influential novels in Western literature.

Dumas was as colorful as the characters he created. He engaged in numerous love affairs and duels, fought in revolutions, and joined Garibaldi's 1860 expedition to Sicily. He produced a vast body of work and spent a great fortune faster than he made it. In 2002, over one-hundred-thirty years after his death, his remains were exhumed and moved to Paris where, in a televised ceremony presided over by President Jacques Chirac of France, he was reinterred in the Pantheon.

"With you, we were D'Artagnan, Monte Cristo or Balsamo, riding along the roads of France, touring battlefields, visiting palaces and castles— with you, we dream."

—JAQUES CHIRAC, IN A SPEECH AT DUMAS'S
REINTERMENT IN PARIS

WATER FOR ELEPHANTS

BY SARA GRUEN

I am ninety. Or ninety-three. One or the other.

ELDERLY JACOB JANKOWSKI languishes in a nursing home and looks back at his life. He was a twenty-three-year-old virgin, getting his veterinary degree at Cornell, when his parents' sudden death left him penniless. A day before finals he walked out of town and jumped a random train that turned out to be carrying the Benzini Brothers Most Spectacular Show on Earth. He talked his way into a job as the show's veterinarian.

Very quickly, he received an education—in every respect. Along with him, the reader is immersed in a world of acrobats, aerialists, sword swallowers, and lion tamers with, as one critic put it, a "bizarrely coded and private world with its own laws, superstitions and vocabulary."

Set during the Depression, the novel tells the stories of Jacob's growing love for Marlena, the beauteous equestrian wife of the hot-tempered, sadistic ringmaster, and of Rosie, the bull elephant with an unquenchable thirst for lemonade, who might be able to save the circus if only Jacob can tame her.

This runaway 2006 bestseller, stuffed with photos and wonderfully arcane details of Depression-era circus life, was Gruen's third novel. She says it was inspired by the photographs of Edward J. Kelty, who followed traveling circuses in the 1920s and 1930s.

"I came into this project loving elephants, but now I'm absolutely besotted."

—SARA GRUEN, *BOOKPAGE* INTERVIEW

OUT OF AFRICA

BY ISAK DINESEN

I had a farm in Africa, at the foot of the Ngong Hills.

IN THIS MEMOIR, Baroness Karen Blixen (pen name: Isak Dinesen) takes the reader on a thrilling trip to her family's farm in Kenya's bush country (then British East Africa), where she lived from 1914 to 1931. Her idyllic existence became increasingly fraught as the coffee crop failed and bankruptcy brought Blixen's hope of living in unity with nature to an abrupt end.

Descriptions of everyday life and of her interactions with the Kenyans are exquisite. It's the small vignettes that enthrall—adopting an infant antelope, the heart-pounding terror of a late-night lion hunt, or watching native children who gathered, waiting for the cuckoo clock to strike noon. What emerges is an elegy to a lost land and to Kenya itself, written by a Danish colonist.

"If I know a song of Africa," she asks, "of the giraffe and the African new moon lying on her back, of the plows in the fields and the sweaty faces of the coffee pickers, does Africa know a song of me?"

The book was published in 1937. Later, Blixen was nominated for the Nobel Prize. Ernest Hemingway, who won the prize instead, complimented Blixen by deferring to her greater claim.

Blixen picked the nom de plume *Isak* because in Hebrew it means "he who laughs." Dinesen, her maiden name, means the same thing in Danish.

"Art, for Isak Dinesen, was not a representation of nature but a triumph over nature; although her work has clearly been an inspiration for a new generation of neo-Gothic writers, in her own attitudes we can see a direct link to the fin-de-siècle decadence which, as a young woman, she admired, and which, in her own life, she intermittently emulated."

—MARGARET DRABBLE, *NEW YORK TIMES*

TRAVELS WITH MY AUNT

BY GRAHAM GREENE

I met my Aunt Augusta for the first time in more than half a century at my mother's funeral.

AT THE FUNERAL for the woman he *thinks* is his mother, Henry Pulling meets Aunt Augusta. The unmarried, retired bank manager and dahlia expert hasn't seen her in over fifty years, but he and the flamboyant seventy-five-year-old dowager, with "her brilliant red hair, monumentally piled, and her two big front teeth which gave her a vital Neanderthal air," form an immediate and powerful bond.

No sooner has she whisked him off in a taxi than he remembers he left his lawn mower out, uncovered. "Forget your lawn-mower," she says. And within fifteen pages she has revealed that, though Henry is his father's child, he's not his mother's.

With barely a look backward, Henry abandons his boring existence. He and Aunt Augusta, together with her black lover, Wordsworth, travel to Brighton Beach and beyond, to Istanbul and Paraguay. Henry learns of his aunt's fascinating and sketchy past while she teaches him how to stop fretting about dahlias and to enjoy life.

Greene, who died in 1991 at the age of eighty-six, wrote twenty-four novels, most of them taut thrillers. He said of *Travels with My Aunt*: "It was the only book I ever wrote for the fun of it."

"The book is much concerned with the inevitable reproach of death and with various ingenious dodges whereby it may be avoided or at least postponed.... But the only successful way to delay death is by living, and this Pulling learns to do."

—RICHARD BOSTON, *NEW YORK TIMES*

ANGLE OF REPOSE

BY WALLACE STEGNER

Now I believe they will leave me alone.

RETIRED HISTORIAN LYMAN Ward is estranged from his wife and bored by his son. His joints are locked by arthritis. From his wheelchair, he undertakes a biography of his pioneer grandparents who, like many others, moved west to strike it rich.

Drawing on his grandmother's letters to a friend, he learns about his grandfather, an engineer who met with repeated failure in mining, irrigation, and construction engineering. His grandmother was a prim, refined homemaker and illustrator. As Lyman reconstructs the past, a vivid portrait emerges of the nineteenth-century American West—one with the myth of paradise and endless opportunity stripped away. The more Lyman learns, the more his ancestors' troubles mirror his own.

"Angle of repose" is an engineering term for the "angle at which dirt and pebbles stop rolling." In the novel, what interests Lyman about his grandparents is "how two such unlike particles clung together, and under what strains, rolling downhill into their future until they reached the angle of repose where I knew them." As he gathers understanding, he redefines the term as "the angle at which a man or woman finally lies down," and by then he's talking about finding that place himself.

The prolific, much-lauded Stegner said that this novel is the single story he was meant to write. Though it won the 1972 Pulitzer for fiction, Stegner faced criticism for failing to acknowledge that Lyman's grandmother's fictional correspondence were based on the letters of nineteenth-century writer Mary Hallock.

"Wally poked a hole in the myth of the West."

—ROBERT REDFORD

March

Manhattan Transfer

BY JOHN DOS PASSOS

The nurse, holding the basket at arm's length as if it were a bedpan, opened the door to a big dry hot room with greenish distempered walls where in the air tinctured with smells of alcohol and iodoform hung writhing a faint sourish squalling from other baskets along the wall.

THIS PORTRAIT OF New York City in the Jazz Age is told in a series of loosely connected stories. From the turn of the century to the eve of the Depression, Dos Passos presents a kaleidoscope view.

The novel opens with the birth of Ellen Thatcher, born to an ailing mother and a poor ambitious father. It ends with Jimmy Herf, briefly Ellen's husband and the father of her child, leaving his job and hitching a ride out of Manhattan. In between, Ellen goes through three failed relationships and turns from stage-struck innocent to embittered realist. She finds success as an actress, but she agrees to marry a lawyer she doesn't love.

The lives of scores of other characters seem to collide at random. A rawboned kid, Bud Korpenning, searches for work he never finds. Gus McNiel, a milkman, finishes his route, stops at a bar for a drink, and gets run over by a train. And so it goes through hundreds of disparate New Yorkers. Overlapping stories take the reader into skyscrapers and tenements, into the lives of the very wealthy and the struggling immigrant poor. The city is exposed for its shallowness and immorality.

The experimental, cinematic style stunned readers when this was first published in 1925. The author was just twenty-four.

"Most stories are made of a few fibres carefully twisted together in a single strand. This story is of many fibres woven into an outspread fabric, almost without design."

—*TIME* MAGAZINE

Moon Tiger

BY PENELOPE LIVELY

"I'm writing a history of the world," she said. And the hands of the nurse are arrested for a moment; she looks down at this old woman, this old ill woman.

CLAUDIA HAMPTON, AN aging historian and former war correspondent, is dying of cancer. She wants desperately to write a history of the world but it keeps turning into recollections of her own life—love affairs, incest, childbirth, and a too-brief romantic encounter in Egypt with Tom Southern, a British World War II tank commander. Her memories come alive as visitors pass through her hospital room and through her mind.

The structure of the novel reflects Lively's fascination with memory. Present and past seem to coexist. Personal and historical episodes intermix and are strung together without regard to chronology, sometimes repeated as seen from a different character's viewpoint.

The novel takes its title from mosquito repellent called Moon Tiger. Claudia watched it as she lay awake with her lover in the wee hours, "a green coil that slowly burns all night, repelling insects, dropping away into lengths of grey ash, its glowing red eye a companion of the hot, insect-rasping darkness." It is an image that anchors a moment of utter contentment in Claudia's memory.

Lively was brought up in Cairo. She came to England after the war, and like her character, was educated at Oxford in history. Known as an author of "women's novels," she creates a meditation on the past that pulls the reader in. *Moon Tiger* won the 1987 Booker Prize.

"[Moon Tiger] is not a small canvas and yet it is worked with exquisite delicacy."

—PENNY PERRICK, *SUNDAY TIMES*

CALL IT SLEEP

BY HENRY ROTH

Standing before the kitchen sink and regarding the bright brass faucets that gleamed so far away, each with a bead of water at its nose, slowly swelling, falling, David again became aware that this world had been created without thought of him.

THE YEAR IS 1911 and David Schearl, a hyper-intense, observant, anguished boy lives on New York's grimy Lower East Side. The city, with its taunting bullies on the street corners and girls who flirt and tease, is a dangerous place for David. But home is no better, the atmosphere there poisoned by a domineering father who can't keep a job. "They look at me crookedly," his father says of his coworkers, "with mockery in their eyes! How much can a man endure? May the fire of God consume them!" But it's his father who is consumed by rage, fueled by suspicion that his wife doesn't love him and that David is another man's son. Only David's saintly mother provides a refuge.

To write the narrator and to tell the rich story of David's inner life, Roth drew on his own immigrant experience. Published in 1934, this was Roth's only novel until the publication of *Mercy of a Rude Stream*, volumes 1–4, from 1994–98. *Herald Tribune* reviewer Lewis Gannett praised the writing but proved prescient in predicting that its stark reality would be unpopular. Thirty years after its publication, the book was largely forgotten. Meanwhile, Mr. Roth worked as a laborer, a substitute teacher, a precision tool grinder, a hospital attendant, and finally raised waterfowl on a farm in Maine.

By the 1960s readers were ready for its bleak landscape. It was reissued and sold over 1 million copies.

"At the end of a novel like Call It Sleep, *one has lived through a completeness of rendered life, and all one need do is silently acknowledge its truth."*

—IRVING HOWE, *NEW YORK TIMES*

A Coney Island of the Mind

BY LAWRENCE FERLINGHETTI

In Goya's greatest scenes we seem to see / the people of the world / exactly at the moment when / they first attained the title of / 'suffering humanity.'

THE BEAT MYSTIQUE infuses this book of verse, first published in 1958. The great poet's words invoke poignant memories ("In the pennycandystore beyond the El . . ."), surreal imagery ("Don't let that horse / eat that violin . . ."), and harsh polemic ("we come we conquer all . . .").

Angry, engaged, perceptive, Ferlinghetti spoke for his own generation and beyond. He compared himself to a social climber, making a difficult downward descent, giving poetry back to the people. With more than 1 million copies in print, this has become the most popular book of poetry ever published. Its title is taken from Henry Miller's *Black Spring*.

Artist, bookseller (City Lights bookstore in San Francisco), and publisher as well as poet, Ferlinghetti was instrumental and courageous in giving young poets a platform from which to speak to American audiences. When he published Alan Ginsberg's *Howl*, he was arrested and tried for obscenity. In 1998 he was named San Francisco's first poet laureate, and in 2000 received the lifetime achievement award from the National Book Critics Circle.

This was his second volume of verse—perfect to read, then reread aloud to jazz accompaniment.

"[A] poem has to have a public surface . . . , a common-sensual surface that anyone can get, and you have to hold people's attention, which is where the comic part comes in, and then, when you get them laughing, you can zap them."

—LAWRENCE FERLINGHETTI, PBS INTERVIEW WITH
ELIZABETH FARNSWORTH

THE AUTOBIOGRAPHY OF ALICE B. TOKLAS

BY GERTRUDE STEIN

I was born in San Francisco, California. I have in consequence always preferred living in a temperate climate but it is difficult, on the continent of Europe or even in America, to find a temperate climate and live in it.

IN THE PERFECT Stein-ian twist, Gertrude Stein uses the voice of her longtime companion, Alice B. Toklas, to write her own autobiography. Speaking as Toklas, she says: "About six weeks ago Gertrude Stein said, it does not look to me as if you were ever going to write that autobiography. You know what I am going to do. I am going to write it for you. I am going to write it as simply as Defoe did the autobiography of Robinson Crusoe. And she has and this is it."

Published thirteen years before her death, Stein takes a look back at her early days. She tells of an exciting literary life in Paris, and of friendships with artists and luminaries like Hemingway, Cocteau, Picasso, and Cézanne.

Compared to most of her other works, this autobiography is easy reading and a model of lucidity. The controversial author often confused her would-be readers who were used to a traditional narrative by picking words for their sound rather than for their sense. For example, from *Tender Buttons* (1914): "Out of kindness comes redness and out of rudeness comes rapid same question, out of an eye comes research, out of selection comes painful cattle."

Autobiography was serialized in *Atlantic Monthly*. In 1933, the year it was published as a book, Stein made the cover of *Time*.

"[O]ne locks Stein into the box of a genre at one's peril. For this Houdini of literature will escape with a chuckle at critical knuckle-headedness."

—CATHARINE R. STIMPSON

THE PRIME OF
MISS JEAN BRODIE

BY MURIEL SPARK

The boys, as they talked to the girls from Marcia Blaine School, stood on the far side of their bicycles holding the handlebars, which established a protective fence of bicycle between the sexes, and the impression that at any moment the boys were likely to be away.

JEAN BRODIE, A subversive teacher at an Edinburgh day school, selects a few girls from each year's class and molds them in her own image. The girls, known as "the Brodie set," may learn little history or arithmetic. But Miss Brodie tutors them in the art of Italian muralist Giotto, the techniques of proper skin care, the poetry of Tennyson, and the politics of fascism.

"I am putting old heads on your young shoulders," Miss Brodie tells them, "and all my pupils are the crème de la crème."

Surely she is one of the most intriguing characters in modern fiction, at once hilarious and sinister. "Give me a girl at an impressionable age and she will be mine for life," she says. The results are disastrous when one of her girls becomes her personal spy and another martyrs herself to a political cause. In the ultimate betrayal, Miss Brodie offers one of her girls to the lover she cannot have.

Spark was born in Edinburgh. In high school she became one of the crème de la crème of students selected for an unorthodox curriculum by teacher Christina Kay, the model for Miss Brodie.

"[Muriel Spark] is a profoundly serious comic writer whose wit advances, never undermines or diminishes, her ideas."

—BARBARA GRIZZUTI HARRISON, *NEW YORK TIMES*

THE AMAZING ADVENTURES OF KAVALIER & CLAY

BY MICHAEL CHABON

In later years, holding forth to an interviewer or to an audience of aging fans at a comic book convention, Sam Clay liked to declare, apropos of his and Joe Kavalier's greatest creation, that back when he was a boy, sealed and hog-tied inside the airtight vessel known as Brooklyn, New York, he had been haunted by dreams of Harry Houdini.

YOUNG SAM CLAY, son of a psychiatric nurse and a vaudeville muscleman, dreams of literary glory as he toils as a clerk for a novelty wholesaler. His cousin, Josef Kavalier, is a magician whose Houdiniesque talents helped him escape Nazi-occupied Prague. Joe yearns for enough money to free the family he left behind.

Sam and Joe conjure masked superhero comic characters and build a comic empire. Joe's glimpse of the voluptuous surrealist artist Rosa Saks, naked and asleep in her bed, inspires a voluptuous girl action hero with "furry antennae hung at playful angles, as if tasting the viewer's desire." Sam invents "The Escapist," a powerful and all-knowing hero who rescues "those languishing in tyranny's chains." This sprawling and enthralling novel, studded with cameo appearances by historical figures such as Salvador Dali and Orson Welles, celebrates the golden age of the adventure comic from the late 1930s to the early '50s. It brings alive the New York of that era to a background of swing music with World War II on the horizon.

To research this book, which won the 2001 Pulitzer, Chabon not only immersed himself in comic book history, New York City, World War II, magic, and Prague's Golem, he also interviewed comic book artists from the 1940s and '50s.

"Mr. Chabon has fashioned a big, ripe, excitingly imaginative novel and set it in the world of his grandfather, a New York City typographer at a plant where comics were printed."

—JANET MASLIN, *NEW YORK TIMES*

FINAL PAYMENTS

BY MARY GORDON

My father's funeral was full of priests.

AT LAST THIRTY-YEAR-OLD Isabel Moore's eleven years of caring for her intensely religious invalid father come to an end. She's nursed him through several strokes, secretly rebelling against his domination in small ways—addressing envelopes for Women's Strike for Peace and escaping to the park instead of attending Mass on Sunday.

Her father's death frees Isabel to emerge from the dimly lit Queens household and live her own life. In short order she sells the house, moves, and falls into an affair with a married man. When the betrayed wife of her lover screams at her, "You're a good person," she's rocked by guilt and flees.

The reader will cringe when Isabel tries to atone by caring for the spiteful, crippled Margaret Casey, her father's one-time housekeeper whom Isabel drove from his house. Only after Isabel has grown fat, idle, and ugly, can she finally free herself from the self-loathing that cripples her spirit. Ultimately she is saved by her own intelligence and good sense.

Though Gordon sets the novel in a working-class, Irish-Catholic Queens neighborhood like the one where she grew up, she has said that Isabel is based more on the experience of her mother's generation—women who were expected to sacrifice their own happiness for the men in their lives. Her literary model was Mary McCarthy, "because she was so glamorous, and so smart, yet Catholic."

In this debut novel, Mary Gordon established herself as one of America's pre-eminent novelists.

"Gordon goes beyond any formulas about sheltered young women entering the churning world and learning through suffering."

—*TIME* MAGAZINE

DAVID COPPERFIELD

BY CHARLES DICKENS

Whether I shall turn out to be the hero of my own life, or whether that station will be held by anybody else, these pages must show.

POOR DAVID SUFFERS the prototypical Dickensian childhood. His father dies and his mother marries brutish Mr. Murdstone. David is sent off to a boarding school with a ruthless headmaster. When his mother dies, his stepfather consigns him to work at a grim London factory. David escapes and walks to Dover in search of his eccentric aunt, Betsey Trotwood, who christens him "Trot."

A picaresque coming-of-age story, this novel gave birth to an enduring array of characters: David's faithful nurse Peggotty, evil headmaster Mr. Creakle, and of course dissolute Mr. Micawber and villainous Uriah Heep.

This 1850 novel, written at Dickens's career midpoint (he wrote seven novels before it and seven after), was serialized first in a magazine, as was typical at the time. In assessing his own novels, Dickens said, "I have in my heart of hearts a favourite child. And his name is David Copperfield." Considered by Tolstoy to be the greatest novelist of the nineteenth century, Dickens's writing is still held up as a standard for modern storytellers.

"Now I am reading David Copperfield *for the Nth time, I'm sucking it like a caramel."*

—LEO TOLSTOY, QUOTED IN *THE DEATH OF IVAN ILYICH: A CRITICAL COMPANION* BY GARY R. JAHN

WAR AND PEACE

BY LEO TOLSTOY

*"Well, Prince, so Genoa and Lucca are now just family estates of
the Buonapartes. But I warn you, if you don't tell me that this
means war, if you still try to defend the infamies and horrors per-
petrated by that Antichrist—I really believe he is Antichrist—I will
have nothing more to do with you and you are no longer my
friend, no longer my 'faithful slave,' as you call yourself!"*

AGAINST A BACKDROP of the Napoleonic invasion of Russia,
this novel opens in 1805 when the major characters are young
adults and the Russian aristocracy is waking up to the threat
posed by Napoleon. It concludes in 1820, when the ideas that
led to the Decembrist uprising aimed at replacing the czarist
monarchy with a republic are first being discussed.

With a cast of hundreds and a sprawling story that defies
encapsulation, the novel takes as its overarching subject death—
mass slaughter in a futile war. Its characters—from impulsive
Natasha Rostov, to haughty Prince Andrey, to the compassionate Pierre Bezukhov who searches for life's meaning, to Napoleon himself—have been picked up and thrust forward by the
brutal force of mortal combat. The battles of Austerlitz and
Borodino leave the reader seared and gasping for breath.

One of the novel's most poignant moments comes when
the youngest Rostov, Petya, is shot in the head and dies during
a battle with French forces at a moment of victory. As Prince
Aubrey says, "War is not a polite recreation, but the vilest thing
in life, and we ought to understand that and not play at war."

E. M. Forster called this monstrously long (1400-plus
pages) novel the greatest ever written.

"To many readers, Tolstoy's War and Peace *is the most intimidating of
literary monuments. . . . But once you cross the border, you discover
that [its] world is more familiar and at the same time more surprising
than the rumors suggested."*

—RICHARD PEVEAR, TRANSLATOR

THE BLUEST EYE

BY TONI MORRISON

Nuns go by as quiet as lust, and drunken men and sober eyes sing in the lobby of the Greek hotel.

NOBEL LAUREATE MORRISON'S first novel tells the heartbreaking story of an eleven-year-old black girl who feels invisible. Pecola Breedlove yearns for the blondest hair and the bluest eye: "But with blue eyes, she thought, everything would be different. She would be so pretty that her parents would stop fighting. Her father would stop drinking. Her brother would stop running away. If only she could be beautiful. If only people would look at her."

When Pecola's drunken father burns down their house, Pecola is left homeless. She's taken in, only to be turned out again. She floats on the periphery of her neighbor's lives, teased and tormented. At the center of the book is her harrowing rape by her father which she only survives by disconnecting and shutting down—creating what Morrison calls a void that is Pecola's "unbeing." Like a splintered mirror, a repeated image that Morrison uses in the novel, Pecola is emotionally shattered. Her own community has failed her, too, denying her safety and solace. Set in the 1940s, the narrative voices that tell the story range from biblical, to down-home, to streetwise and bluesy, always more like poetry than prose.

Morrison, who emerged as a major novelist in the wake of the 1960s, was born in Lorain, Ohio, the steel mill town in which this novel is set.

"I am not like James Joyce; I am not like Thomas Hardy; I am not like Faulkner . . . my effort is to be like something that has probably only been fully expressed in music."

—TONI MORRISON, INTERVIEW PUBLISHED IN
CONTEMPORARY LITERATURE

MEMOIRS OF A GEISHA

BY ARTHUR GOLDEN

Suppose that you and I were sitting in a quiet room overlooking a garden, chatting and sipping at our cups of green tea while we talked about something that had happened a long while ago, and I said to you, "That afternoon when I met so-and-so . . . was the very best afternoon of my life, and also the very worst afternoon."

DISGUISED AS A memoir of one of Japan's most celebrated geishas, this tour-de-force novel is written by a man. It tells the story of Chiyo, born in the 1920s to a desperately poor fisherman and his invalid wife. Chiyo is nine when a wealthy businessman offers to adopt her and her sister. Instead, she is whisked off to Kyoto where she is installed in a geisha house. She tries to escape and return home but fails.

By day, she learns the exacting art of being a geisha. By night she is introduced to potential patrons. Her virginity is auctioned off to the highest bidder.

Transformed into the intoxicatingly beautiful Sayuri, she works for years to pay back the price of her purchase. Along the way she acquires a generous tutor and a dangerous rival, the envious Hatsumomo. She dreams of fairy-tale love and happiness—of one day being swept off her feet by the man who once charmed her with his kindness.

In her way, Chiyo/Sayuri is a twentieth-century Moll Flanders, a survivor who reinvents herself and uses every feminine asset at her disposal to get what she wants. The *New York Times* called this 1997 first novel "a bold act of ventriloquism."

Golden studied Japanese art and history. As part of his research, he interviewed one of Japan's most famous geishas, Mineko Iwasaki. She later sued him for defamation of character.

"I couldn't believe that [an American] man wrote this book about the life of a woman . . . with such detail about a little-known Japanese subculture."

—ZIYI ZHANG, ACTRESS WHO PLAYED SAYURI
IN THE MOVIE ADAPTATION

THE METAMORPHOSIS

BY FRANZ KAFKA

One morning, as Gregor Samsa was waking up from anxious dreams, he discovered that in bed he had been changed into a monstrous verminous bug.

THE FIRST LINE of this novella, published in 1915, says it all. Having discovered upon waking that he's a bug, Gregor Samsa seems oddly unconcerned. He examines his messy room. He checks the weather. He laments his traveling-salesman job. But he has a tough time getting out of bed and soon realizes he can no longer speak.

Kafka soon dispels the impression that this is a nightmare: "It was no dream." Initially Samsa's family cares for him. But gradually he's seen as a burdensome nuisance that his relatives are eager to squash.

After his transformation, Samsa still maintains his human consciousness and reveals to the reader the stultifying emptiness of his regimented former life, the stifling power exerted over him by parents and family, and the meaninglessness of his job. He is an intensely unheroic hero. Overwhelmed by forces he cannot control, his solace lies in his own intellect, moral integrity, and the certainty of death. His is a bone-chilling world of existential isolation.

This is a dark comedic masterpiece from the consummate pessimist of the twentieth century. The Jewish Czech writer's biographer Frederick R. Karl called Kafka's work a "tragic vision, leavened by wit, mockery and irony."

Kafka died of tuberculosis in 1924 at the age of forty-one, and it wasn't until the 1940s that this novella took its place among the great works of the twentieth century.

"[If you] think of Samsa as someone trapped in an insane hallucination, then you will not be on the right wave length to receive the full impact of the story."

—PHILIP ROTH, *NEW YORK TIMES REVIEW OF BOOKS*

ANNE FRANK: THE DIARY OF A YOUNG GIRL

BY ANNE FRANK

*It's really a wonder that I haven't dropped all my ideals, because
they seem so absurd and impossible to carry out. Yet I keep
them, because in spite of everything I still believe that people are
really good at heart.*

ANNE FRANK WAS an extraordinary, bright, spunky young
girl, and her story has become part of the Zeitgeist. She turned
thirteen in 1942, three weeks before the German invasion of
Holland, when she and her family were forced into hiding in
the attic of her father's office building in Amsterdam. There they
remained hidden for more than two years until they were
betrayed and captured when the Nazis raided their hideout.

Her diary ends there, but the true story continued. Anne
Frank died at the Bergen-Belsen concentration camp in Germany, in 1945, shortly before the war's end. But before the
Nazis ransacked the Franks' hiding place, Anne's five notebooks
and more than 300 loose sheets of paper were rescued by neighbors who had helped keep the Franks hidden. Later, they were
given to Otto Frank, Anne's father and the family's lone survivor, and he labored to bring them to publication.

The book, based on diary extracts addressed to Anne's
imaginary friend "Kitty," was first published in 1947. It immediately caught the attention of readers worldwide and remains
a simple, eloquent testament to the sustaining power of hope
in the face of evil.

*"The difference between Anne Frank and the men and women who
shared my experience is that the tragedy began at the point at which
Anne Frank's journal ended."*

—ELIE WIESEL, IN *HOPE AGAINST HOPE*, BY
EKKEHARD SCHUSTER AND
REINHOLD BOSCHERT-KIMMING

NIGHT

BY ELIE WIESEL

They called him Moishe the Beadle, as if his entire life he had never had a surname.

RAISED IN AN Orthodox household, at twelve years old Nobel laureate Wiesel lived with his parents and sister in Sighet, a small town in the mountains of Romania. When he and his family were rounded up, they didn't even know what the word *Auschwitz* meant.

Wiesel never saw his mother and sister again after they were separated from him on his first day at Auschwitz. Without any histrionics, Wiesel chronicles the Nazi Holocaust, searing the full realization of what he experienced into his readers' collective consciousness. He lets the details of concentration camp life speak for themselves—the constant hunger, the sadistic doctors, and the Kapos who beat their fellow Jews. He tells of his guilty relief when finally his father died after a prolonged illness and repeated beatings. He writes of his own crisis of faith in the face of consummate evil.

Wiesel was liberated four years later from the Buchenwald camp, his family's only survivor. In this memoir, he speaks out, reliving the horrors of the concentraton camp.

When Wiesel completed *Night* in 1956, the only holocaust literature published to date was *The Diary of Anne Frank*. More than fifteen publishers turned down Wiesel's manuscript, deeming the book's stark reality too morbid. Finally it was published by a small press, Hill & Wang. The book spent eighty weeks on the *New York Times* bestseller list, sold more than 10 million copies, and started a new genre of holocaust survivor literature.

"I understood what had first drawn me to [Elie Wiesel]: that look of Lazarus risen from the dead, yet still a prisoner within the grim confines where he had strayed, stumbling among the shameful corpses."

—FRANÇOIS MAURIAC IN THE PREFACE TO *NIGHT*

THE GULAG ARCHIPELAGO: 1918–1956

BY ALEKSANDR SOLZHENITSYN

How do people get to this clandestine Archipelago? Hour by hour planes fly there, ships steer their course there, and trains thunder off to it—but all with nary a mark on them to tell of their destination.

THIS WORK TELLS the true story of another twentieth-century holocaust—the Soviet government's systematic imprisonment and extermination of tens of millions of Soviet citizens from 1929 to 1953. They were incarcerated in an "Archipelago" of forced labor camps scattered about the country and run by the secret police. *GULAG* is an acronym for the bureau that administered those penal camps.

Nobel laureate Solzhenitsyn was a survivor of these camps. He based this narrative on his own experiences and those of more than 200 other survivors. He paints a damning picture of a secret country within a country. "Gradually it was disclosed to me that the line separating good and evil passes not through states, nor between classes, nor between political parties, but through the human heart."

Solzhenitsyn wrote the book over a decade, 1958 to 1968. He authorized Western publication only after the Soviet secret police seized the manuscript in 1973. Even after the dissolution of the Soviet system, the government has acknowledged only some of its actions and taken no responsibility in regard to these labor camps.

"From the first pages the angry, bitter, and sarcastic narrative created the grim world of gray camps surrounded by barbed wire, the offices of the investigators and the torture chambers bathed in merciless light, the Stolypin railroad cars, the icy mines of Kolyma and Norilsk—this was the plight of many millions of our citizens, the reverse side of the enthusiastic unity and labor achievements celebrated in songs and presented in newspapers."

—ANDREI SAKHAROV, QUOTED IN *THE WORLD OF ANDREI SAKHAROV* BY GENNADY GORLIK

PADDY CLARKE HA HA HA

BY RODDY DOYLE

We were coming down our road. Kevin stopped at a gate and bashed it with a stick. It was Missis Quigley's gate; she was always looking out the window but she never did anything.

THE VOICE OF the narrator in this poignant and at times horrifying 1993 novel is ten-year-old Paddy Clarke. The year is 1968, and Paddy lives in a tough working-class Dublin neighborhood with Ma and Da and younger brother Sinbad. He observes in acute detail—wet cement, fire, hot tar bubbles, a beloved hot-water bottle, a widowed father who howls at the moon—but his understanding is only surface deep.

Though he says he wants to be a missionary and talks with Father Moloney about heaven, Paddy is anything but angelic in the way that he tortures his little brother, forcing a lighter-fuel capsule into Sinbad's mouth and lighting it. This and other apparently unconnected events of childhood take place against the backdrop of Paddy's parents' unhappy, violent marriage. "Ma and Da had gone way past Round Fifteen. . . . One of them would soon fall over."

This complex, engaging story, told with a child's vocabulary and in Irish dialect, is filled with earthy humor. Doyle's fourth novel (after *The Commitments*, *The Snapper*, and *The Van*), it won the Booker Prize.

"Perhaps no one has done so much to create a new set of images for the Ireland of the late twentieth century as Roddy Doyle."

—MARY GORDON, *NEW YORK TIMES*

THE LIAR'S CLUB

BY MARY KARR

My sharpest memory is of a single instant surrounded by dark.
I was seven, and our family doctor knelt before me where I sat on
a mattress on the floor.

KARR IS ONLY seven when this harrowing memoir of childhood opens in the early 1960s. Reluctantly, she shows the doctor her bruises.

In the swampy, toxic East Texas oil town where Karr grew
up (appropriately, she calls it "Leechfield"), the "liar's club"
members were Karr's dad and his drinking buddies. Her father's
whoppers, filled with oversized characters and terrifying drama,
were easier to bear than a reality replete with alcoholism, squa-
lor, rape, and illness.

She tells of a family in a state of gradual breakdown.
Grandma carried a hacksaw in her purse. Her mother, who had
been married six times before marrying Karr's father, was
impulsive and erratic. In a fit of madness, she set fire to her
daughters' toys and clothes and threatened them with a knife.
When Karr's sister, Lecia, broke her collarbone, the family was
so dysfunctional that no one took her to a doctor.

Karr became a fearless score-settler ("I was small-boned
and skinny, but more than able to make up for that with sheer
meanness."). She needed her every ounce of meanness in order
to survive.

Karr's story unfolds in a series of flash-forwards and flashbacks, remembered from an adult's viewpoint. As painful as
events are, Karr tells them with compassion, unsparing candor,
and in the voice of a poet.

"After I grew up, the only man ever to punch me found himself awak-
ened two nights later from a dead sleep by a solid right to the jaw, after
which I informed him that, should he ever wish to sleep again, he
shouldn't hit me."

—MARY KARR

THE HOUSE OF MIRTH

BY EDITH WHARTON

Selden paused in surprise. In the afternoon rush of the Grand Central Station his eyes had been refreshed by the sight of Lily Bart.

WHARTON WRAPS AN astringent satire of a "society of irresponsible pleasure-seekers" around a tragic Cinderella story. The lovely Lily Bart is wealthy, privileged, and "brought up to be ornamental." Soon after her opulent debut into New York society, her father announces that the family is "ruined." He and Lily's mother die, and Lily's penurious aunt, Mrs. Peniston, reluctantly takes Lily in. Determined to find her Prince Charming, for eleven years Lily searches. But the only charmers she finds aren't rich enough.

Wharton unleashes her acid tongue on her heroine, showing Lily to readers through the eyes of the one man she loves: "He had a confused sense that she must have cost a great deal to make, that a great many dull and ugly people must, in some mysterious way, have been sacrificed to produce her."

Naive and far too passive, Lily falls victim to her own avarice. The appearance of impropriety irreparably compromises her reputation, and Lily is ostracized from polite society. At twenty-eight, she ends up disheveled and destitute, addicted to drugs, making her living the only way she can on the street.

"It will be acclaimed largely because of its moral side—its vivid, pitiless portrait of the folly which pervades a newly builded, imperfectly founded, social structure; and it will have great vogue because the sins and shortcomings of New York's fashionable life are set forth in it by one who can speak of them, with a sophisticated utterance of first-hand knowledge."

—1905 *NEW YORK TIMES BOOK REVIEW*

THE BEGINNING OF SPRING

BY PENELOPE FITZGERALD

In 1913 the journey from Moscow to Charing Cross, changing at Warsaw, cost fourteen pounds, six shillings and threepence and took two and a half days.

THIS COMEDY OF manners is set in czarist Russia in 1913, on the eve of the Revolution. Frank Reid is a decent, stolid fellow who runs a Moscow-based printing business that he inherited from his father. His pedestrian life derails when his wife abruptly leaves him. Initially she takes their three children with her; a day later, Frank retrieves the kids from the train station.

With his wife in absentia, Frank scrambles for child care. He is almost desperate enough to consign them (and himself) to Miss Kinsman, recently dismissed from a position. "Miss Kinsman was dowdy, another of the words that couldn't be translated into Russian, because there was no way of suggesting a dismal unfashionableness which was not intentional, not slovenly, not disreputable, but simply Miss Kinsman's way of looking like herself."

Just in time, Frank finds the beautiful, serene peasant girl, Lisa Ivanovna, who turns out to be perfectly suited to the job—and to him and his intelligent children, who are far more clear-sighted than their father.

Though Fitzgerald came from a family of much-lauded writers, she didn't begin her literary career until she was nearly sixty. She is one of only a handful of authors who has had four novels, including this one, nominated for the Booker Prize.

"Not for Fitzgerald the American rough-and-tumble, the I-go-at-life-freestyle-and-contain-multitudes approach to the novel, none of our straining after the bold experiment . . . : instead her fiction possesses an uncanny stillness."

—MICHAEL DIRDA, COMMENTING ON FITZGERALD'S WRITING, IN HIS BOOK *BOUND TO PLEASE*

LET US NOW PRAISE FAMOUS MEN

BY JAMES AGEE AND WALKER EVANS

All over Alabama, the lamps are out.

IN 1936, JOURNALIST James Agee (1909–55) and photographer Walker Evans (1903–75), on joint assignment for *Fortune* magazine, befriended three cotton sharecroppers and won the trust of their families in Depression-ravaged Alabama. The result is a kaleidoscopic mélange of Agee's intense writing (poetry, prose, essay, confessional reveries, and lengthy sermons) and Evans's stark portraits.

In his introduction to the 1988 edition of the book, John Hersey describes Evans's unusual way of preparing to take these pictures: "In setting up a group photograph, Evans would let his subjects assemble and arrange themselves in any way they wished, and he would take his picture only when they were at ease and fully conscious of the camera eye staring straight at them, at home in their setting and in command of themselves." The resulting pictures lend his subjects an unadorned dignity, capturing both the pathos and the reality of their lives.

Fortune rejected the finished piece. Subtitled "Three Tenant Families," it was finally published in book form in 1939. By then the Depression was over and a war loomed on the horizon. Evans's photographs received a much warmer critical reception than Agee's prose.

By 1948 it was out of print, having sold only 1,025 copies. Reprinted in 1960, it ignited a social conscience by revealing a rampant, abject poverty that had been hidden from sight. Now it is considered a classic of American social reportage.

> *"[Agee's] aim was nothing less than a celebration of human fraternity, like Beethoven's Ninth Symphony. But instead of composing an 'ode to joy,' this vibrant and anguished prose-epic would honor the wretched of the earth, opening with Walker Evans's stark, unflinching . . . photographs."*
>
> —MICHAEL DIRDA, *CLASSICS FOR PLEASURE*

THE RED AND THE BLACK

BY STENDHAL

The little town of Verrières could pass for one of the prettiest in the Franche-Comté.

THIS NOVEL PRESENTS a damning portrait of post-Napoleonic French society as hypocritical and self-serving, at all levels. The main character, Julien Sorel, is one of literature's most psychologically complex and interesting characters. Neither villain nor hero, he is a clear-eyed intellectual, an opportunist who manipulates others in a relentless quest for wealth and power. At the same time he's arrogant and impulsive, a hopeless romantic who becomes embroiled in liaisons. When those passions destroy him and he stands accused of shooting the woman he loves, he is forced to come to terms with his own nature.

Critics have argued about whether we are meant to take at face value what Julien says near the end of the novel: "two steps away from death, I am still a hypocrite." Fraudulent or authentic, he is a character imbued with alienation and disaffection. At the end, the reader is left to ponder whether it's possible to achieve worldly success without sacrificing integrity.

Stendhal is the pen name of Henri-Marie Beyle. He was inspired to write this 1830 novel by an 1827 newspaper account of a man charged with attempting to murder a married woman. By the time of his death, his books were largely out of print. Generations later this work is ranked alongside the best of Balzac and Flaubert.

"Sir, I am an observer of the human heart."

> —STENDHAL'S REPLY TO A MAN WHO ASKED
> HIM WHAT WAS HIS BUSINESS

DARKNESS AT NOON

BY ARTHUR KOESTLER

The cell door slammed behind Rubashov.

THE SETTING IS prison, the time Stalinist Russia. Nicholas Rubashov, an ardent, loyal Bolshevik, has been arrested. He was a close associate of Lenin, a leader in the Civil War, and head of the Commissariat. Now he stands accused of acts of treason, though his only treason is his disdain for the Stalinist regime.

Over the course of six weeks, Rubashov is arrested, questioned, tried, and convicted. Not so much tortured—he suffered worse at the hands of the Gestapo—as beaten down by solitary confinement and continuous questioning, he confesses to fantastic crimes that he did not commit. It's what he has always done for the Party: what he was told to do. An ideologue, he goes willingly to his death, harboring the hope that Russia will industrialize and right itself, and Communism's promise will be fulfilled.

Koestler, once a member of the German Communist Party, was inspired to write this novel by Nicolai Bukharin, a revolutionary leader who confessed to the most improbable crimes during the Stalinist show trials of the late 1930s. Like other surviving revolutionary leaders and along with hundreds of thousands of others, he was executed.

Published in 1941 and translated from German, the novel's title echoes lines from a 1671 poem by Milton on the blindness of Samson: "O dark, dark, dark, amid the blaze of noon, / Irrecoverably dark, total eclipse / Without all hope of day!"

"[Koestler's] main theme is the decadence of revolutions owing to the corrupting effects of power, but the special nature of the Stalin dictatorship has driven him back into a position not far removed from pessimistic Conservatism."

—GEORGE ORWELL

Sons and Lovers

BY D. H. LAWRENCE

'The Bottoms' succeeded to 'Hell Row.'

THIS COMING-OF-AGE STORY tells of Paul Morel, the artist son of a coal miner, growing up in the north of England near Nottingham. It's a grim life with men who work in dark mines for subsistence pay.

Paul's mother, Gertrude Morel, is strong and sensitive. Based on Lawrence's mother, she adores Paul but can barely stand her coarse husband. One of a long line of literary Gorgon mothers who devour their sons, Mrs. Morel stands squarely between her son and any woman to whom Paul would be attracted—first Miriam Leivers, a lovely intelligent woman who would be devoted to Paul if only he could return her passion; and then Clara Dawes, a married woman who is every bit Paul's match sexually but who loves her husband. But Paul is stymied; "his soul could not leave" his mother.

This was Lawrence's third novel, and the first English novel to give an insider's look at ordinary working-class life. It was rejected by publishers who deemed it too long, too outspoken, and of course, too steamy. An editor at the London publisher Duckworth cut it down, cleaned it up, and published it in 1913, when Lawrence was twenty-eight years old. By then, Lawrence's mother had been dead for three years. Decades later an unexpurgated version was published.

"[My mother and I] have loved each other, almost with a husband and wife love, as well as filial and maternal. . . . It has been rather terrible, and has made me, in some respects, abnormal."

—D. H. LAWRENCE, *LETTERS*

ONE HUNDRED YEARS OF SOLITUDE

BY GABRIEL GARCÍA MÁRQUEZ

Many years later, as he faced the firing squad, Colonel Aureliano Buendía was to remember that distant afternoon when his father took him to discover ice.

THIS 1967 MASTERPIECE from the Colombian Nobel laureate follows 100 years in the village of Macondo, the lives of its founder, José Arcadio Buendía, his wife Ursula, and generations of their descendents.

José is curious, inventive, engaged in project after project to (among other things) make gold, discover the ocean, and photograph God. Eventually he goes crazy and, for his own safety, must be tied to a giant chestnut tree outside the family's house.

Long-suffering Ursula survives, sharp and strong, until she is 114 (or 122, no one knows which). A monument to sheer force of will, she tidies and mends after disasters strike and raises youngsters long after her children are grown.

Scores of their offspring populate the pages of the novel in a continuum of life, surviving thirty-two revolutions, an invasion of gypsies, and government corruption. Comedy and tragedy are suffused with magical realism as daisies fall on lovers from the sky, an entire town is struck with insomnia, it rains for four years, eleven months, and two days, and a woman ascends to heaven while hanging laundry.

"Here the synthesis of straightforwardness and artifice, realism and magic and myth, political passion and nonpolitical artistry, characterization and caricature, humor and terror, are so remarkably sustained that one recognizes with exhilaration very early on, as with Don Quixote and Huckleberry Finn, that one is in the presence of a masterpiece not only artistically admirable, but humanly wise, lovable, literally marvelous."

—JOHN BARTH, *THE FRIDAY BOOK: ESSAYS AND OTHER NONFICTION*

I, Claudius

BY ROBERT GRAVES

I, Tiberius Claudius Drusus Nero Germanicus This-that-and-the-other (for I shall not trouble you yet with all my titles) who was once, and not so long ago either, known to my friends and relatives and associates as "Claudius the Idiot," or "That Claudius," or "Claudius the Stammerer," or "Clau-Clau-Claudius.". . .

THIS HISTORICAL NOVEL is written as the clandestine diary of Claudius, who lived from 10 B.C. to A.D. 54. Graves imagines a clever, wise Claudius who survives through the reigns of successive emperors—first Augustus who championed the works of Horace and Virgil and was done in by his wife Livia so she could ascend to the throne upon his death, then the sadistic and licentious Tiberius, and finally the incestuous Caligula with his debauched orgies.

In A.D. 41 Claudius becomes emperor himself. He follows the advice of historian Pollio: "exaggerate your limp, stammer deliberately, let your wits wander, jerk your head, and twitch your hands on all public or semi-public occasions." With his limp and stutter and self-effacing manner, his relatives and rivals dismiss him as inconsequential. He is anything but.

After reading the ancient Roman historian Suetonius, the idea for *I Claudius* came to Graves in a dream. Historians may argue with the likelihood of Graves's suppositions about a character whose real diaries are lost to us, but literature has found a charming, decent, heroic underdog, a wise fool to champion.

The scholarly Graves was, above all, a poet who wrote novels so he could write poems. The proceeds from this book, published in 1934 and followed by a sequel, *Claudius the God*, must have sustained him through many lines of verse.

"Prose books are the show dogs I breed and sell to support my cat."
—ROBERT GRAVES, *NEW YORK TIMES*

AN AMERICAN TRAGEDY

BY THEODORE DREISER

Dusk—of a summer night. And the tall walls of the commercial heart of an American city of perhaps 400,000 inhabitants—such walls as in times may linger as a mere fable.

IN 1907, THEODORE Dreiser told friends that he wanted to get "inside the skin of a murderer." He began writing, abandoned several attempts, then started over, basing his characters loosely on the 1906 murder of young pregnant garment worker, Grace "Billy" Brown. Seduced by Chester Gillette and pregnant with his child, Grace had begged him to marry her. But Chester, who'd moved on to mingling with a richer social set, rowed poor Billy out into the middle of an Adirondack lake and whacked her overboard with a paddle. The case was a media sensation, on a par with our own O. J. Simpson trial.

In Chester Gillette, Dreiser saw echoes of his former callow, aimless self. He too had grown up poor, envious of wealth and social status. Clyde Griffiths is the Gillette/Dreiser character who grows up poor in a religious household. Dreiser takes us through his youth and sexual awakening.

Clyde flees Kansas City and his job as a hotel bellboy. His wealthy uncle befriends him and gives him a job in a New York shirt factory. There he meets Roberta Alden and seduces the doomed young factory worker. Her demand of marriage comes after Clyde has taken up with wealthy Sondra and begun to insinuate himself into her higher social set.

Though Dreiser tells without moralizing, the novel is a scathing indictment of an America bound in a class system that breeds the kind of yearning for wealth that leads to murder.

"An American Tragedy *is a novel about a murder that not only illuminated the dark regions of the criminal mind, but plays a searchlight across the landscape of American society.*"

—RICHARD LINGEMAN,
INTRODUCTION TO THE 2000 EDITION

INVISIBLE MAN

BY RALPH ELLISON

I am an invisible man. No, I am not a spook like those who haunted Edgar Allan Poe; nor am I one of your Hollywood-movie ectoplasms. I am a man of substance, of flesh and bone, fiber and liquids — and I might even be said to possess a mind. I am invisible, understand, simply because people refuse to see me.

THE NOVEL'S NAMELESS narrator is a gifted black man who grows up in a black southern community. A talented orator and high school valedictorian, he earns a scholarship to a southern Negro college. His naiveté as he gives a rich white philanthropist trustee a campus tour gets him thrown out. Inadvertently, he reveals an underground black world that the trustee never should have seen. That event reveals the hollowness and cynical hypocrisy of the college president, a man the narrator had deeply admired. Expelled, he leaves for New York, where his prospects are sabotaged. He becomes increasingly marginalized, invisible to his fellow New Yorkers, and increasingly angry about it. When he gives a rousing speech at a Harlem eviction, he's noticed and drawn into the "Brotherhood"—Ellison's euphemism for the Communist Party. He asks the reader: "Being invisible and without substance, a disembodied voice, as it were, what else could I do?" But he finds no yearned-for identity, respect, or recognition with these new brothers. The book's climax is a night of rioting in Harlem.

This novel shocked readers and awed critics. It won the 1953 National Book Award, beating Hemingway's *Old Man and the Sea* and Steinbeck's *East of Eden*. Ellison struggled in vain to write another novel as brilliant as this one.

"For Ellison has an abundance of that primary talent without which neither craft nor intelligence can save a novelist: he is richly, wildly inventive; his scenes rise and dip with tension; his people bleed, his language stings. No other writer has captured so much of the confusion and agony, the hidden gloom and surface gaiety of Negro life."

—IRVING HOWE, *DISSENT*

NATIVE SON

BY RICHARD WRIGHT

Brrrrrriiiiiiiiiiiiiiiiiiinng! An alarm clock clanged in the dark and silent room. A bed spring creaked. A woman's voice sang out impatiently: "Bigger, shut that thing off!"

SET IN CHICAGO in the 1930s, the ringing alarm clock that opens the book was a wake-up call for Americans to pay attention to the hopelessness and hatred that was being nurtured by widespread racism.

Wright said he set out to write a book "no one would weep over," and in the crude, brutish, barely educated character of Bigger Thomas, he created a man few find sympathetic. Bigger is enraged by the way whites treat blacks ("They don't let us do *nothing*.").

Through the welfare office, Bigger gets a job chauffeuring a wealthy white family—"liberals" who own run-down tenements. He's supposed to drive young Mary Dalton to her college class, but she gets him to drive her and her Communist boyfriend to a club. Later, massively drunk, she clings to him as he carries her to her room. Mary's blind mother comes in, and Bigger is terrified that she'll misconstrue the situation. He tries to keep Mary quiet and accidentally suffocates her with a pillow.

Bigger panics and one bad thing leads to another. Arrested, tried, and sentenced to death, he refuses to be dismissed by the Daltons as a "boy," by the prosecutor as a "worthless ape," or by his attorney as a victim of racial inequality: "What I killed for, I am!"

The son of a Mississippi sharecropper, with this first novel Wright became America's first bestselling black writer. For insight into his work, read his often reprinted 1940 essay "How Bigger Was Born."

"Wright could imagine Bigger, but Bigger could not possibly imagine Richard Wright."

—RALPH ELLISON, *SHADOW AND ACT*

THE AGE OF INNOCENCE

BY EDITH WHARTON

*On a January evening of the early seventies, Christine Nilsson
was singing in* Faust *at the Academy of Music in New York.*

WELCOME TO OLD New York in the Gilded Age. Wealthy
lawyer Newland Archer is a dilettante who longs for more.
"Something he knew he had missed: the flower of life." Engaged
to the drab but devoted May Welland, he finds his passion in
her cousin, the glamorous Countess Ellen Olenska.

Countess Olenska has returned to New York after decades
abroad, and it's no coincidence that Archer and his fiancée are
attending the opera *Faust* when he first lays eyes on her. The
Countess is everything May is not.

Olenska flaunts convention, buying a home in the artists'
area, attending parties on Sundays on the arm of a man who is
not only married but Jewish. But the outcry from her family
grows when she announces she will divorce her Polish husband.
Her only hope for respectability, her family believes, is if Newland can convince her not to proceed with the divorce. Instead,
he falls in love with her and finds his conservative, conformist
beliefs about what constitutes "polite" society challenged.

The novel was published in 1920 and won the Pulitzer
in 1921.

Like the countess of this novel, Wharton met the love of
her life after she was already married. She divorced her husband
and moved to Paris to be with her lover, and though they never
married, she was buried by his side.

*"Wharton's remarkably detailed memory enabled her to recreate the
New York of the early 1870s with a richness of color that justified
Edmund Wilson's description of her as the pioneer and poet of interior
decoration."*

—LOUIS AUCHINCLOSS, FOREWORD TO THE 1962 EDITION

THE NATURAL

BY BERNARD MALAMUD

Roy Hobbs pawed at the glass before thinking to prick a match with his thumbnail and hold the spurting flame in his cupped palm close to the lower berth window, but by then he had figured it was a tunnel they were passing through and was no longer surprised at the bright sight of himself holding a yellow light over his head, peering back in.

TO BE "THE best that there ever was" is Roy Hobbs's dream. At nineteen, a scout brings him to a major-league training camp. But his career is cut short and he drops out of sight after a woman, obsessed with killing the best player in baseball, shoots him in a hotel room.

Out of nowhere, Hobbs resurfaces at the age of thirty-four, once again a rookie with the last-place National League New York Knights. He pinch hits for slumping team star Bump Baily. The coach tell him he's got to knock the cover off the ball, and he does. A few days later, Bump runs into the outfield wall and dies. Roy takes his place. With the help of a bat (Wonderboy) hewn from the wood of a tree struck by lightning, Roy can hit anything they throw at him. For the first time ever the team has a shot at the pennant.

In talking about his hero, Malamud said that Hobbs "is an enormously talented baseball player . . . who does not comprehend what it means to be a hero."

This mythic allegory, published in 1952, was Malamud's first novel. He would go on to win a Pulitzer.

"It is a baseball story disconcertingly out of Ring Lardner by T. S. Eliot. . . . The Natural creates a magical universe—in which white witch and black witch struggle for the soul of a secular savior, who will restore the Waste Land to fertility, by winning the pennant for the home team."

—LESLIE A. FIEDLER, *LOVE AND DEATH IN THE AMERICAN NOVEL*

April

ALICE'S ADVENTURES IN WONDERLAND

BY LEWIS CARROLL

Alice was beginning to get very tired of sitting by her sister on the bank, and of having nothing to do: once or twice she had peeped into the book her sister was reading, but it had no pictures or conversations in it, "and what is the use of a book," thought Alice, "without pictures or conversations?"

IN A BOOK loaded with "pictures" and "conversations," there's also plenty of inspired silliness as Alice chases the elusive white rabbit down the rabbit hole. "Down, down, down. Would the fall *never* come to an end!" she wonders as a jar of marmalade floats by.

Alice shrinks to the size of a key, she grows into a giantess, she sups with the Mad Hatter and the March Hare, asks directions from the Cheshire Cat, watches the Lobster Quadrille, and plays a deadly game of croquet with the Red Queen. She asks the Cheshire Cat if he thinks she's mad. "You must be," he answers, "or you wouldn't have come here."

The flights of fancy are delightful and the language enthralls. First published in 1865, this book written for children was an instant hit.

Lewis Carroll was the pen name of English author Charles Lutwidge Dodgson. Though he wrote this book for his young friend, Alice Liddell, it is full of political satire and in-jokes that his contemporaries would have appreciated. The version with the original Sir John Tenniel illustrations is a classic. The annotated version explains the jokes, games, tricks, and parodies. Read the sequel, *Through the Looking-Glass*, to find Tweedledee and Tweedledum and the Jabberwock.

"I always call him Lewis Carroll Carroll because he was the first Humbert Humbert."

—VLADIMIR NABOKOV, WHO TRANSLATED *ALICE* INTO RUSSIAN

LOLITA

BY VLADIMIR NABOKOV

Lolita, light of my life, fire of my loins. My sin, my soul. Lo-lee-ta: the tip of the tongue taking a trip of three steps down the palate to tap, at three, on the teeth. Lo. Lee. Ta.

THIS NOVEL TELLS the sad story of middle-aged Humbert Humbert and his doomed obsession for young girls perched on the brink of puberty. He becomes hopelessly smitten with twelve-year-old Dolores Haze, his "Lolita." He marries her widowed mother, Charlotte, in order to be near his beloved. When Charlotte arranges for Lolita to be sent away so she and Humbert can enjoy their time alone together, what can he do? He contemplates murder.

But "McFate," as Humbert calls it, is on his side. Charlotte is killed in an accident. Soon, Humbert and Lolita have set off on a cross-country trip. Humbert fully indulges his fantasies and, at the same time, spirals down into insanity. He's never fully satisfied because, though he has Lolita's body, he never fully possesses her soul.

Appropriately, Lolita runs off with an even more despicable cad. Humbert goes after her but ends up in a sanitarium. Lolita contacts him later when he's settled in as a scholar at an academy. By now, she's seventeen, pregnant, and broke. He becomes enraged and, armed with a gun, goes after the (other) pedophile and pornographer who destroyed her.

Shocking? Pornographic? Immoral or amoral? When Graham Greene named this 1954 work one of the three best he'd read that year and a Scottish newspaper editor called it "the filthiest book I have ever read," sales soared.

"The first time I read Lolita *I thought it was one of the funniest books I had ever come on. The second time I read it, uncut, I thought it was one of the saddest."*

—ELIZABETH JANEWAY, *NEW YORK TIMES*

ONE FLEW OVER THE CUCKOO'S NEST

BY KEN KESEY

They're out there. Black boys in white suits up before me to commit sex acts in the hall and get it mopped up before I can catch them.

A DEFIANT, CHARMING, congenial trickster, Randle Patrick McMurphy thinks it will be easier to serve time for an assault conviction in a mental hospital than on a prison farm. Wrong. Once inside the looney bin, the Korean War vet locks horns with tyrannical Nurse Ratched, aka Big Nurse, and quickly discovers that the system has lost its mind.

The novel's narrator is McMurphy's schizophrenic friend, Chief Broom, who keeps his head down by perennially sweeping the ward. Wise and observant, he describes the futility of McMurphy's battle: "The thing he was fighting, you couldn't whip it for good. All you could do is keep on whipping it, till you couldn't come out any more and someone else had to take your place."

Kesey was twenty-three years old when he wrote this novel based on some of his own experiences working in a war veterans' psychiatric hospital. Published in February 1962, the book became the rebel's manifesto for the 1960s. He never wrote another book to match this one. His later exploits with the Merry-Pranksters cohorts were immortalized in Tom Wolfe's *The Electric Kool-Aid Acid Test.*

It seemed to many as if Jack Kerouac was passing the torch of iconoclasm in American fiction to Kesey when he praised him as "a great new American novelist."

"*[One Flew Over the Cuckoo's Nest] preceded the university turmoil, Vietnam, drugs, the counterculture. Yet it contained the prophetic essence of that whole period of revolutionary politics going psychedelic. Much of what it said has entered the consciousness of many—perhaps most—Americans.*"

—PAULINE KAEL, *NEW YORKER*

WEST WITH THE NIGHT

BY BERYL MARKHAM

How is it possible to bring order out of memory?

BERYL MARKHAM WAS a pioneer aviator and the first person to fly solo across the Atlantic Ocean. This memoir, published in 1942, is known for the hypnotic, philosophical poetry of its prose.

Markham tells of growing up in Kenya on her parents' horse farm outside Nairobi. As a child she was clawed by a lion and bitten by a baboon—perhaps inoculating her against fear. Her pet was a zebra. She picked up several African languages from farm workers, learned to hunt with a spear, and became a passionate horsewoman. She sealed her reputation as a trainer and breeder when one of her horses won a prestigious race.

Markham became Kenya's first woman to earn a commercial pilot's license. As a bush pilot she delivered supplies, passengers, and mail to the country's remote regions and scouted elephants from the air. In 1936, after some false starts, she completed a daring solo flight from England to America in a single-engine, 120-horsepower airplane with no radio, navigation equipment, or speedometer, wearing an inner tube around her neck . . . just in case. She landed nose-first in Nova Scotia, becoming the first ever to fly east to west across the Atlantic.

According to Markham's biographer Errol Trzebinski, this fascinating book was probably written by her third husband, journalist Raoul Schumacher.

"*[West with the Night] is the sort of book that makes you think human beings can do anything.*"

—*NEW YORK TIMES BOOK REVIEW*

MIDDLE PASSAGE

BY CHARLES JOHNSON

*Of all the things that drive men to sea, the most common disaster,
I've come to learn, is women. . . .*

IN THIS HISTORICAL novel, it's 1830 when Rutherford Calhoun, a well educated, freed slave from Illinois, desperate to avoid marrying a prissy, cat-loving schoolmarm and eager to evade his financial debts, stows away on a slave ship bound for the Gulf of Guinea.

The ship takes on a cargo of mythic Allmuseri tribesmen who are said to heal themselves, feel sick if they wrong anyone, and have unlined palms, no fingerprints, and two brains ("a second brain, a small one at the base of their spines"). They perform a lethal, unarmed, dancelike combat.

Inadvertently, the ship also takes on their many-faced god. Packed in an insecure crate, it seethes and churns, a divine force that threatens to unbalance not only the ship itself but the entire ocean.

As a former slave and an American patriot, Calhoun is torn between loyalty to his white shipmates and empathy for the souls in torment in the hold. When tensions boil over, he must negotiate each group's competing claims to freedom, personhood, and justice.

Johnson began his career as a successful cartoonist. His second passion was philosophy, and even this novel's bigoted Captain Ebenezer Falcon is a philosopher. (Falcon observes: "Slavery, if you think this through, forcing yourself not to flinch, is the social correlate of a deeper, ontic wound.")

In 1991, this book won the National Book Award.

"I wanted to tell a rousing sea-adventure story and I wanted it to be philosophical."

—CHARLES JOHNSON

ALL QUIET ON THE WESTERN FRONT

BY ERICH MARIA REMARQUE

We are at rest, five miles from the front.

IT WAS ON this date in 1917 that the United States entered World War I. in 1916, author Erich Maria Remarque had been conscripted into the German army at the age of eighteen and served on the Western front.

First published in Germany in 1929 as *Im Westen Nichts Neues*, the novel's stark description of the agonies of battle cry out with anger and grief at the plight of conscripted soldiers. The book chronicles the horrors of war and the residue of alienation it leaves in its wake, killing the spirits of soldiers who survive.

Paul Bäumer, the novel's Everyman, is inspired by his teacher to join the German army. He is inducted into its realities by fellow soldier Stanislaus Katczinsky. His idealism confronts reality: "I see how peoples are set against one another and in silence, unknowingly, foolishly, obediently, innocently slay one another."

Speaking for the common soldier, Mr. Remarque has one of his characters say: "We are forlorn like children, and experienced like old men; we are crude and sorrowful and superficial—I believe we are lost."

The ironic title comes from a phrase often found in the Kaiser's official statements—"All quiet on the western front"— glossing over the harsh reality of war. The Nazis condemned the book and the 1930 film based on it by throwing both into a huge bonfire of "objectionable" literature in front of Berlin University on May 10, 1933.

"[All Quiet on the Western Front *was] unquestionably the best story of the World War.*"

—H. L. MENCKEN

THE WOMAN IN WHITE

BY WILKIE COLLINS

This is the story of what a Woman's patience can endure, and what a Man's resolution can achieve.

ON HAMPSTEAD HEATH on a moonlit night, drawing teacher Walter Hartright encounters a "solitary Woman, dressed from head to foot in white garments, her face bent in grave inquiry on mine, her hand pointing to the dark cloud over London, as I faced her." He later discovers that she'd escaped from a nearby asylum.

Who is the mysterious woman in white? In the days before DNA testing, answering a simple question of identity was not easy. Her identity will determine whether Hartright will find the happiness he seeks with his young pupil, the lovely Laura Fairlie. Aided by Laura's half-sister, the "admirable" but "ugly" Marian Halcombe, Hartright investigates.

The theme of identity pervades this novel, and in the tradition of great mystery novels, characters are disguised or misrepresent themselves, consciously or unconsciously hiding secrets—including, of course, the charming and devious villain, the scheming baronet Count Fosco.

This complicated tale of murder, madness, and mistaken identity is narrated from multiple viewpoints and was inspired by a true crime. One of the most popular novels of the nineteenth century, it is considered by many to be the first true mystery novel. It made Collins famous as a master of suspense and precise plotting.

"No sooner was [The Woman in White] finished than I received a number of letters from single gentlemen, stating their position and means, and their wish to marry the original Marian Halcombe at once."

—WILKIE COLLINS

A Stillness at Appomattox

BY BRUCE CATTON

The end of the war was like the beginning, with the army marching down the open road under the spring sky, seeing a far light on the horizon.

THIS BOOK JOURNEYS through the final year of the Civil War, day by day, from Wilderness to Appomattox and the surrender. Grant, Meade, Sheridan, and "the courtly" Lee live on the pages of this, the final volume of Catton's Civil War trilogy, *Army of the Potomac*.

The events of that year explain why Ulysses S. Grant is considered a great hero, and how lax command contributed to Union failures at Spotsylvania, Cold Harbor, and Petersburg. The true heroes were common soldiers, those who volunteered and re-enlisted in 1964. Their bravery saved the Union.

The finale at Appomattox (April 8, 1865) is spellbinding. Soldiers, who might have been wild with the joy of victory, seemed dazed instead as they "sat on the ground and looked across at the Confederate army and found themselves feeling as they had never dreamed that the moment of victory would make them feel."

Catton, who became a senior editor of *American Heritage* magazine five years after this book was published, is known for a historian's evenhandedness and for the beauty of his prose. Read this book to hear the guns roar, to smell the burning powder, and to feel the exhaustion of the troops and the suffering of the wounded.

A Stillness won the 1954 National Book Award and the Pulitzer Prize.

"*Writing from the point of view of the citizens who found themselves soldiers, [Mr. Catton] has reaffirmed the great American tradition of a peace-loving people who, faced with necessity, can also produce greatness in war.*"

—NATIONAL BOOK AWARD CITATION

THE CANTERBURY TALES

BY GEOFFREY CHAUCER

When that Aprilis, with his showers swoot,
The drought of March hath pierced to the root,

GEOFFREY CHAUCER, A fourteenth-century poet about whom little is known, bequeathed to world literature these classic tales. The Narrator rents a room at the Tabard Inn during his journey to the Saint Thomas à Becket shrine in Canterbury. Fellow pilgrims arrive at the inn. The Host at the inn suggests that each pilgrim relate two tales along their journey to Canterbury and two more tales on the journey back. The best storyteller will be rewarded with a sumptuous dinner.

The pilgrims' stories comprise *The Canterbury Tales*. Best loved among these often bawdy tales include the salacious, earthy "Miller's Tale," "The Nun's Priest's Tale" with its multiple interpretations of the cock Chanticleer's dream, and the ebullient "Wife of Bath's Tale" in which a knight seeks to discover what women most desire.

Chaucer died in 1400 before finishing *The Canterbury Tales*. The thousands of lines he penned have been hailed as one of the great works of literature.

"*When we studied* The Canterbury Tales *in graduate school at Virginia Tech, I was struck with the idea of grassroots canonization. Thomas Becket had been a Saxon in Norman England—in other words, a redneck. . . . I was sure that the common people of England viewed Becket as a homeboy saint—their man in heaven.*"

—SHARYN MCCRUMB

Midnight in the Garden of Good and Evil

BY JOHN BERENDT

He was tall, about fifty, with darkly handsome, almost sinister features: a neatly trimmed mustache, hair turning silver at the temples, and eyes so black they were like the tinted widows of a sleek limousine—he could see out, but you couldn't see in.

THE OPENING LINE introduces the reader to antique dealer Jim Williams. He lives alone in one of Savannah's grand mansions, Mercer House (built by an ancestor of Johnny Mercer). But he's no blue blood, he tells the reader in a "drawl as soft as velvet."

Later, when he stands accused of murdering young hustler Danny Hansford, the case throws staid, upper-crust Savannah society into a tailspin. What will they do without his annual Christmas parties? Williams pleads self-defense and throws a party anyway.

The murder fictionalizes a true crime of the 1980s. As in the real case, it ends in an acquittal. The torrid details of the case hold residents spellbound and peel away the town's veneer of gentility.

Berendt revels in one outrageous character after another—a voodoo priestess, a flamboyant black drag queen, piano-playing con men, and a failed inventor who "walks" flies by gluing threads to their backs. The Syracuse-born Berendt was living in New York when he visited Savannah on a whim and stayed for eight years.

Published in 1994, this book did for Savannah tourism what Shakespeare did for Stratford-upon-Avon.

"Not since William Tecumseh Sherman spared Savannah from the torch has this city been so indebted to a Yankee."

—KEVIN SACK, *NEW YORK TIMES*

GRAVITY'S RAINBOW

BY THOMAS PYNCHON

A screaming comes across the sky.

THAT "SCREAMING" SOUND is a V-2 rocket hurtling toward London in 1944. The "rainbow" of the title is the rocket's arc—a symbol of death—and the characters in the book move about under it as if they were "its children." Turns out the rockets hit precisely where and when, most inconveniently for him, U.S. Army Lieutenant Tyrone Slothrop gets an erection.

The novel is set in England, France, and Occupied Germany in 1944 and 1945. The plot is complex with over 400 characters and multiple intertwined subplots including flashbacks to World War I, America in the 1920s and 1930s, and Germany's earliest experiments with concentration camps and genocide in German Southwest Africa in the early 1900s.

This is German history steeped in paranoia. The central character is German lieutenant Weissmann (SS code name: "Captain Blicero" or "white death"). He creates those powerful and deadly V-2 rockets.

Even coming on the heels of a spate of blackly comic anti-war novels of the 1950s and 1960s (*Catch-22* and *Cat's Cradle* for example), no one had seen anything quite like this long, difficult, and ambitious novel. It was Pynchon's third.

"Complex." "Bonecrushingly dense." "Brilliant." "Impenetrable." To those terms readers have used to describe this 1973 novel, add "controversial." When it won the National Book Award, the intensely private Pynchon neither acknowledged nor accepted the award. Pulitzer Prize jurors unanimously recommended it for that year's award for fiction, but the Pulitzer board rejected the recommendation.

"No work of fiction published in 1973 begins to compare in scale, originality and sustained intellectual interest with Mr. Pynchon's book."

—PULITZER PRIZE JURY SPOKESMAN BENJAMIN DEMOTT

THE BONFIRE OF THE VANITIES

BY TOM WOLFE

*At that very moment, in the very sort of Park Avenue co-op that
so obsessed the Mayor . . . twelve-foot ceilings . . . two wings,
one for the white Anglo-Saxon Protestants who own the place
and one for the help . . . Sherman McCoy was kneeling in his
front hall trying to put a leash on a dachshund.*

MASTER OF THE Universe bond trader Sherman McCoy's
black Mercedes takes a wrong turn in the East Bronx. Stopped
at a makeshift barricade, two young black men approach him
and a fight starts. Our hero leaps back into the car and his
mistress guns the engine. As the car races off, it hits the skinnier
of his two assailants. Another character sums up his situation:
"The guy hit the wrong kind of kid in the wrong part of town
driving the wrong brand of car with the wrong woman, not his
wife, in the bucket seat next to him. . . ."

What follows is a media nightmare. Crooks, cops, a Hasidic
landlord, a politically connected black minister, a white mayor,
and a gleeful Bronx DA who's running for re-election pile on
to take advantage.

Wolfe, a brilliant stylist and satirist, has said that this novel's main character is New York City. This huge bestseller certainly captured the city in a money-hungry era. Wolfe was well
known for powerful works of nonfiction (*The Right Stuff* for
example). This was his first novel. Chapters were first published
serially in *Rolling Stone* magazine.

*"In the real 'bonfire of the vanities' Savonarola sent his 'Red Guard'
units into people's homes to drag out their vanities—which were anything from false eyelashes to paintings with nudes in them, including
Botticellis. This bonfire is more the fire created by the vain people
themselves, under the pressure of the city of New York."*

—TOM WOLFE

LUCKY JIM

BY KINGSLEY AMIS

"They made a silly mistake, though," the Professor of History said, and his smile, as Dixon watched, gradually sank beneath the surface of his features at the memory.

IN AMIS'S FELICITOUS first novel set in postwar Britain, the protagonist is hapless academic Jim Dixon, who considers his own scholarly research the epitome of "niggling mindlessness"—a "funeral parade of yawn-enforcing facts" that throw "pseudo-light . . . upon nonproblems." It's a job he's drifted into after the war. With his taste for pop music and pubs, he doesn't fit in stodgy academia. With good reason, he's worried about losing his job and his bumbling department head can't or won't clue him in on his future prospects.

Dixon has a girlfriend, Margaret Peel, a university colleague with terrible taste in clothing and an annoying laugh. He more or less inherited her and her neuroses after her feeble suicide attempt. If only the lovely Christine Callaghan, the girlfriend of Professor Welch's artist-son Bertrand, would give him a tumble.

To further torture himself, Dixon gets roped into singing tenor at a group recital. The coup de grâce comes when he wakes up from a debauched night of drinking and carousing, "spewed up like a broken spider-crab on the tarry shingle of the morning."

This comic campus novel heralded the arrival of a literary generation of 1950s writers sometimes called The Angry Young Men. Through their writings, they vigorously proclaimed their contempt for British life.

"Lucky Jim—you remember when you read it, like Pearl Harbor and the death of FDR."

—RUSSELL FRASER, *MODERNS WORTH KEEPING*

THE ODYSSEY

BY HOMER

Tell me, O Muse, of that ingenious hero who travelled far and wide after he had sacked the famous town of Troy.

THIS EPIC POEM in twenty-four books begins on the Greek island of Ithaca. The Trojan War has been over for ten years and Odysseus has not returned. His wife, Penelope, is being courted by suitors who have overrun and pillaged the palace and threaten to kill their son, Telemachus.

Neither Penelope nor Telemachus knows that Odysseus is alive and being held captive by the nymph Calypso on her island. At the behest of the goddess Athena, Calypso agrees to let Odysseus go. But first, he tells her the story of his journey thus far: The harrowing tale of his trip to the Land of the Lotus-Eaters, his battle with the Cyclops, his love affair with the witch-goddess Circe, his temptation by the deadly sirens, his journey into Hades, and his battle with the sea monster Scylla.

Meanwhile, Athena is also helping Telemachus stand up to his mother's suitors and undertake a voyage to find his father.

Dressed as a beggar, Odysseus finally reaches home, where he and his son are reunited. Together they wreak vengeance on the men who have been trying to usurp their places.

Like all stories of Greek mythology, this one was passed down through generations of oral storytellers. It tells the classic hero's journey.

"A hero ventures forth from the world of common day into a region of supernatural wonder: fabulous forces are there encountered and a decisive victory is won: the hero comes back from this mysterious adventure with the power to bestow boons on his fellow man."

—JOSEPH CAMPBELL DEFINES THE MONOMYTH
IN *THE HERO'S JOURNEY*

HOUSE OF SAND AND FOG

BY ANDRE DUBUS III

*The fat one, the radish Torez, he calls me Camel because
I am Persian and because I can bear this August sun longer
than the Chinese and the Panamanians and even the little
Vietnamese Tran.*

IT'S JUST A modest bungalow in the California hills, but when it's mistakenly seized for back taxes it becomes the object of desire. For the former owner, recovering addict Kathy Nicolo who has lost everything else and is estranged from her family, it represents a last hope for the future. For her married lover, the cop who evicted her and then quickly fell into her bed, winning it back is a chance to win her love.

Massoud Amir Behrani, who supports his family by working on a California road crew by day and by night as a convenience store clerk, buys the house at auction. For this educated, once wealthy ex-fighter-jet pilot, in exile from the Shah's Iran, the house represents his family dignity.

The authorities admit that an administrative error has been made, but it's too late to correct it. Wills collide with tragedy for all. This page-turner is a full-blown tragedy and a cautionary tale for our greedy times.

Dubus is the son of Andre Dubus, the celebrated short-story writer and essayist. With this, his third novel and a finalist for the National Book Award, he stepped out from his father's shadow.

"From the moment that one starts to read their story, one has no choice but to stay with these characters until the heartbreaking end."

—GILL HORNBY, *TIMES* (LONDON)

Why We Can't Wait

BY MARTIN LUTHER KING

The bitterly cold winter of 1962 lingered throughout the opening months of 1963, touching the land with chill and frost, and then was replaced by a placid spring.

IN A MOVING introduction, Dr. King shows us "a young Negro boy . . . sitting on a stoop in front of a vermin-infested apartment house in Harlem." He sees "a young Negro girl . . . sitting on the stoop of a rickety wooden one-family house in Birmingham. Some visitors would call it a shack." Though these youngsters live hundreds of miles apart, they share a common struggle against segregation in 1963. In this book, he says, he tells their story and "why we can't wait."

Dr. King explains what he calls the "Negro Revolution," drawing on three centuries of black oppression to express the growing frustration of many African Americans. He points to both political parties' neglect of civil rights. "Freedom is never voluntarily given by the oppressor," he observes, "it must be demanded by the oppressed."

Several dramatic chapters focus on the nonviolent crusade he led, fighting for civil rights in Birmingham. He remembers Bull Connor, the racist commissioner in a city where "brutality directed against Negroes was an unquestioned and unchallenged reality." Bombings, burnings, hangings, and castration were common—the brutal photographs tell it all.

King's "Letter from Birmingham Jail," dated April 16, 1963, when King was incarcerated on charges of civil disobedience, is ostensibly addressed to eight of the city's white clergymen with whom he had hoped to find common ground. "There comes a time when the cup of endurance runs over, and men are no longer willing to be plunged into the abyss of despair."

"It is the triumph of Reverend Dr. Martin Luther King Jr.'s life and legacy that the ceilings have been lifted off of our dreams."
—REVEREND JESSE L. JACKSON SR., FROM THE
AFTERWORD TO THE 2000 EDITION

THE AMBASSADORS

BY HENRY JAMES

Strether's first question, when he reached the hotel, was about his friend; yet on his learning that Waymarsh was apparently not to arrive till evening he was not wholly disconcerted.

IN THIS NOVEL, which Henry James considered his best, puritanical New Englanders meet the French and *vive la difference*.

Middle-aged Lambert Strether is sent as an "ambassador" from Boston to Paris to track down Chad Newsome, the wayward son of a wealthy widow. Strether presumes Chad has fallen prey to the wiles of some femme fatale who is after his money. When he finally finds Chad, whom he hasn't seen for five years, he's struck by the transformation: "It was as if, in short, he had really, copious perhaps but shapeless, been put into a firm mould and turned successfully out."

The femme turns out to be the enchanting Countess de Vionnet, with her "rare unlikeness to the women he had known." Later, Strether is astonished to find that the countess is as helplessly in love with Chad Newsome "as a maidservant crying for her young man."

As Strether's sympathy toward Chad grows, Mrs. Newsome dispatches a new group of emissaries. They include Chad's rigid sister, Sarah Pocock, with her "consistency of chill," a counterpoint to Vionnet's "warm splendour."

In the end, Strether may go back to America but he can never go back to being the man he once was.

"[T]he subject does not invite discussion at tea parties. But without any doubt [James] has woven a delightful story about it. He is not to be blamed if he found the subject altogether too irresistible to be resisted, and except by Sarah Pocock he will be acquitted of an intention to corrupt anybody's morals."

—*NEW YORK TIMES* 1903 REVIEW

COLD MOUNTAIN

BY CHARLES FRAZIER

At the first gesture of morning, flies began stirring.

INMAN, A CONFEDERATE soldier wounded at the battle of Petersburg, wakes up in a hospital ward. Flies buzz around the long wound in his neck that after months has finally started to heal. Disillusioned by the war, he's learned "how frail the human body is against all that is sharp and hard." Yearning for "a life so quiet he would not need ears," he leaves the hospital and begins the long, arduous walk home to Cold Mountain in North Carolina. There he hopes to find Ada Monroe, the woman he has barely embraced but loves.

Ada, meanwhile, is on a parallel journey. She's a city girl, educated but ill prepared for the daunting task of taking over her father's farm. Still, she has no desire to return to Charleston. Her future lies with the farm and with the man she hopes will return. She's helped along by Ruby, a tiny woman who becomes her friend and teacher.

This debut novel took Frazier seven years to write. Its narrative voice rings of the nineteenth-century Blue Ridge Mountains, an area where Frazier spent his boyhood. In 1997 it was a surprise pick for the National Book Award.

"Stephen Crane's The Red Badge of Courage *is perhaps the most famous literary examination of one man's view of this war's particular hell; Charles Frazier's powerful first novel, set in North Carolina in 1865, sees him making his own mark on Crane's scarred territory."*

—ERICA WAGNER, *TIMES* (LONDON)

BELOVED

BY TONI MORRISON

124 was spiteful. Full of a baby's venom. The women in the house knew it and so did the children.

A SINGLE HORRIFYING event lies at the core of this novel, so terrible that it can barely be spoken of. Eighteen years earlier Sethe, a runaway slave, slit her baby's throat rather than give her up to her white tormentor. Death was a better fate than suffering as Sethe had.

Now, Sethe is an outcast, living in a house with her other daughter at the edge of her own community. Handprints appear in the icing of a birthday cake and mirrors shatter as the angry spirit of the murdered baby girl, "Beloved," haunts the home.

When Paul D., an old friend returns to town, Sethe allows herself to contemplate the tantalizing possibility of starting afresh, of enjoying an ordinary, happy life. But soon another visitor arrives—an odd, quiet teenaged girl who says she is Beloved.

This powerful, unforgettable novel, set in Ohio at the terrible time of Reconstruction, makes slavery a palpable truth. It's one of those books that burrows its way in and takes up residence in a dark place in your soul.

Two months after the novel failed to win the National Book Award, forty-eight black writers and critics wrote a letter to the *New York Times Book Review*, attributing the failure to "oversight and harmful whimsy." The novel went on to win the 1988 Pulitzer Prize and American Book Award.

"It seems to me there's an enormous difference in the writing of black and white women. Aggression is not as new to black women as it is to white women. Black women seem able to combine the nest and the adventure.... They are both safe harbor and ship; they are both inn and trail. We, black women, do both."

—TONI MORRISON, INTERVIEW FROM *BLACK WOMEN WRITERS AT WORK*, EDITED BY CLAUDIA TATE

THE ODD WOMAN

BY GAIL GODWIN

On a mid-January morning in the early nineteen-seventies, at 2 A.M., Central Standard Time, Jane Clifford lay awake in a Mid-western university town, thinking about insomnia: traditions of insomnia, all the people she knew who had it, the poets and artists and saints who left written testimonies of their sleeplessness.

JANE CLIFFORD ATTENDS her grandmother's funeral and takes stock of her own life. As she gazes at Edith, a "regal," "queenly," "invulnerable" figure, she observes: "Achieving death, Edith had rid herself at last of troublesome womanhood."

The eponymous "odd" (unpaired) woman, Jane is a professor of nineteenth-century literature, engaged in an ongoing affair with a married man. She yearns for the passion and romance of the century she studies. As stale as her real world is, her inner life is rich with fantasies straight out of gothic romance.

Light and witty, the novel takes place primarily in Jane's head. The women in her world (relatives, friends, and colleagues, both dead and alive) speak as voices in her mind, each promoting another feminine ideal. Aunt Edith shakes a bony virtual finger (through one of her fourteen pairs of white gloves), exhorting Jane to avoid the excesses indulged in by her great aunt Cleva who ran off with a villainous actor and died giving birth to his illegitimate daughter.

Unexpected sexual fulfillment brings Jane an epiphany and suddenly she knows that she wants more out of life—out of real life, that is.

"A hundred years from now, the current outpouring of feminist-inspired fiction will be of interest chiefly to social historians, who will wonder how we could have been so backward as to need so much instruction. . . . If one of those books is still being read for pleasure and enlightenment, I think it will be Gail Godwin's The Odd Woman."

—KATHA POLLITT, *NEW YORK TIMES*

A Clockwork Orange

BY ANTHONY BURGESS

What's it going to be then, eh? There was me, that is Alex, and my three droogs, that is Pete, Georgie, and Dim, Dim being really dim, and we sat in the Korova making up our rassoodocks what to do with the evening, a flip dark chill winter bastard though dry.

WELCOME TO THE future—the nightmare fantasy world of vicious, depraved delinquent Alex and his hoodlum friends, monsters who crave violence and kink it to suit their mood. In his world, space has been conquered but a profound social malaise lingers. Burgess creates a lexicon for his thugs, inventing terms like *rassoodock* (mind), *droogs* (gang members), *britva* (knife), *krovvy* (blood), and *cancers* (cigarettes).

Alex and his droogs select victims on a whim. At one point he rapes two ten-year-old kids, just for kicks. After one of his victims dies, he's put in prison where he becomes a Bible-thumping model prisoner, but reverts to type when he and his cellmates kill a new arrival.

Identified as the ringleader, Alex is forced to watch horrifying scenes of filmed violence until the mere whiff of aggression makes him sick. By the time he's "reconditioned," he can't even stand the Bible. Turned loose, he becomes a political pawn as he goes from being unthinkingly bad to being unthinkingly good. The moral: Evil occurs when the state robs citizens of their capacity for choice.

A reviewer aptly called the novel "a tour-de-force in nastiness." It is the best-known work of a prolific and versatile author.

"I call myself a serious novelist who is attempting to extend the range of subject matter available to fiction and a practitioner who is anxious to exploit words much as a poet does."

—ANTHONY BURGESS, *PARIS REVIEW* INTERVIEW

SILENT SPRING

BY RACHEL CARSON

There was once a town in the heart of America where all life seemed to live in harmony with its surroundings

WITH THIS NONFICTION, Rachel Carson rang alarm bells. We are slowly poisoning ourselves and Earth, she said, because "every human being is now subjected to contact with dangerous chemicals, from the moment of conception until death."

Once a marine biologist for the Fish and Wildlife Service, Carson's interest in the topic was sparked by a 1958 letter from a friend, telling of massive bird kills on Cape Cod after DDT sprayings. She could find no magazine interested in assigning her the story but she spent four years writing it anyway. In the book's most haunting chapter, "A Fable for Tomorrow," all life in a nameless town has been "silenced" by DDT.

When the book was serialized in 1962 in the *New Yorker*, the pesticide lobby threatened to sue. Failing that, they spent big bucks trying to discredit Carson's science. But in a 1963 report from President Kennedy's Science Advisory Committee, Carson's work was vindicated and that led to the banning of DDT. She became a sort of patron saint of the nascent environmental movement.

"Silent Spring *came as a cry in the wilderness, a deeply felt, thoroughly researched, and brilliantly written argument that changed the course of history. Without this book the environmental movement might have been long delayed or never developed at all.*"

—AL GORE, INTRODUCTION TO THE 1994 EDITION

THE GINGER MAN

BY J. P. DONLEAVY

Today a rare sun of spring. And horse carts clanging to the quays down Tara Street and the shoeless white faced kids screaming.

THIS RAUCOUS LITERARY autobiography introduced the world to the red-bearded Ginger Man, Sebastian Balfe Dangerfield, a roguish ex-GI studying law at Dublin's Trinity College. He's a barroom brawler and a hedonist who, according to one reviewer, gives "moral turpitude a new lease on life."

Dangerfield is a lecher who lives a squalid life with his wife, an upper-class Englishwoman, and his daughter. He's flunking out, up to his neck in debt, and drinks himself under the table nightly. The couple separate and he moves to London, a place much more to his liking.

This is a hilariously funny novel, rich with sexual adventures and misadventures. Despite the wild humor and zany situations, there's a serious core and commentary about the meaning of life and the power of sex.

Like his character, Bronx-born Donleavy flunked out of law school at Trinity where he was studying under the GI Bill after World War II. With this work, Donleavy achieved his avowed artistic goal: "To make your mother and father drop dead with shame." First published in 1955 after being rejected by more than thirty publishers, it came out in America in 1958, heavily censored. In 1965 an unexpurgated American edition was published. Never out of print, it has sold an estimated 50 million copies.

"The picaresque novel to stop them all."

—DOROTHY PARKER, *ESQUIRE*

THE MAGNIFICENT AMBERSONS

BY BOOTH TARKINGTON

Major Amberson had "made a fortune" in 1873, when other people were losing fortunes, and the magnificence of the Ambersons began then.

THE AMBERSONS ARE the richest of the rich, the most aristocratic family of any in their small midwestern town. The novel tells of George Amberson Minafer, grandson and only heir to Major Amberson's considerable fortune. He's heir, as well, to the family's considerable hubris.

At eight, when we first meet George, he is already full of himself and looking down his aquiline nose at his neighbors. Worshipped by a mother convinced of his heroic nobility, he is allowed to do whatever his little heart desires.

No surprise, he grows into an arrogant twenty-year-old with a prodigious sense of entitlement. Returning home on vacation, he falls deeply and disastrously in love with Lucy Morgan, an "independent, masterful, self-reliant little American" who is the daughter of his mother's friend. By then, more than a few wish fervently that one day he'll get "his comeuppance." And in the end, he does. Symbolically, with his downfall, the town itself grows increasingly industrialized and seems to become tarnished.

Tarkington wrote forty novels, many of them bestsellers, and about twenty plays. Raised in Indiana, he was brilliant at creating the world of small-town America (*Penrod*) and at capturing the love affairs of the young (*Seventeen*). In 1919, this novel was awarded the Pulitzer Prize. Two years later, he would win again for *Alice Adams*.

"Tarkington's an extraordinary writer. . . . He deserves to be taken much more seriously. If the movie of Ambersons *has any quality, a great part of it is due to Tarkington."*

—ORSON WELLES, INTERVIEW WITH PETER BOGDANOVICH, IN *THIS IS ORSON WELLES*

THE BONE PEOPLE

BY KERI HULME

*In the beginning, it was darkness, and more fear, and a howling
wind across the sea.*

SET IN NEW Zealand, this novel tells of despairing artist
Kerewin Holmes who can no longer create art. She builds herself a tower on the beach and crawls into its protective shell,
dreaming and drinking. She finds a discarded child's sandal on
the beach, and into her life comes Simon, a mute, silver-haired
little boy who was shipwrecked and rescued by locals. Young
Simon's body is covered with keloid scars from where his
embittered Maori foster father, Joe, has beaten him.

This unusual novel is woven through with dreams, myth,
magic, the world of the dead, and the traditions of ancient cultures. The subject matter can be harrowing—as in a grimly
detailed assault on this autistic child. But ultimately the message
is one of hope, as Kerewin, Simon, and Joe find common ground
in a bond of support and interdependence.

Hulme explains what she was about in writing this very
unusual novel: "I . . . was getting my head straight on questions
like what happens to outcasts, outsiders. What would happen
if a Maori spiritual presence was resurrected in this land of
ours?"

Hulme spent twelve years writing this novel and then was
unable to find a mainstream press to publish it. Published by a
small feminist New Zealand publishing collective, it sold out
its initial print run in six weeks and went on to become the most
successful novel in New Zealand publishing history.

"Novel no one wanted takes the Booker Prize."
—*GUARDIAN* HEADLINE, NOVEMBER 1, 1985

THE WORLD ACCORDING TO GARP

BY JOHN IRVING

Garp's mother, Jenny Fields, was arrested in Boston in 1942 for wounding a man in a movie theater.

THE HERO OF this novel is novelist T. S. Garp, a Job upon whom every version of disaster rains. He is the bastard son of a nurse who wants to live alone and support herself. Even more suspect, she says, "I wanted a baby, but I don't want to share my body or life to have one."

Known around the hospital where she works as Virgin Mary Jenny, she gets a dying, nearly comatose war veteran to impregnate her. Later she turns into a feminist hero. In one of the novel's many imaginative scenes, Garp gets himself up in drag to attend her funeral.

At the novel's core is a horrifying car crash that destroys a child, partially blinds another, and leaves the bodies and memories of all those involved permanently scarred. Though Garp's one overwhelming wish has been to make his family and the world safe, his own reckless driving is at fault.

In an interview Irving explained, "My idea was to subject likeable characters with their worst fears, which is the height of paranoia. The stupid randomness of violence makes us all vulnerable."

The novel has been hailed for its wild inventiveness and rude humor. Is it a feminist tract? An allegorical horror story? The National Book Critics deemed it a stellar work, nominating it for its fiction award in 1978.

"I kept reading to find out what would happen next and when it had all finally happened I didn't want it to stop. So I read it again, and it seemed just as true the second time around, as full of the hilarity of survival as the pain, an X-rated soap opera that runs from the ridiculous to the sublime."

—WILLIAM McPHERSON,
WASHINGTON POST BOOKWORLD

THE BERLIN STORIES

BY CHRISTOPHER ISHERWOOD

My first impression was that the stranger's eyes were of an unusually light blue.

TWO INTERRELATED novellas are bound together into a single volume. They share characters and are both set in Berlin in early 1930s Weimar Germany. Each is narrated by a pleasant enough English fellow, a writer who makes his living by giving language lessons.

In *The Last of Mr. Norris*, William Bradshaw is on a train when he meets Mr. Norris, a prissy Englishman with a taste for bad hairpieces. Norris, who runs a sketchy import-export business, initiates Bradshaw into Berlin's murky nightlife including mistresses of S&M, Anni and Olga. As the Nazis rise to power, Norris beats a hasty retreat to South Africa with his blackmailing secretary Schmidt in hot pursuit.

Goodbye to Berlin is a series of vignettes centered in the narrator's rooming house where Fraulein Schroeder presides over a cast of colorful residents that include, of course, Sally Bowles. A modestly talented, naively optimistic nineteen-year-old nightclub singer, Sally is an English expat and an easy mark. She yearns for a big break and, in the meanwhile, would settle for a very rich man. As one critic remarked, "A better short study of a woman deliberately destroying herself would be hard to find." The novel was adapted into the musical and movie *Cabaret*.

The narrator watches: "I am a camera with its shutter open, quite passive, recording, not thinking." He records a brief flowering of culture and freedom before the Nazis ended what they considered decadence and vice.

"Just as much as his literary fame, Christopher Isherwood's personal candor qualifies him for his unsolicited role as Hero Emeritus of the modern gay movement."

—ARMISTEAD MAUPIN, *VILLAGE VOICE*

THE KON TIKI EXPEDITION

BY THOR HEYERDAHL

Once in a while you find yourself in an odd situation.

NORWEGIAN SAILOR/SCIENTIST/ANTHROPOLOGIST Thor Heyerdahl undertook a great adventure and captured the world's imagination when he embarked on a 4,300-mile sail across the Pacific on a primitive raft made of balsa wood. His aim was to prove that ancient people from pre-Columbian times *could have* settled Polynesia. If they had, he argued, the knowledge the pyramid builders would have brought with them accounts for the mysterious stone statues on Easter Island.

Heyerdahl christened his vessel *Kon Tiki*, after the Inca sun god. On April 28, 1947, he and five other men and a green parrot sailed from Peru. A hundred and one days later, their raft crash-landed on the Polynesia coral island of Raroia. He'd proved his point.

The book reads more like a novel than a true-life adventure, and its success transformed Heyerdahl into a popular hero. Later he sailed a papyrus boat across the Atlantic and a reed boat across the Indian Ocean to "prove" his controversial theories of early seafaring migrations.

When novelist William Styron was a young, poorly paid reader for McGraw-Hill, he rejected this classic adventure story. Stingo, the narrator of Styron's *Sophie's Choice*, repeats the gaffe.

"Their saga, told by the expedition's organizer, is a revelation of how exciting science can become when it inspires a man with the heart of a Leif Ericsson and the merry story-telling gift of an Ernie Pyle."

—HARRY GILROY, *NEW YORK TIMES*

ALL THE PRETTY HORSES

BY CORMAC McCARTHY

The candleflame and the image of the candleflame caught in the pierglass twisted and righted when he entered the hall and again when he shut the door.

WHEN HIS GRANDFATHER dies, sixteen-year-old John Grady Cole has no reason to stay in Texas. His parents are separated, his invalid father has bidden him goodbye, and his grandfather's ranch is about to be sold. Grady convinces his buddy Lacey Rawlins to ride on horseback with him to Mexico. They are joined, for a while, by young sharpshooter Jimmy Blevins, whose hot temper and stolen horse foreshadow trouble.

The pair ride on to the Hacienda de Nuestra Señora de la Purísima Concepción. There, Grady's talent for breaking and understanding horses earns him his keep, but his innocence and ignorance get him into trouble. He falls for the lovely rebellious Alejandra, daughter of the hacienda's owner. But it's a hopeless match. Her father, the aristocratic Don Hector, and his austere aunt will have none of it. They conspire to have Grady and Rawlins arrested for murder and horse theft, crimes Blevins committed.

This dark, pessimistic story explores the nature of good and evil. Reviewers compare McCarthy's literary themes of masculinity to Hemingway's and his lush prose to Faulkner's. McCarthy's sixth novel and the first volume in his "Border Trilogy," this won the 1992 National Book Award and the National Book Critics Circle Award.

"The deity that presides over Mr. McCarthy's world has not modeled itself on humanity; its voice most resembles the one that addressed Job out of the whirlwind."

—MADISON SMARTT BELL, *NEW YORK TIMES*

A TREE GROWS IN BROOKLYN

BY BETTY SMITH

APR.
30
ARBOR DAY

Serene was a word you could put to Brooklyn, New York.

FRANCIE NOLAN GROWS up in impoverished, turn-of-the-century Williamsburg. It's the first two decades of the twentieth century, and like her Irish and German and Italian immigrant neighbors, her family struggles for survival. Francie and her brother forage in garbage, looking for something they can exchange for a few pennies at the pawnshop.

This novel is Francie's story, and it teems with unforgettable characters. There's Francie's father, the doomed Johnny Nolan, singing waiter and hopeless drunk; her mother, the steely Katie, who scrubs floors and makes stale bread into a glorious meal; easy Aunt Sissy, who calls all her men John; and Francie, who buries herself in books, hungering for beauty and yearning for a better life. Francie is like this novel's repeating image, the "Tree of Heaven" that grows out of a crack in the sidewalk in front of the family home. "Some people call it the tree of heaven. It grows in boarded-up lots and out of neglected rubbish-heaps. . . . It is the only tree that grows out of cement."

This autobiographical novel paints a grim, unsparing picture of immigrant life. Death, failure, violence, alcoholism, and the daily grind of poverty get their due. And yet there is humor, love, understanding, and courageous vitality in this family.

Published in 1943, the book was a success, rocketing to instant celebrity an unknown divorcée who was struggling to raise two daughters and pay her rent.

"Literary justice has at last been done to Brooklyn, at least the Williamsburg section of Brooklyn."

—ORVILLE PRESCOTT, *NEW YORK TIMES*

May

THE AMERICAN

BY HENRY JAMES

On a brilliant day in May, in the year 1868, a gentleman was reclining at his ease on the great circular divan which at that period occupied the centre of the Salon Carré, in the Museum of the Louvre.

THE AMERICAN OF the title, an innocent abroad, is Christopher Newman. He's an awkward, wealthy, fundamentally goodhearted, recently retired businessman. He goes to Paris, eager to absorb the culture. At the Louvre, his attention is caught by the pretty but trifling Noémie Nioche, but he falls in love with elegant, aristocratic Claire de Cintré, whom he meets at a friend's home.

Claire's younger brother, Valentin, approves of the match. But her mother and her brother Urbain strongly disapprove. They can tolerate Newman's money but not his common American ways. His efforts to win them over by appealing to their good nature with his own go for naught.

Claire enters a convent, forever to be walled off from the man who loves her. Meanwhile, her brother Valentin is killed during a duel over the flighty Noémie. At his death, Valentin reveals to Newman that his mother and brother murdered his father. Newman finds documents incriminating the pair. At the last moment, rather than sacrifice his essential goodness, he turns away from vengeance against those who robbed him of his beloved.

James wrote this novel when he was living in France. It was published as a book in 1877 and extensively revised and published again in 1907.

"Romance? Melodrama? Balzac novel? Comedy of manners? Tragedy? Black farce? Like Newman's eye, you can find in [The American] almost anything you look for."

—ADRIAN POOLE, INTRODUCTION TO THE
1991 (OXFORD UNIVERSITY PRESS) EDITION

DELIVERANCE

BY JAMES DICKEY

*It unrolled slowly, forced to show its colors, curling and snapping
back whenever one of us turned loose.*

FOUR MIDDLE-AGED GUYS from the suburbs are determined
to prove their manliness by pitting themselves against nature
in this 1970 novel. Two of them—a mutual-fund salesman and
a soft-drink executive—are spectacularly unprepared for what
would be even the fittest athlete's worst nightmare. Only Lewis
is experienced and physically prepared for what they are about
to undertake. Whitewater is the test.

They embark on a canoe trip through a lawless wilderness.
The treacherous, soon-to-be-dammed river with its boiling currents seem to pull a boat in several directions at once. On the
second day out, a pair of hillbillies saunter out of the woods
with shotguns and perpetrate the kind of mayhem that would
delight good old Alex of *Clockwork Orange*. A bad situation
grows hopeless with rapids crashing and bullets flying between
gorgeous cliffs of sheer granite.

Dickey mused about this masterpiece of suspense: "A snake
can bite you and you can die before you could get treatment.
There are men in those remote parts that'd just as soon kill you
as look at you. And you could turn into a counter-monster
yourself, doing whatever you felt compelled to do to survive."

This was the first novel from the author of twenty volumes
of poetry. The *New York Times* called him a "two-fisted poet."
Dickey also wrote the screenplay for the stunning 1972
movie.

*"Unless you're a natural-born sourpuss—or maybe resent the notion
that a celebrated poet could one day up and write a novel and produce
a crackerjack—you'll suspend disbelief, you'll buy the story and you'll
love it."*

—CHRISTOPHER LEHMANN-HAUPT, *NEW YORK TIMES*

LOVING

BY HENRY GREEN

Once upon a day an old butler called Eldon lay dying in his room attended by the head housemaid, Miss Agatha Burch.

THIS UPSTAIRS-DOWNSTAIRS TALE opens with the head butler crying out for "Ellen" as he lies dying in his bedroom in a cavernous Irish castle. Outside the castle walls, peacocks strut and screech; outside the butler's door lurks First Footman Charley Raunce, eager to nip in and make off with the dying man's treasured notebooks that reveal how to skim wealth from the castle's guests and finances.

"And the wicked shall flourish even as a green bay tree," declares the housekeeper as Mr. Raunce, the notebooks procured, takes the old butler's place at the head of the servants' table.

Liaisons are revealed—upstairs and down. Mrs. Jack, daughter of the English owner Mrs. Tennant, is involved in a passionate affair with Captain Davenport. Downstairs, apprentice footman Albert is lovesick for housemaid Edie who, in turn, has set her beady little eyes upon Raunce, while housemaid Kate is obsessed with the idea of being in love.

Fifty years ago, the pseudonymous Henry Green (Henry Yorke) was one of the best-known fiction writers around. *Loving*, his seventh novel, is considered one of his best. A wealthy, intensely private British aristocrat, he said he chose the name Green for its blandness.

"[He] is there at the center of what he writes, but in effect his identity has turned into fiction. And while you, the reader, know nothing of Mr. Henry Green's life, as he has taken good care to see to, in the long run a life's confidence is what you feel you have been given."

—EUDORA WELTY

THE SEA, THE SEA

BY IRIS MURDOCH

The sea which lies before me as I write glows rather than sparkles in the bland May sunshine.

CHARLES ARROWBY, AN esteemed but arrogant man of London's theater world, retires and sequesters himself at his seaside home on the south coast of England. Intending to "abjure magic and become a hermit," he leaves all vestiges of his former life behind. Every day he swims in the "blessed northern sea," hoping to be washed clean.

Instead of finding seals frolicking by the shore, he is haunted by a strange sea monster. Instead of finding solitude, he is visited by a steady stream of friends, former lovers, and actors still awed by his power and bullying presence, many of whom he's invited to come.

His thoughts turn back to Hartley, the woman who was his first love. When he was twenty, she jilted him. Now, forty years later, he stumbles upon her in a nearby town. Determined to save her and her son from ordinary pain and ordinary lives, he holds her against her will, threatens to kill her husband, and indirectly causes her son to drown. Only by giving up his delusion and relinquishing power can he find peace.

The prolific British novelist's nineteenth novel, this is considered her major work. It won the 1978 Booker Prize.

"[Iris Murdoch] was beautifully patient with stuff [of life], putting it all down in a steady harvest, a student of philosophy and the classics, alert to the ripples and quirks of contemporary life, a word child who, confident of being loved, could afford to lavish her attention on everything around her."

—JOHN UPDIKE, *NEW YORKER*

LIKE WATER FOR CHOCOLATE

BY LAURA ESQUIVEL

Tita was so sensitive to onions, any time they were being chopped, they say, she would just cry and cry; when was still in my great-grandmother's belly her sobs were so loud that even Nacha, the cook, who was half-deaf, could hear them easily.

WORDS SEEM TO literally smolder on the page of this Mexican author's exuberant first novel. A tribute to the senses, it combines magical realism, seething eroticism, and food to concoct a sensual feast.

Set in turn-of-the-century Mexico at a ranch near the Texas border, this is the story of Tita, the youngest of three sisters. It is narrated by Tita's grand-niece in monthly chapters that each begin with an extravagant recipe. The one for turkey mole starts: "Fifteen days before the turkey is to be killed, begin feeding it small walnuts."

The novel opens with Tita's premature birth on a table in a kitchen redolent with the smell of onions and simmering noodle soup. Tita's life will center around the kitchen, the domain of her guardian angel, Nacha the cook. As the youngest, she cannot marry until her older sisters are hitched, and the thankless job of caring for their termagant mother in her old age falls to her. When Tita discovers that her mother has cruelly promised her beloved Pedro to her sister Rosaura, she becomes unhinged.

Wildly imaginative, this was honored in 1994 as the novel ABA booksellers most enjoyed recommending.

"Cooking is a sacred activity. It is an act of lovemaking."

—LAURA ESQUIVEL

Sense and Sensibility

BY JANE AUSTEN

The family of Dashwood had been long settled in Sussex.

"*THERE WERE NEVER such devoted sisters. . . . *" This is a tale of two heroines, sisters of opposite temperament. Marianne Dashwood ("I must feel—I must be wretched.") is afflicted by a surfeit of "sensibility." Her older sister Elinor's sensibility is straitjacketed with a surfeit of "sense."

Austen's first novel, published in 1811 with "A Lady" as the author on the title page, it tells of Mrs. Dashwood and her daughters. They are summarily turned out of their home when Mr. Dashwood dies. Rescued and provided for by distant relative Sir John Middleton, they move to Devonshire to live in Barton Cottage. (Austen and her sisters were rescued from a similar plight and given lodging by Edward Knight.)

Both fall in love and are inexplicably forsaken. Unbeknownst to Elinor, her beloved, Edward Ferrars, long ago rashly promised himself to the unsuitable and vulgar Lucy Steele. His mother finds out and promptly disinherits him. Despite this, Edward vows to make good his promise to Lucy. Marianne's beloved is the charming, worldly John Willoughby. She tumbles down a hill on the grounds of his estate and he becomes her knight in shining armor, carrying her home.

It turns out that affairs of the heart can be as easily capsized by rationality as by emotion. Elinor pretends she feels nothing for Edward. When Willoughby returns Marianne's beseeching letters and she discovers that he is engaged to a wealthy heiress, she nearly dies in a downward spiral of sickness and despair. Only her own good sense and her family's love save her.

"*In Jane Austen's novels . . . women don't faint unless they have real reason to.*"

—CAROL SHIELDS, *JANE AUSTEN*

POSSESSION: A ROMANCE

BY A. S. BYATT

The book was thick and black and covered with dust.

THIS NOVEL IS a double-decker love story—a pair of star-crossed Victorian poets and a pair of modern-day academicians—wrapped up in a literary mystery.

The Victorian poets are Randolph Henry Ash and Christabel LaMotte (think: Robert Browning and Christina Rossetti). He is a major literary icon. She is a "fairy poet" whom modern feminist scholars have tried to elevate into a lesbian role model.

The modern academics are Roland Mitchell and Maud Bailey. He's a struggling scholar, toiling in the London Library. There he uncovers drafts of two letters sent by Ash to an unknown woman. The letters suggest a tantalizing what-if: Could these be Ash's love letters to the legendary LaMotte? Were the two engaged in a clandestine love affair? The major discovery could breathe life into Mitchell's academic career.

A feminist academic and the leading LaMotte scholar, Bailey is intrigued by the possibility that LaMotte was neither a lesbian nor the chaste spinster she claimed to be. Bailey joins Mitchell, and the pair become "possessed" by their discovery. They soon find that they have more in common than a love of Victorian poetry.

To make this fictional world believable, Byatt penned more than a thousand lines of "Victorian" poetry and scores of period letters and journal pages. Surprisingly, it's a page-turner. Published in 1990, it won Britain's prestigious Booker Prize.

"I'm interested in feminist themes, women's freedom. Literary feminism is a much more dubious thing."

—A. S. BYATT

THE SHELTERING SKY

BY PAUL BOWLES

He awoke, opened his eyes. The room meant very little to him; he was too deeply immersed in the non-being from which he had just come.

IN THIS NOVEL of dislocation published in 1949 and set in the shadow of World War II, a trio of New York intellectuals journey to North Africa seeking oblivion. Port Moresby wants to escape to a part of the world untouched by war, somewhere free of the "taint" of Europe. There he hopes to find respite from "infinite sadness" and despair. His neurotic wife Kit accompanies him, hoping to rekindle the love that she believes they once had for one another. Their shallow friend, Tunner, comes along, hoping to seduce Kit.

Their journey begins in Oran, the Algerian city that is the setting for Albert Camus's *The Plague*. They walk Saharan Africa's dark streets and into its scorching deserts and immerse themselves in alien landscapes and cultures. The vast emptiness of the place echoes the emptiness of their souls.

At just the moment when Port and his wife may be finally reconnecting, he contracts typhoid fever. Kit abandons him as he nears death, and wanders on like a sleepwalker. On her own now, she encounters violence and finally madness.

This was the well-known composer's first novel, written when he was thirty-eight. Bowles first visited Tangier in 1931 at the suggestion of Gertrude Stein and lived there for fifty years. Christopher Isherwood borrowed his name for his character, Sally Bowles.

"I suspect that a good many people will read this book and be enthralled by it without once suspecting that it contains a mirror of what is most terrifying and cryptic within the Sahara of moral nihilism, into which the race of man now seems to be wandering blindly."
—TENNESSEE WILLIAMS, *NEW YORK TIMES BOOK REVIEW*

WINESBURG, OHIO

BY SHERWOOD ANDERSON

The writer, an old man with a white mustache, had some difficulty getting into bed.

THIS CELEBRATED BOOK presents a series of devastating, loosely connected short stories and sketches. The fulcrum is George Willard, a young reporter, who becomes the confidant of the town's odd assortment of inhabitants. The result is an episodic portrait of life in small-town rural Midwest.

These are stories of wasted lives and wasted loves as Anderson's "grotesques," isolated from their communities, undertake their own idiosyncratic search for meaning. In "Paper Pills," for example, we meet Doctor Reefy, an isolated physician who prescribes medication for himself. He scribbles his innermost thoughts and feelings on rolled-up papers that he squirrels away in his pockets. He calls these "paper pills" his "pyramids of truth."

The book was first published in 1919 at the opening of the "machine age." With it, Anderson dramatized, in intensely personal terms, the impact of the shift from farm to industry in middle America and a yearning for lost community. (Sinclair Lewis's *Main Street* would be published a year later.)

Winesburg is modeled after Clyde, Ohio, where Anderson grew up. Though linked with the greats of his era like Sinclair Lewis and Theodore Dreiser, Anderson is less well remembered. Ray Bradbury credited *Winesburg, Ohio* as the inspiration for his *Martian Chronicles*.

"Into his brief pages Anderson not only gets brilliant images of men and women who walk in all the colors of reality; he also gets a profound sense of the obscure, inner dramas of their lives."

—H. L. MENCKEN, *SMART SET CRITICISM*

White Noise

BY DON DeLILLO

*The station wagons arrived at noon, a long shining line that
coursed through the west campus.*

HITLER, POISONOUS SNAKES, and above all, the specter of
death cavort across the nightmarish pages of this satiric 1985
novel. This is the story of the Gladneys. Jack Gladney chairs
the Hitler Studies department at a small college and teaches
courses like "Advanced Nazism." His son, whom he named
Heinrich, has a best friend who is trying to break the Guinness
World Record for time spent sitting in a cage full of deadly
snakes. Jack's friend Murray is trying to get a department of
Elvis Studies started. And Jack's wife Babette, who tends the
children from their assorted previous marriages, lectures adults
on good posture.

The Gladneys' life rolls off its bizarre but pedestrian rails
when a tanker in a nearby railyard is punctured. Nyodene
Derivative is released, growing quickly into an "airborne toxic
event." Jack is exposed to the poisonous gases when he has to
fill up the car in order to evacuate his family to an abandoned
Boy Scout camp. Contaminated and now "tentatively scheduled
to die," he becomes obsessed with death.

Babette admits that death terrifies her, too. She's become
addicted to a fear-allaying experimental drug, Dylar. To ensure
a supply, she's been having sex with Willie Mink, the drug company salesman. Jack is desperate to take the drug, too, but
Babette won't reveal her source.

What would you give, the novel asks us to imagine, to be
freed from the fear of death?

*"Don DeLillo has . . . supplanted both Pynchon and Mailer as chief
shaman of the paranoid school of American fiction. Beginning as a
fantasist, he has moved stealthily toward realism while retaining a dark
and at times prophetic vision of occult conspiracies and correspon-
dences and technology-gone-mad."*

—ROBERT TOWERS, *NEW YORK REVIEW OF BOOKS*

MAMA DAY

BY GLORIA NAYLOR

You were picking your teeth with a plastic straw—I know, I know, it wasn't really a straw, it was a coffee stirrer.

OPHELIA (COCOA) BRINGS George—her New York citified husband, who spent his childhood in a homeless shelter in Harlem and worked his way through school—home with her on her annual summer holiday to the Georgia sea island of Willow Springs. The isolated black community is connected to the mainland by a bridge so rickety that it frequently washes out in storms.

Mama Day, a modern-day "conjure woman," awaits them there. She is nearly a hundred years old, knows the secrets of herbal healing, and lightning does her bidding. She is a direct descendant of Sapphira Wade, a full-blooded African who married her master, bore him seven sons, then killed him and escaped, "laughing in a burst of flames." Cocoa is the only daughter born to those seven sons. Mama Day senses a grave danger for Cocoa, one that only great sacrifice can avert.

In chapters written alternately from Cocoa's and George's point of view, this sassy, spirited, wise book transports the reader into a world of ritual and mysticism, black folk and spiritual lore, leading inexorably to a devastating finish.

Naylor credits Toni Morrison's *The Bluest Eye* with giving her the courage to write. This 1988 novel was her third, and is far more complex and dark than her award-winning first novel, *The Women of Brewster Place*.

"Recent novels like Mama Day . . . *resonate with the genuine excitement of authors discovering ways, for the first time it seems, to write down what had only been intuited or heard."*

—BHARATI MUKHERJEE, *NEW YORK TIMES*

THE COLOR OF WATER

BY JAMES McBRIDE

I'm dead. You want to talk about my family and here I been dead to them for fifty years.

THIS IS BIOGRAPHICAL and autobiographical work by a black musician, composer, and writer. In a profound and nuanced story about race and survival, he tells of his own upbringing and his mother tells of her fierce struggle to raise her family and assure her children's success.

Ruth McBride Jordan, once known as Rachel Deborah Shilsky, was the daughter of an Orthodox rabbi. She grew up in a violently racist and anti-Semitic Virginia town in a household dominated by her father. She fled north to the Jewish Bronx, and then to Harlem to marry black musician, Andrew D. McBride. In 1940s New York, she began a new life as a Christian. She and her husband founded an all-black Baptist church in a Brooklyn project. Her reception in the black community was tentative and muted, at best.

James was the youngest of their eight children. After his father died, his mother married again—this time to a kindly, stolid black fireman who worked for the housing authority. They had four more children before she was widowed again.

McBride was six years old when he asked his mother if she was black. She replied, "I'm light-skinned," and changed the subject. He says, "I just desperately wanted her to be black like all my friends' mothers, and she wasn't. And on top of that, she was just peculiar. She did weird things. She spoke Yiddish. . . ."

Confused, he asked his mother, "What color is God's spirit?" Her answer: "It doesn't have a color. God is the color of water."

"I hope that people will see through her life what the possibilities are when you just forget about the differences and deal with the commonalities."

—JAMES McBRIDE

GROWING UP

BY RUSSELL BAKER

At the age of eighty my mother had her last bad fall, and after that her mind wandered free through time. . . .

RUSSELL BAKER'S CHILDHOOD was, by any measure, harrowing. From profound adversity, Baker developed that sense of humor that informed all of his writing.

His parents were married after he was conceived. After a round of drinking, his stonemason father fell into a diabetic coma and died. Baker was only five years old. His mother reluctantly gave his younger sister to childless in-laws and moved young Russell and another sister in with an odd assortment of relatives in Newark. Later, the family moved to a Baltimore apartment above a funeral parlor that gave off a powerful smell of boiled shrimp and embalming fluid and where Baker survived threats and beatings from bullies.

With gentle wit and fondness, the great satirical commentator remembers his small town boyhood and especially his mother. Determined that he not grow up like his father "and his people, with calluses on their hands, overalls on their backs, and fourth-grade educations in their heads," she found Baker a job selling the *Saturday Evening Post* door to door. He detested it. When he brought home an A on a seventh-grade composition, she decided that maybe he could be a writer. And so he was. His droll "Observer" column appeared regularly in the *New York Times*.

This book won the Pulitzer in 1983 and went on to become one of those rare award winners that people read just for the fun of it.

"[Growing Up is] a classic book about growing up in the Depression, demonstrating that a good memoir is also a work of history, catching a distinctive moment in the life of both a person and a society."

—WILLIAM ZINSSER, INTRODUCTION TO
INVENTING THE TRUTH

THE STONE DIARIES

BY CAROL SHIELDS

My mother's name was Mercy Stone Goodwill. She was only thirty years old when she took sick, a boiling hot day, standing in her back kitchen, making Malvern pudding for her husband's supper.

MASQUERADING AS A diary complete with period photos and a family tree, this 1993 novel tells of Daisy Stone Goodwill's life. The "diary" leaps forward in decade-wide bounds, revealing Daisy's home-centered life. Her mother dies when she's an infant, and Daisy goes to live with Clarentine Flett, a botanist as obsessed with the western ladyslipper as Daisy's mother was with food in general and Malvern pudding in particular.

Her foster mother dies. Daisy's first husband, a young botanist who finds his passion in cataloging orchids and with whom she has three children, kills himself. Daisy takes over writing his horticulture column. She loves writing as Mrs. Green Thumb and adores her marvelous home garden ("English in its charm, French in its orderliness, Japanese in its economy.").

The author tells us, over and over, this is an average, ordinary life. Despite tragedy on tragedy, through marriages, motherhood, widowhood, work, and finally illness, this is a cheerful tale, imbued with the hope of Daisy's lists, like her "Must Do's Long Term." At sixty, she realizes with a pang, "Somewhere along the line she made the decision to live outside of events; or else that decision was made for her."

This understated story of a woman's life, told in gorgeous prose and through the accretion of vivid detail, won the 1995 Pulitzer and the 1994 National Book Critics Circle awards.

"[T]he heroine of this novel passes through her life without ever fully occupying it—an absence that this beautiful and haunting book attempts to redeem."

—PENELOPE LIVELY

THE JOY LUCK CLUB

BY AMY TAN

My father has asked me to be the fourth corner at the
Joy Luck Club.

IN THIS TAPESTRY of interwoven stories of four Chinese
immigrants and their first-generation Chinese American daughters, seven characters narrate, celebrating the joys and frustra-
tions of a generational and cultural gap.

When Suyuan Woo dies, her daughter June reluctantly
takes her place in the Joy Luck Club and at the mahjong table
with her mother's three aging "aunties." They are among the
millions of dislocated Chinese, part of the diaspora cut off from
the mainland after 1949 and the Communist triumph. June
feels odd and out of place at the table with these women in their
"funny Chinese dresses." The old customs they maintain make
her uncomfortable. But soon, June suspects there are "unspeakable tragedies they had left behind."

With the help of the Joy Luck Club, June journeys to China
to complete a mission her mother could not.

The book began as a short story that Tan wrote when she
was working as a technical writer. It was published in a literary
magazine, then in *Seventeen*, and found its way into the hands
of a literary agent. Tan wrote a proposal for a novel based on
the story and traveled to China with her mother to discover a
heritage that had destroyed much of its own past. In 1989 this
was nominated for the National Book Award.

"While we as readers grope to know whose mother or grandmother is
getting married in an unfamiliar ceremony, or why a concubine is com-
mitting suicide, we are ironically being reminded not just of the night-
marishness of being a woman in traditional China, but of the enormity
of the confusing mental journey Chinese emigrants had to make."

—ORVILLE SCHELL, *NEW YORK TIMES*

HOUSEKEEPING

BY MARILYNNE ROBINSON

My name is Ruth. I grew up with my younger sister, Lucille, under the care of my grandmother, Mrs. Sylvia Foster, and when she died, of her sisters-in-law, Misses Lily and Nona Foster, and when they fled, of her daughter, Mrs. Sylvia Fisher.

THIS NOVEL OPENS with a "spectacular derailment"—a train plunges into a lake in the town of Fingerbone. "The train, which was black and sleek and elegant, and was called the Fireball, had pulled more than halfway across the bridge when the engine nosed over toward the lake and then the rest of the train slid after it into the water like a weasel sliding off a rock."

One of three women widowed in the wake of the crash is the grandmother of sisters Ruth and Lucille. The tragedy echoes years later when their mother abandons the girls on their grandmother's front porch and drives her car into the same lake.

Grandma is ill equipped to care for the girls. Aunt Sylvie, their mother's sister who appears and takes over, is even less so. Her notions of childrearing and housekeeping are eccentric in the extreme, and soon the house is overrun with newspapers, small animals, and leaves. The girls are terrified that Sylvie will disappear, too, since she "seldom removed her coat, and every story she told had to do with a train or bus station."

This eloquent novel about transience challenges the virtues of domestic order and suggests that homelessness isn't necessarily about not having a home. It won the 1981 Hemingway Foundation/PEN award.

"Housekeeping *is very definitely going somewhere—that is, has a plot and characters to carry it out. But author Marilynne Robinson uses the language so exquisitely, we would have to say that this book dances all the way.*"

—CAROLYN BANKS, *WASHINGTON POST BOOK WORLD*

ALL OVER BUT THE SHOUTIN'

BY RICK BRAGG

My mother and father were born in the most beautiful place on earth, in the foothills of the Appalachians along the Alabama-Georgia line.

IN THIS MEMOIR of a hardscrabble youth, a poor Southern white boy commemorates a mother who went eighteen years without buying herself a new dress so that her kids would be well fed and have decent clothes to wear to school.

When Bragg was a toddler, his mother picked cotton. She dragged him through the fields behind her on a burlap bag, riding "the back of a six-foot-long sack like a magic carpet." He recalls her guiding spirit: "Of all the lessons my mother tried to teach me, the most important was that every life deserves a certain amount of dignity, no matter how poor or damaged the shell that carries it."

The memoir begins in Bragg's boyhood in the foothills of Appalachia. He was the kind of little boy who buried bits of crumpled tinfoil under the family shack so he could dig them up again as treasure. His father, a tormented Korean War vet, was a hard drinker with a violent temper who rarely kept his promises to the family that depended on him.

Sheer talent, prodigious hard work, and good luck got Bragg through a stint at Harvard, a job at a local newspaper, and ultimately a career at the *New York Times*. His feature writing won him the Pulitzer Prize in 1996 at the age of thirty-six. Published a year later, this book will have you laughing between the sobs.

"Pulitzer prize-winning journalist and Southern writer Rick Bragg writes memoirs that read like music—Southern music that he makes powerfully universal."

—TOM ASHBROOK, *ON THE POINT*, NPR

LIFE OF PI

BY YANN MARTEL

My suffering left me sad and gloomy. Academic study and the steady, mindful practice of religion slowly brought me back to life.

THIS IS ONE of literature's more bizarre, surprising, enchanting, and ultimately profound novels. Its protagonist is Piscine Molitor Patel, a boy growing up in Pondicherry, India. Fed up with the nickname "Pissing," he christens himself "Pi." His parents run the zoo.

In Part 1, Pi searches for God. To his father's exasperation, he becomes a religious seeker. "We're a modern Indian family: we live in a modern way; India is on the cusp of becoming a truly modern and advanced nation—and here we've produced a son who thinks he's the reincarnation of Sri Ramakrishna." (Ramakrishna was the nineteenth-century Hindu leader who demonstrated the essential unity of all religions.) Pi becomes a devout disciple of Hinduism, Christianity, and Islam, until the pandit, the priest, and the imam get wise.

Pi's father has difficulties with the new Gandhi government, and when the zoo closes the family sets sail for Canada with animals destined for zoos around the world. Part 2 begins, "The ship sank."

Pi is cast adrift on a lifeboat, "three and a half feet deep, eight feet wide and twenty-six feet long, exactly," with a zebra, a hyena, an orangutan, and a huge Bengal tiger named Richard Parker. Only his animal training expertise saves him from becoming tiger food during the ensuing 227-day struggle for survival.

This was Canadian author Martel's third book and won the 2002 Booker Prize.

"Martel writes with such convincing immediacy, seasoning his narrative with zoological verisimilitude and survival tips about turtle-fishing, solar stills and keeping occupied, that disbelief is suspended, like Pi, above the terrible depths of the Pacific Ocean."

—JUSTINE JORDAN, *GUARDIAN*

LONESOME DOVE

BY LARRY McMURTRY

When Augustus came out on the porch the blue pigs were eating a rattlesnake—not a very big one.

THIS POPULAR NOVEL with a heart as big as the Texas sky is no clichéd myth of the American West. In it, a pair of aging antiheroes leads an 1870s cattle drive to Montana from the Texas town of Lonesome Dove, a widish spot in the road near the Mexican border.

A pair of retired Texas Rangers—white-haired, easygoing, hard-drinking Augustus McCrae and stiff, formal, solitary Captain Woodrow Call—have been living a quiet life, running a livery stable when Jake Spoon shows up with a proposition. Their charming but unreliable friend, who's running from murder charges in Arkansas, wants them to help him with a cattle raid south of the border and then drive the herd north.

They agree to what they suspect will be their last joint adventure. Traveling northward, hoping to tame yet another frontier, they encounter Lorena Wood, a world-weary but vulnerable prostitute, and Comanche Blue Duck, a character as evil as any in the pages of fiction. Their epic journey is fraught with danger and death as well as comic brawls and a scourge of locusts.

The prolific McMurtry (*Hud*, *The Last Picture Show*, and *Terms of Endearment*) comes from a large west Texas family that he has described as "cowboys first and last." This novel was published in 1985 and went on to win the Pulitzer.

"It occurred to me in Lonesome Dove *that the men who drove the cattle up the trail were in the process of killing the very thing they loved. They knew it, and the knowledge lent poignancy to what they were doing, and their memories of it."*

—LARRY McMURTRY

THE KITE RUNNER

BY KHALED HOSSEINI

I became what I am today at the age of twelve, on a frigid over-cast day in the winter of 1975.

THIS STORY OF betrayal is set in Afghanistan against the fall of the Afghan monarchy, the Soviet invasion, the mass exodus of refugees, and the rise of the Taliban. Amir, a privileged Afghan youth, owes his triumph in an annual ritual of battling kites to Hassan, his kite runner, who is also his best friend and loyal servant. Hassan tracks and intercepts opponents' damaged kites as they drift to earth. Afterward, when Hassan is brutalized by local bullies, Amir runs off to hide rather than stand up to the attackers.

Years later, Amir and his family are living well in California, having fled the country at the fall of the monarchy and the Soviet invasion. Amir is still haunted by his own cowardice and "the past claws its way out." He returns to Afghanistan, now under Taliban control, hoping to help Hassan and his family, hoping it's not too late to make amends.

Published in 2003, just two years after the United States had gone to war in Afghanistan, this novel turned into a blockbuster when it came out in paperback and became a favorite of reading groups. Hosseini is an Afghan immigrant, son of an Afghan diplomat and a high-school teacher. He grew up in Kabul, Tehran, and Paris. After spending years as a physician in California, he began to write. His books have yet to be published in Afghanistan.

"In The Kite Runner, *Khaled Hosseini gives us a vivid and engaging story that reminds us how long his people have been struggling to triumph over the forces of violence—forces that continue to threaten them even today."*

—EDWARD HOWER, *NEW YORK TIMES*

DO ANDROIDS DREAM OF ELECTRIC SHEEP?

BY PHILIP K. DICK

A merry little surge of electricity piped by automatic alarm from the mood organ beside his bed awakened Rick Deckard.

IN A FALLOUT-SHROUDED San Francisco after "World War Terminus" has destroyed much of Earth, empathy boxes and mood organs keep the populace docile. "Electric sheep," robotic replicas of animals, are given to survivors who can't afford to own a real member of the endangered species.

Bounty hunter Rick Deckard hunts down renegade androids—robots that look just like humans and believe they *are* human. They were created to serve families emigrating to colonies on Mars and to make them feel less isolated. Indistinguishable from humans, these droids are perfectly fine as long as they stay in their places. But of course, they don't. It's up to Deckard to round up and destroy any that try to escape. His challenge is how to tell an android from a human, and his crisis of consciousness comes when he begins to feel empathy for one of his quarry.

This classic cyberpunk novel, published in 1968 before the term *cyberpunk* was coined, is set in 1992. It was the inspiration for the movie *Blade Runner.*

Dick grew up reading magazines like *Startling Stories* and *Fantastic Universe,* and when he dropped out of college, he began writing stories for them. "The words come out of my hand, not my brain," he said of his manic writing binges. The resulting work, at its best as in this novel, is visionary and surreal.

"Throughout his work this literary shaman returns, again and again, to the same pair of existential questions: What is it to be human? What is real?"

—MICHAEL DIRDA, *CLASSICS FOR PLEASURE*

ANIMAL FARM

BY GEORGE ORWELL

Mr. Jones, of the Manor Farm, had locked the hen-houses for the night, but was too drunk to remember to shut the pop-holes.

IN THIS ALLEGORICAL tale from 1946, the animals on Manor Farm revolt. One weekend when Farmer Jones is in a drunken stupor and forgets to feed them, they rise up and run him off the farm. A pair of pigs lead the rebellion—Napoleon who is "not much of a talker but with a reputation for getting his own way," and Snowball who is more eloquent and lively but "not considered to have the same depth of character." Using the philosophy and rhetoric espoused by Major, a pig now deceased, they set up a Bolshevik-style commune.

Despite the commune's first commandment, "All animals are equal," the leaders soon assign themselves special rations and quarters. Dictatorial Napoleon (Orwell's stand-in for Stalin) takes over, driving Snowball (Lenin) off the farm. Napoleon tells the farm animals that Snowball is a traitor, and he soon has them believing Snowball is secretly in cahoots with Farmer Jones.

The bewildered animals have no choice but to bow to Napoleon's rules; dissenters are executed. After many years the pigs learn to walk on two legs and carry whips. Their commandment has become: "All animals are equal, but some animals are more equal than others."

In the end, the animals can't tell the pigs from humans.

"[Orwell] writes absolutely without coyness or whimsicality and with such gravity and charm that Animal Farm *becomes an independent creation, standing quite apart from the object of its comment. The qualities of pathos in the tale of the betrayal of the animals . . . would compel the attention of persons who never heard of the Russian Revolution."*

—ARTHUR M. SCHLESINGER JR., *NEW YORK TIMES*

THE CALL OF THE WILD

BY JACK LONDON

Buck did not read the newspapers, or he would have known that trouble was brewing, not alone for himself, but for every tide-water dog, strong of muscle and with warm, long hair, from Puget Sound to San Diego.

WHEN "MEN, GROPING the Arctic darkness," find gold, there's a rush northward. The Klondike strike needs strong, heavy dogs with thick coats to pull the sleds. Buck, a Saint Bernard/Scotch shepherd mix, is snatched from the lap of luxury on a ranch in the Santa Clara Valley and sold to a dog agent. He's shipped to the harsh frozen Yukon where, after a two-day ride in a tiny crate, he's brutally "broken in." Fundamentally transformed, he becomes part of a train of sledge dogs that carry mail to Dawson.

Buck is repeatedly challenged and must prove himself to the pack. He clashes with the lead dog Spitz, each fighting for survival itself. "Mercy was a thing reserved for gentler climes."

The hardship and savagery to which Buck is subject awaken his innate wildness, calling him back to the kind of life that was bred out of him. The book ends with the unforgettable image of Buck, running wild, leading a wolf pack through pale moonlight.

The book was first published serially in 1903 in the *Saturday Evening Post*. The magazine paid London three cents a word. It has remained in print ever since.

"The Call of the Wild *is the greatest dog story ever written and is at the same time a study of one of the most curious and profound motives that play hide-and-seek in the human soul.*"

—CARL SANDBURG

AMERICAN TABLOID

BY JAMES ELLROY

He always shot up by TV light.

THIS DARK CRIME novel has three protagonists—though the term seems strange in this context. Kemper Boyd, "still too handsome to live," spies on the Kennedys for Hoover. He ends up also on the payroll of the CIA and the United States Senate Select Committee on Investigations. Ward Littell, Boyd's friend, has what turns out to be a lethal admiration for Bobby Kennedy. Pete Bondurant is a vicious Canadian hit man and extortionist who has killed, among others, his own parents and brother.

As with all of Ellroy's novels, this is savagely gripping. But far from his usual California crime story, there's no grisly murder or feverish police investigation. The subject matter here is political greed and corruption. Instead of a war of good and evil, there's a conflagration among Teamsters boss Jimmy Hoffa, Howard Hughes, J. Edgar Hoover, Joe Kennedy, and mobsters Santo Trafficante, Carlos Marcello, and Sam Giancana. It ends with the Kennedy assassination.

When this first came out in 1995, readers of crime fiction had never seen anything quite like it. One reviewer called it "brilliant and appalling." Ellroy's unique writing style—staccato sentences; disembodied dialogue; caustic humor; spare powerful prose—influenced a raft of modern thriller writers.

"It's a book, for all the family," Ellroy said in an interview with the *Guardian*, "if your family's name happens to be Manson."

"Oliver Stone's J. F. K. looks like the Disney version beside Mr. Ellroy's web of triple-dealing operatives, hapless thugs and public figures . . . whose private activities are freely imagined and embroidered here."

—JANET MASLIN, *NEW YORK TIMES*

CAPTAIN BLOOD

BY RAFAEL SABATINI

Peter Blood, bachelor of medicine and several other things besides, smoked a pipe and tended the geraniums boxed on the sill of his window above Water Lane in the town of Bridgewater.

A PIPE-SMOKING, GERANIUM-TENDING bachelor of medicine? Feels like an odd start for what is probably the single best known work of swashbuckling fiction. Yes, the mild-mannered but aptly named English gentleman turns into the infamous pirate Captain Blood.

In the beginning, Dr. Peter Blood is trying to mind his own business, living the quiet life of a physician in Bridgewater in Somersetshire. The Monmouth Rebellion breaks out between the forces of the Duke of Monmouth and King James II. Blood refuses to fight, but he's captured anyway when he tends to the wounded on the battlefield. In short order, he's convicted of treason by a corrupt judge and sentenced to die.

The king commutes Blood's sentence and ships Blood and his fellow convicts to Barbados. Blood is sold to the malevolent Colonel Bishop. When Spanish forces attack his Caribbean island, Blood and other slave-convicts escape. They capture one of the Spanish vessels and sail off.

Blood's only alternative now is to become a buccaneer. Until his triumphant return to England, he remains a gentleman pirate. He keeps his ship clean and disciplined and never harms women who fall into his clutches.

This swashbuckling fantasy for the ages was published in 1922 and made Sabatini a household name after twenty-five years of writing. Contemporaries called him "the modern Dumas."

"Sabatini's pure-hearted heroes are forced into piracy but never sink to the level of the brutish brigands around them."

—JAN ROGOZINSKI, *PIRATES! BRIGANDS, BUCCANEERS, AND PRIVATEERS IN FACT, FICTION, AND LEGEND*

THE ONCE AND FUTURE KING

BY T. H. WHITE

On Mondays, Wednesdays and Fridays it was Court Hand and Summulae Logicales, while the rest of the week it was the Oragon, Repetition and Astrology.

THESE ENCHANTED PAGES are a modern retelling of the legend of King Arthur. Published as a single volume in 1958, it is comprised of four books that Terence Hansbury White wrote over a twenty-year period.

The first book tells of Arthur's remarkable education at the knee of necromancer Merlyn. He learns to live within the skin of fish, bird, and beast. In the second book, Arthur consolidates his kingdom, establishes the Round Table, and along the way inadvertently sleeps with his half-sister. The child of their union is a son, Mordred. In the third book, the great knight Lancelot ("an ugly young man who was good at games") falls in love with Arthur's wife Guenever, and Arthur's hopes for the Round Table crumble. The final book finds Arthur and the Round Table in shambles as Arthur awaits what will be his last battle.

When Harry Potter pulled the Sword of Gryffindor from the Sorting Hat, surely J. K. Rowling was paying homage to the moment in the medieval Arthurian legend when young Arthur pulls the magic sword from a stone, revealing himself to be the rightful king of England. The musical play and movie *Camelot* are based on White's book, and Disney adapted it into the movie *The Sword in the Stone*.

"*[Once and Future King] is a glorious dream of the Middle Ages as they never were but as they ought to have been . . . compounded of . . . fantasy, farce, fable, parable, fairy story and wonderfully learned lore about falconry, boar hunting, jousting, archery, birds, beasts and fishes. There are also great and little magics, mythological monsters, knightly battles and horrible wars.*"

—ORVILLE PRESCOTT, *NEW YORK TIMES*

THE MALTESE FALCON

BY DASHIELL HAMMETT

Samuel Spade's jaw was long and bony, his chin a jutting v under the more flexible v of his mouth. . . . He looked rather pleasantly like a blond satan.

WITH THIS CLASSIC mystery, Dashiell Hammett (born May 27, 1894) introduced the world to Sam Spade and defined literature's iconic hard-boiled American private dick—dispassionate and jaded, a hard drinking man's man who'd rather outthink 'em than out-shoot 'em.

It opens with the trusty girl Friday (Effie Perine) announcing that there's a girl, Miss Wonderly, who wants to see Spade. "You'll want to see her; she's a knockout," Effie says.

In slinks a tall, slender, soft-spoken femme fatale with cobalt eyes. She pleads with Spade to find her sister who ran away from New York with an older man, Floyd Thursby. Spade's partner and friend, Miles Archer, agrees to stake out Thursby at his hotel in hopes of finding the sister and getting her away from him.

When Archer is found shot dead, Spade is determined to find his killer. Soon he discovers that "Miss Wonderly" has been lying to him. Her real name is Brigid O'Shaughnessy, and there is no sister. Brigid pleads with Spade to help her recover an invaluable and centuries old, gem-encrusted statue, the Maltese Falcon, which she and Thursby stole. Spade finds himself literally in a den of thieves, trying to stay alive and find his friend's killer.

Spare, raw, and understated, Hammett's writing is compared to Hemingway. The story is said to be based on the Sonoma Gold Specie case to which he was assigned as a Pinkerton detective before becoming a writer. A sensation when it was published in 1930, within a decade it had been made into three films.

"Hammett took murder out of the Venetian vase and dropped it into the alley."
—RAYMOND CHANDLER, "THE SIMPLE ART OF MURDER," *ATLANTIC MONTHLY*

A LESSON BEFORE DYING

BY ERNEST J. GAINES

I was not there, yet I was there. No, I did not go to the trial, I did not hear the verdict, because I knew all the time what it would be.

THE NOVEL IS set in segregated, rural Louisiana in the late 1940s. Jefferson, a slow, uneducated field worker, has been wrongly convicted of murder. His mistake: accepting a ride from a pair of men and being the lone survivor of their gun battle with a liquor store owner. Gaines expresses anger at the outcome: "Twelve white men say a black man must die, and another white man sets the date and time without consulting one black person. Justice?"

Even the public defender calls the uneducated Jefferson a "dumb animal." While he's held in a squalid, segregated jail cell awaiting execution, his godmother begs Grant Wiggins, a local black teacher, to teach Jefferson to read: "I don't want them to kill no hog. I want a man to go to that chair, on his own two feet."

Wiggins hopes to marry a beautiful, intelligent fellow teacher, but he is depressed by the hopelessness of his work, teaching children in the same segregated school he once attended. Inevitably they seem to get sucked into a cycle of poverty and racism.

In this unforgettable human drama, the teacher and the condemned man teach each other about human dignity.

Gaines was born and raised on a Louisiana plantation where his understanding of American life was shaped. He has said that he wanted to create the kinds of characters who are absent from the stories he'd read. This was his eighth book and won the 1993 National Book Critics Circle Award.

"Gaines is admired for his compassionate portrayal of ordinary people whose most heroic qualities are strength of character and unshakable dignity in humiliating and dehumanizing circumstances."

—ROBERT BAIRD SHUMAN, *GREAT AMERICAN WRITERS*

MAUS: A SURVIVOR'S TALE

BY ART SPIEGELMAN

I went out to see my father in Rego Park. I hadn't seen him in a long time—we weren't that close.

WITH ITS BLACK-AND-WHITE drawings of Jews as mice, Poles as pigs, Nazis as cats, and wartime Europe as a giant mousetrap, Spiegelman commented on the aptness of the metaphor: "I found that the gas Zyklon B (the gas used to exterminate Jews) was originally rat poison. And once the mouse part of it was clear, it seemed to be appropriate to make it a cat and mouse chase." Probably the first bestselling graphic novel, despite the comic-book format the story is told with chilling realism.

In it, Spiegelman's father narrates his own experiences as a Jewish Holocaust survivor. Spiegelman himself is a mouse in the strip ("I know this is insane, but I somehow wish I had been in Auschwitz . . . so I could really know what they lived through").

Spiegelman first published these strips in the internationally acclaimed magazine *Raw*. Many publishers rejected the manuscript in book form. Later recognized as a powerful exploration of the Jewish experience, in 1992 it won a Pulitzer Prize Special Award.

No stranger to the power of graphic satire, Spiegelman was once creative consultant for Topps Inc., and in the mid-'70s he created Wacky Packages bubble gum cards parodying "Neveready" batteries, "Rice-a-phony," and the like, and drew the infamous Garbage Pail Kids satirizing the ultra-cutesy Cabbage Patch dolls.

"By casting Jews as mice and Nazis as cats, Spiegelman taps the reservoir of sentiment usually reserved for Bambi, but inverts it—instead of cute animal high jinks, one is confronted with fathomless human sorrow. Images sear: a Jewish child smashed into a wall by a German soldier; a father and son hanged and left on display in a public square."

—ROBERT PFEIFFER, *WASHINGTON POST*

Remembrance of Things Past

BY MARCEL PROUST

For a long time I used to go to bed early.

THIS VERY CHALLENGING book—a 3,000-page novel that was once dismissed as the work of a self-indulgent neurotic dilettante—left one critic complaining that Proust had devoted fifty pages to "how he turns over and over in his bed before getting to sleep." How many of us have read more than the classic evocative passage with the madeleine cookies in which memories are preserved through remarkable use of language, giving the mundane activities of life the permanence and redemptive beauty of art?

It was the death of Proust's beloved mother that drove him to the realization that we only experience things in retrospect, and only by losing something do we realize what we had. The book tells of a sensitive, spoiled child who, like Proust, is morbidly dependent on his mother. He grows older and falls in love. Later he takes up with a woman with whom he is desperately unhappy. She runs away and is killed in an accident. During the war he finds refuge in a sanitarium. When he emerges, he finds his social world has aged and his friends are ready for death.

Proust began the book in 1907. He wrote in solitude, lying in bed in a room lined with cork to shut out the distractions of Paris. Once a celebrated intellectual and man about town, he turned into reclusive invalid. He died in 1922. This novel is revered as one of the great modernist works.

"I wouldn't have wanted to write like Proust, but I could see what you could do with memory. I could see what you could do with incidents. It was after reading Proust that I found I rather liked writing prose."

—MURIEL SPARK, *NEW YORK TIMES* INTERVIEW

PALE HORSE, PALE RIDER

BY KATHERINE ANNE PORTER

She was a spirited-looking young woman, with dark curly hair cropped and parted on the side, a short oval face with straight eyebrows, and a large curved mouth.

"PALE RIDER" IS the figure of death that accompanies protagonist Miranda Rhea in her dreams in this 1939 collection of three short novels.

In *Old Mortality,* Miranda is a child, home from boarding school with her sister Maria. The two live a cosseted childhood. Fascinated by a beautiful young cousin and enthralled by the story of Aunt Amy who made a loveless marriage and died as a result, the sisters begin to emerge from the past that has swaddled them.

Noon Wine seems to be narrated by Miranda—or perhaps by the author—and tells a story remembered from childhood. Mr. Thompson, a Texas dairy farmer, hires the taciturn Mr. Helton to help out. Helton turns out to be an escaped lunatic, and Thompson inexplicably murders a man.

In the third novella, *Pale Horse, Pale Rider,* Miranda is a disillusioned reporter, bitter and angry about World War I and madly in love with a young soldier who lives in her boarding house. A vividly portrayed 1918 flu epidemic grips the city. Miranda survives, only to discover that though the war has ended, the man she loves has died.

The writing of these bittersweet stories is rich in wit and humor.

"In writing Pale Horse, Pale Rider, *Katherine Anne had transmuted into art and mythologized her experiences of near-death during the 1918 flu epidemic and her pacifism in conflict with anti-German hysteria and wartime patriotism."*

—DARLENE HARBOUR UNRUE, PORTER'S BIOGRAPHER

June

THREE JUNES

BY JULIA GLASS

Paul chose Greece for its predictable whiteness: the blanching heat by day, the rush of stars at night, the glint of the lime-washed houses crowding its coast.

THREE INTERRELATED STORIES all taking place in the month of June comprise this critically acclaimed 2002 novel. In the first June, grieving husband and father, Paul McLeod, travels to Greece with a tour group in 1989, trying to get over his wife Maureen's death. He becomes captivated by Fern, an American painter who fails to return his attentions. Along the way, we learn of Paul's and Maureen's early years, her precious dogs and their three sons.

The next June is six years later. Paul is dead. His son Fenno, a failed graduate student nearing middle age, is gay and has opened a bookstore in Manhattan's West Village. He has to journey to the family home south of Glasgow to arrange his father's funeral. Fenno's complicated relationship with his father and with his twin brothers come into focus as Fenno must decide whether to donate sperm to help his brother's wife conceive a child. He must finally come to terms with disappointing his father, who'd wanted him to take over the family newspaper.

The final June is years later. The protagonist is Fern, a pregnant widow, who met Paul in Greece in the novel's first section.

For readers who revel in rich prose, this debut novel delivers in brilliantly rendered moments. It won the 2002 National Book Award.

"Masterfully, Three Junes *shows how love follows a circuitous path, how its messengers come to wear disguises."*

—KATHERINE WOLFF, *NEW YORK TIMES*

A MAP OF THE WORLD

BY JANE HAMILTON

I used to think if you fell from grace it was more likely than not the result of one stupendous error, or else an unfortunate accident.

ALICE GOODWIN AND her husband Howard live on a dairy farm in rural Wisconsin. Owning it has been Howard's dream, but their neighbors consider them outsiders. Alice has to fight all her natural instincts as she strives to be the perfect farm wife and mother.

This 1994 novel opens with unbearable tragedy. On a hot summer day, Alice is supposed to be watching her friend Theresa's two children. Instead, she's looking at her map of the world—one she labored over after her mother's death. As a girl, she would look at it and imagine an ideal place, an Arcadia to which she could escape. In that moment during which her attention is distracted, one of Theresa's children wanders off to the nearby pond and drowns.

Once that boundary between Alice's safe life and unthinkable tragedy has been breached, Alice's life spins out of control. The eponymous world map affords no protection from the witch-hunt that targets her. Alone and vulnerable in jail awaiting trial, she yearns for the punishment she feels she deserves.

Named a *New York Times* Notable Book of the Year, it was also named one of the top ten books of the year by *Entertainment Weekly*, *Publishers Weekly*, the *Miami Herald*, and *People* magazine.

"Jane Hamilton opens her second novel . . . by posing the question: Is there any pain more terrible than the death of one's child? It seems impossible, but yes, there is one step further into hell."

—CAROL SHIELDS, *WASHINGTON POST*

ANNAPURNA

BY MAURICE HERZOG

The day fixed for our departure was close at hand.

PRIOR TO JUNE 3, 1950, when Maurice Herzog led a group of French climbers to the summit of the 8,000-meter peak in the Himalayas known as Annapurna, no one had climbed that high. In this true adventure story, Herzog takes his readers on the historic expedition.

The ascent, with no maps to guide them or supplemental oxygen to offset the effects of altitude, is spellbinding. Their five-week descent is a spine-chilling nightmare of avalanche, frostbite, and snow-blindness.

Herzog survived with only stumps where he had once had fingers. As he recuperated in a hospital, the euphoric state that had overcome him upon reaching the summit persisted. He began to dictate this book. That transcendental optimism pervades it.

"This freedom," he wrote, "which I shall never lose, has given me the assurance and serenity of a man who has fulfilled himself."

Annapurna immediately became a classic; it was translated into more than forty languages and has sold over 10 million copies. Though Herzog says, in the book's introduction, "I conceived it to be my duty to give a plain truthful account of what happened," later books (*True Summit*, for example) raise questions about Herzog's version of events.

> "When I put down [Annapurna]—swallowed in one sitting, as I recall— I wanted more than anything to become a mountaineer."
> —DAVID ROBERTS, *TRUE SUMMIT: WHAT REALLY HAPPENED ON THE LEGENDARY ASCENT OF ANNAPURNA*

THE TIN DRUM

BY GÜNTER GRASS

Granted: I am an inmate of a mental hospital; my keeper is watching me, he never lets me out of his sight; there's a peep-hole in the door, and my keeper's eye is the shade of brown that can never see through a blue-eyed type like me.

THIS NOVEL IS framed as the autobiography of Oskar Matzer-ath, written from a mental hospital in the early 1950s. His memory begins with his own birth. From that moment, he understands adult conversation. His great gift is a "glass demol-ishing scream."

At three he receives a tin drum and determines "that I would stop right there, remain as I was—and so I did; for many years I not only stayed the same size but clung to the same attire." He stays three feet tall until, in his late teens, he wills himself to grow to four feet one.

A symbol perhaps of the German Everyman of the Nazi era, he steals, commits adultery, murders, and betrays without hesi-tation. He takes in the horror of Nazism and the slaughter of World War II without blinking.

The allegorical, picaresque, 600-page long German novel, fraught with violence and blasphemy, presents a horrifying, clear-eyed insider's view of a corrupt World War II Germany. The furor the novel created when it was published in 1959 still reverberates today.

Long seen as modern Germany's moral conscience, the Nobel Prize-winning author published his memoir (*Peeling the Onion*) in 2006, at the age of 78. In it, he revealed that he had served in the Waffen SS during the war.

"At the ages of 14 and 15, I had read Great Expectations *twice—Dick-ens made me want to be a writer—but it was reading* The Tin Drum *at 19 and 20 that showed me how. . . . Grass wrote with fury, love, derision, slapstick, pathos—all with an unforgiving conscience."*

—JOHN IRVING, *NEW YORK TIMES*

A PRAYER FOR OWEN MEANY

BY JOHN IRVING

I am doomed to remember a boy with a wrecked voice—not because of his voice, or because he was the smallest person I ever knew, or even because he was the instrument of my mother's death, but because he is the reason I believe in God; I am a Christian because of Owen Meany.

THE NARRATOR OF the tale is John Wheelwright, and the "instrument of my mother's death" in the novel's first line is a baseball. It's hit by Owen Meany during a Little League game, a hard foul down the third base line that strikes Wheelwright's beautiful mother in the head, killing her. Like the carelessly thrown snowball loaded with a rock in Robertson Davies's *Deptford Trilogy*, the baseball sets off a complex and mythic chain of events.

Wheelwright remembers Owen in flashbacks to the 1950s and 1960s. At age eleven, Owen is the size of a five-year-old. In adulthood, he's barely five feet tall. This unlikely diminutive and endearing hero has such a high-pitched voice that he can only scream (Irving renders his words in capital letters). The fateful baseball convinces Owen that he is "GOD'S INSTRUMENT."

Owen has visions—he sees an angel of death, and later his own tombstone, complete with the date of his death. He knows that he will die heroically and, like Christ, his death will serve a great purpose. It does—but not the way the reader or he expects.

Comic and heartbreaking, this 1989 work was Irving's seventh novel.

"No one has ever done Christ in the way John Irving does Him in A Prayer for Owen Meany. *This is big time, friends and neighbors.*"

—STEPHEN KING

BAND OF BROTHERS

BY STEPHEN AMBROSE

*The men of Easy Company, 506th Parachute Infantry Regiment,
101st Airborne Division, U.S. Army, came from different back-
grounds, different parts of the country.*

MILITARY HISTORIAN STEPHEN Ambrose brings to the
pages of this 1992 book the heroism and humanity in the day-
to-day lives of a company of World War II paratroopers. This
is no romantic tale of war heroics, but the story of "citizen soldiers" who, when pushed to the limit, showed they were capable of great courage and selflessness.

Their basic training was under Captain Herbert M. Sobel,
who drove recruits to exhaustion. He made them run faster, drill
longer, and work harder. He was so detested that his men argued
over who'd shoot him. After they were dropped into France on
D-Day, June 6, 1944, they realized that they owed their survival
to Captain Sobel's severity. When Hitler's forces came unexpectedly roaring back six months later, Easy Company was again
rushed to the front—this time without adequate winter clothing,
equipment, food, or ammunition. They held out until C-47s
dropped supplies and they were able to fight back.

The war in Europe ended and Easy Company reached Hitler's hideout. Pressure released, they drank themselves comatose
on Hitler's wine. Of the 140 paratroopers that had formed the
outfit, 48 had been killed and more than 100 were wounded.
All of them, as Ambrose puts it, had given "the best years of
their lives."

Ambrose bases his book on the soldiers' journals and letters
and on interviews. He writes their stories in their voices.

*"Stephen Ambrose came to our reunion in New Orleans around
1989. . . . When he saw he had forty to fifty men from one company,
he was interested in how we stayed together for almost fifty years. He
knew he had gold."*

—WILLIAM GUARNERE AND EDWARD HEFFRON (EASY COMPANY
PARATROOPERS), *BROTHERS IN BATTLE, BEST OF FRIENDS*

LORD OF THE FLIES

BY WILLIAM GOLDING

The boy with fair hair lowered himself down the last few feet of rock and began to pick his way toward the lagoon.

THIS ALLEGORICAL NOVEL tells of a very different "band of brothers" and reveals the much darker side of human nature.

As an atomic war rages, a plane evacuating a group of children crashes. They are stranded on an island. The book's title is the name they give to a wild pig they slaughter for food—they impale its head on a stick and it becomes infested with a horde of flies.

These well-brought-up preteen boys, freed from social constraints and festering in the hot humidity of the jungle, discard their clothes and paint their bodies. They try to govern themselves, with horrifying results. Two opposing tribes are formed and only one child, a fat boy who is nearly blind, retains his sense and integrity. He saves the surviving boys but cannot save himself.

This work presents a pessimistic view of humankind, precariously perched on the brink of savagery. Apparently, what we call civilization is only skin-deep.

Nobel laureate Golding's first novel, it was published in 1954 after being rejected by twenty-one publishers. Golding had been in the British Royal Navy in World War II and took part in the 1944 Normandy landings.

"World War II was the turning point for me. I began to see what people were capable of doing. Anyone who moved through those years without understanding that man produces evil as a bee produces honey, must have been blind or wrong in the head."

—WILLIAM GOLDING

Humboldt's Gift

BY SAUL BELLOW

*The book of ballads published by Von Humboldt Fleisher in the
Thirties was an immediate hit.*

IN THIS EXUBERANTLY funny 1975 novel, the underlying
theme is death. Its characters—Pulitzer Prize-winning historian
Charlie Citrine and the once-great poet Von Humboldt
Fleisher—have a complicated friendship. Charlie has revered
Humboldt ever since a pilgrimage years earlier to Greenwich
Village. During that trip, Humboldt introduced young Charlie,
fresh out of Chicago, to New York's best talkers. Charlie recalls,
"Under their eloquence, I sat like a cat in a recital hall."

In the '40s, as Humboldt's star falls and Charlie's rises,
Humboldt becomes increasingly erratic and jealous. In a final
insult, Humboldt takes a blank check that Charlie has given
him for emergencies, writes in a large amount and cashes it. It's
not robbery, but a jab at his friend for writing what Humboldt
considers a third-rate though successful Broadway play.

Humboldt dies in a squalid Times Square hotel leaving
Charlie two screenplays that promise to make him wealthy.
Charlie, literally haunted by Humboldt and by the guilt he feels
over dodging a final encounter with the old man, finds a way
to redeem their friendship.

An intensely autobiographical novelist, Bellow based the
story on his own relationship with the poet Delmore Schwartz
who died forgotten in the gutter at around the time Bellow was
achieving worldwide fame. Though the reader may not like the
characters, as one critic put it, "Life bursts from the page."

*"The characters in Bellow's novels all seem to be saying, with a mixture
of horror and fascination, 'What's the world coming to?'"*

—MICHAEL IGNATIEFF

O Pioneers!

BY WILLA CATHER

One January day, thirty years ago, the little town of Hanover, anchored on a windy Nebraska tableland, was trying not to be blown away.

WILLA CATHER, ONE of the most popular writers of her time, wrote about strong women and their triumphs over adversity. Her books celebrate the European immigrants who settled the American West.

This 1913 novel, which she considered one of her two "first" novels, was published when Cather was forty. It tells of seventeen-year-old Alexandra Bergson and her Swedish immigrant family arriving at desolate Hanover, a town "anchored on a windy Nebraska tableland."

When Alexandra's father dies, she devotes her life to the daunting task of making the farm financially viable. While Alexandra's father envisioned the land as something to "tame," Alexandra learns to live "without defiling the face of nature any more than the coyote that had lived there before him had done."

To paint this vivid portrait of the harsh realities of immigrant life on the plains—part family saga of survival, part love story—Cather drew on her own experiences. Cather's family could not eke out a living from the land.

With its title borrowed from a Walt Whitman poem, this was the first of Cather's three prairie novels.

"Clearness, warmth of feeling, a sense of an artist who could be trusted, this is still my impression of [Willa Cather's] books; one could read in perfect confidence—not even the prose attracted your attention from what the writer meant to tell you."

—KATHERINE ANNE PORTER

THE HANDMAID'S TALE

BY MARGARET ATWOOD

We slept in what had once been the gymnasium.

IN THIS RICH story of a dystopian future, the Republic of Gilead is an oppressive, underpopulated, Christian theocracy ruled by men. Right-wing fundamentalists set up the repressive state in the 1980s (the novel was published in 1986) after murdering the U.S. president and members of Congress. It is a bleak place. Women have been disenfranchised and are prevented from working or having money or learning to read. Homosexuals, Jews, old women, and nonwhites have been sent to the Colonies to clean up toxic waste.

The novel opens in the "re-education center." The narrator is being held there, separated from her family after trying to escape to Canada. She becomes known only by the cipher "Offred" (property of Commander Fred). Her only purpose is to bear her owner's children.

Scrawled on the ceiling of her bedroom where Commander Fred's previous wife committed suicide, Offred finds, "Nolite te bastardes carborundorum" (Don't let the bastards grind you down). She tries not to, and the ambiguous ending holds out tantalizing hope that perhaps she succeeds.

This cautionary tale is celebrated for its gorgeous prose and controversial for its forthright feminism. Atwood reminds the reader that all of the horrifying ways in which women are oppressed in this novel have been played out in history.

"The daughter of an entomologist at the University of Toronto, with a master's degree in Victorian literature from Harvard (1962), Atwood would seem to have an instinct for taxonomy; for the casting of a cold but not unsympathetic eye upon the strategies by which individuals present themselves to others in order to confirm their identity or, simply, like the desperate captive in The Handmaid's Tale, . . . *to survive."*

—JOYCE CAROL OATES, *NEW YORK TIMES*

DON QUIXOTE

BY MIGUEL DE CERVANTES SAAVEDRA

In a village of La Mancha, the name of which I have no desire to call to mind, there lived not long since one of those gentlemen that keep a lance in the lance-rack, an old buckler, a lean hack, and a greyhound for coursing.

THIS CLASSIC WORK of over 1,000 pages was originally published in Spanish in two separate volumes early in the seventeenth century. Cervantes tells the enduring saga of Alonso Quijano, a man who lives modestly in a village in La Mancha and who sells off farm acreage to expand his book collection. From "little sleep and too much reading," his brain "dries up." He dons rusty armor and a cardboard helmet and transforms himself into Don Quixote de la Mancha, a knight who strives to redress "all manner of wrongs."

His quest gets off to a rocky start. He's beaten up and neighbors carry him home. His book collection is burned to dissuade him from his quest. But a local laborer, Sancho Panza, joins him and becomes his squire. This time out, he battles windmills that he thinks are giants.

Sansón Carrasco, a man from Don Quixote's village, tries to rescue him from his delusions. But he's convinced to go along to Toboso where Don Quixote intends to pay his respects to Dulcinea, a local farm girl. There Don Quixote defeats the Knight of the Mirrors (Carrasco in disguise).

On Don Quixote goes to further adventures—meeting with the Knight in the Green Topcoat, descending into the Cave of Montesinos, and taking Master Peter's puppet show a bit too seriously. More battles and ultimately defeat and humiliation ensue. After a long slumber, he announces that he is, once again, Alonso Quijano, and dies.

"Those of us who toil through Cervantes, I suspect, after an initial jolt, chortlingly habituate ourselves to the 'infinite drubbings' meted out and sustained by the gaunt hidalgo."

—MARTIN AMIS

MAYTREES

BY ANNIE DILLARD

It began when Lou Bigelow and Toby Maytree first met.

MEET LOU AND TOBY. She's a painter. He's a poet and house mover. He is instantly smitten with her direct intensity and beauty. He courts her, and soon they find themselves "shipwrecked on the sheets," blindsided by love's intensity.

They marry, and life goes on for the bohemian pair and their circle of intellectual friends. They have a child, Petie, and Toby strays into the arms of a friend, Deary, a femme fatale with a penchant for sleeping in the dunes. She carries him off to Maine for a twenty-year love affair.

Abandoned, Lou tries not to fall apart. She simplifies her life, shedding chores she doesn't need to do and friends she's only tolerated. She devotes herself to raising Petie. Through compulsive cleaning and treks to Pilgrim Monument, she holds her life together. She finds solace in nature and in her work. Decades later, Lou and Toby find their way back to one another.

Originally subtitled "A Romantic Comedy about Light Pollution," this 2007 book was Dillard's second novel. Its oceans and sandy beaches, sky and stars are as richly drawn as its characters. It came three decades after her Pulitzer Prize–winning nonfiction book, *Pilgrim at Tinker Creek*.

"Annie Dillard's books are like comets, like celestial events that remind us that the reality we inhabit is itself a celestial event, the business of eons and galaxies, however persistently we mistake its local manifestations for mere dust, mere sea, mere self, mere thought."

—MARILYNNE ROBINSON, *WASHINGTON POST*

PEACE LIKE A RIVER

BY LEIF ENGER

From my first breath in this world, all I wanted was a good set of lungs and the air to fill them with—given circumstances, you might presume, for an American baby of the twentieth century.

THIS ENGAGING, FEEL-GOOD first novel serves up magical realism, American-style. In it, eleven-year-old Reuben Land comes of age in rural Minnesota in the early 1960s. His life takes a violent turn when his father, Jeremiah (a poetry-loving school janitor), saves a high-school girl from rape only to be hounded by the two goons whom he thwarted. The pair invade the family's house and Reuben's brother Davy shoots them dead. Davy is arrested. He breaks out of jail and flees.

Reuben, his father, and his tomboy sister Swede take off into the Badlands of North Dakota to find Davy. From the outset, the hand of the Divine seems to be at their back. Miracles are nothing new to the Lands. Reuben Land, dead for twelve minutes after his birth, breathed when his father Jeremiah ordered him to do so "in the name of God." Jeremiah was once carried four miles by a tornado without suffering a scratch. While airborne, he encountered a higher power. Now he can walk on air or heal the scarred face of his enemy by touching it. A meager soup pot becomes bottomless when hungry visitors arrive. Reuben, who barely survived his own birth and is severely asthmatic, believes his purpose in life is to serve as witness.

A reporter and producer for Minnesota Public Radio from 1984, Enger took six years to write this novel. Published right after the September 11 terrorist attacks, its themes of faith, family, the pioneering spirit, and the loss of innocence struck a chord.

"When I was starting [Peace Like a River] . . . , my son was fighting a terrible case of asthma. He was just fighting for breath. . . . As a parent you want to work a miracle."

—LEIF ENGER, *BOOKPAGE* INTERVIEW

FLAGS OF OUR FATHERS

BY JAMES BRADLEY WITH RON POWERS

*In the spring of 1998 six boys called to me from half a century
ago on a distant mountain, and I went there.*

JOE ROSENTHAL'S PULITZER Prize–winning photo of six
marines raising a flag on Iwo Jima during World War II is iconic.
One of those men was John Bradley, who lived out his quiet life
as a funeral director in the small town of Antigo, Wisconsin. He
never talked about his military exploits, and that silence led his
son James to unearth the true story after his death.

The book presents a graphic, unvarnished portrait of men
at war on one of history's most savage battlefields. The Japanese defended the island of Iwo Jima with 22,000 dug-in soldiers. Their orders: Kill ten Americans each and then die. Of
the 70,000 American Marines who invaded on February 19,
1945, 26,000 were killed or wounded. By the time it was over,
21,000 Japanese soldiers had died.

Bradley highlights the irony that an accidental, relatively
meaningless act (they were replacing a smaller flag that had
been raised earlier by others) captured on film rendered those
six soldiers heroes. He writes of his father, "no matter how
many millions of people thought otherwise, he understood that
this image of heroism was not the real thing." Reality was far
more horrific—marines who saw their buddies literally sliced
into pieces on the battlefield.

Bradley explores the impact of "the Photograph" on the
three men pictured who came home, and on the families of the
three men who didn't. Surrounded by unspeakable bravery,
their own images captured performing a meaningless act
aroused the American populace to a frenzy of patriotism.

*"The best battle book I ever read. These stories, from the time the six
men who raised the flag at Iwo Jima enlisted, their training, and the
landing and subsequent struggle, fill me with awe."*

—STEPHEN AMBROSE

BURGER'S DAUGHTER

BY NADINE GORDIMER

Among the group of people waiting at the fortress was a school-girl in a brown and yellow uniform holding a green eiderdown quilt and, by the loop at its neck, a red hot-water bottle.

ROSA BURGER GROWS up white and South African. When we meet her, she is fourteen years old and standing in line outside prison waiting to give her incarcerated mother a quilt and a hot-water bottle. As she waits to find out whether she will be admitted, she gets her first period.

Rosa's communist, antiapartheid activist father dies in prison. Her mother dies, too. Rosa tries to numb herself to the horrors around her and steer clear of politics. But a scene of cruelty in the streets of Soweto drives her from the country.

In self-imposed exile on the French Riviera, trying to sort out her feelings, she seeks out her father's first wife who left him because she was not a "born revolutionary." She falls in love, but love fails to change her in the way she'd hoped. Finally, she finds the strength to return to her homeland and join the fight her parents left unfinished.

Gordimer grew up in a small town outside of Johannesburg. This, her second novel, was published in 1979 and banned by the South African government's directorate of publications. In 1991 she became the first woman in twenty-five years to win the Nobel Prize for Literature.

"Burger's Daughter *is both a political novel and a love story, one that suggests that there is no politics without love or love without politics. Neither side . . . is sacrificed to the other. Hers is a democracy of the passions."*

—ANATOLE BROYARD, *NEW YORK TIMES*

ULYSSES

BY JAMES JOYCE

There was no hope for him this time; it was the third stroke.

TOLD AS AN extended interior monologue, *Ulysses* encompasses a single day—June 16, 1904—in the lives of Leopold Bloom, Jewish advertising canvasser who is an average Everyman, and Stephen Dedalus, scholar-philosopher. Nothing, however seemingly trivial or personal, is omitted, and the rough life of Dublin is vividly portrayed. Joyce said of this novel, "I want to give a picture of Dublin so complete that if the city one day disappeared from the earth, it could be constructed out of my book."

Full of bawdy humor, the novel is an homage to Joyce's favorite hero from childhood, Odysseus. In this allegorical retelling of Homer's great tale, Bloom and Dedalus play the father-and-son roles of Odysseus (Ulysses) and Telemachus. Over the course of a long day, their paths cross in a labyrinth of wandering. Eventually they converge at the Holles Street lying-in hospital.

As true today as when the *New York Times* reviewed it in 1922, "It requires real endurance to finish *Ulysses*." Its so-called "stream of consciousness" style—dropping the reader right into a character's head—was revolutionary. It definitively replaced the omniscient narrator of the nineteenth-century novel.

First published in book form in 1922, *Ulysses* was deemed obscene and barred from circulation in America until 1933. As a 1922 *New York Times* reviewer pointed out, "It reeks of lust and of filth, but Mr. Joyce says that life does, and the morality that he depicts is the one he knows."

"[James Joyce] stood the world of literature on its noodle when he wrote Ulysses.*"*

—MALACHY MCCOURT, *VOICES OF IRELAND: CLASSIC WRITINGS OF A RICH AND RARE LAND*

ALL THE PRESIDENT'S MEN

BY BOB WOODWARD AND CARL BERNSTEIN

June 17, 1972. Nine o'clock Saturday morning. Early for the telephone. Woodward fumbled for the receiver and snapped awake.

A PAIR OF brash young *Washington Post* reporters bring down a president. In this book, Bob Woodward and Carl Bernstein tell all—at least all that was known by the time they finished writing the book a little over a year after the evidence they uncovered about the Watergate break-in led to the revelation of the Nixon tapes.

The book takes us from their initial wariness of working together—the more mercurial Bernstein and the calm methodical Woodward are a study in opposites—to appreciating one another's strengths. Investigating a simple burglary at the Democratic National Headquarters leads them to uncover massive spying and sabotage that reaches up to President Nixon's inner circle. Accounts of secret underground meetings between Bernstein and his informer, the mysterious Deep Throat (so-called because his information was always "deep background," and could never directly or indirectly be quoted) read like pulp fiction. Their triumph comes when White House Press Secretary Ron Ziegler issues a formal apology for castigating their paper.

Published in 1974 while Watergate was still unfolding, the book turned the investigative team into celebrities.

"The suspense in All the President's Men *is more pervasive and finally more terrifying than a suspense story . . . because the setting is sunny Washington, D.C., a familiar place suddenly made unfamiliar by overwhelming fear."*

—DORIS KEARNS GOODWIN

THE RISK POOL

BY RICHARD RUSSO

*My father, unlike so many of the men he served with, knew just
what he wanted to do when the war was over. He wanted to
drink and whore and play the horses.*

THIS TALE OF fractured families is set in Mohawk, a small
town in upstate New York where "most everybody . . . lived
pretty near the edge—of unemployment, of lunacy, of bankruptcy, of potentially hazardous ignorance, of despair."

Narrator Ned Hall's mother quits her job and virtually
disappears into a Librium-induced fugue after an affair with a
priest. Ned's father, a gambler and good ol' boy who has peri-
odically drifted in and out of the boy's life, drops back in and
whisks him away from a relatively ordered, antiseptic suburban
existence. The two live in a squalid apartment. Ned learns to
shoot pool, play cards, handicap horses, pilfer, and lie. Ned's
best friend is a hell-raising teen who rages around town on a
motorcycle in a self-declared war on the rich.

Then Ned falls in love with Tria, a girl from a privileged
home who, like him, is damaged goods and terrified of turning
out like her dad.

This 1988 book is an excellent introduction to Russo, a
modern master at capturing flawed characters in a blue-collar
landscape.

*"[Russo] brilliantly evokes the economic and emotional depression of
a failing town, a place where even the weather is debilitating and the
inhabitants seem to struggle merely to stay in place."*

—HILMA WOLITZER, *CHICAGO TRIBUNE BOOKS*

MRS. DALLOWAY

BY VIRGINIA WOOLF

Mrs. Dalloway said she would buy the flowers herself.

WRITTEN IN STREAM-OF-CONSCIOUSNESS style and published three years after James Joyce's *Ulysses*, this novel is a day in two lives. In the tragic aftermath of the Great War, a sense of loss pervades each of these characters as, in the background, a clock strikes the hours.

On a June day in 1923, Clarissa Dalloway is buying flowers for a party she will give that night. Like her friends, she is glad that the war has ended. Aging and lonely, plagued with regrets and beset by petty grievances, she is preoccupied with last-minute details of her party when the man she wonders if she should have married shows up. He's just returned from India.

Meanwhile, Septimus Warren Smith, a shell-shocked military hero of the war, sits in the park listening to sparrows he believes are singing to him in Greek. On the night that Clarissa has her party, Septimus ends his own life.

Published in 1925, this study of sanity and suicide explores the subjectivity of truth. It foreshadows Woolf's own suicide in 1941. Despite periods of depression and insanity, Woolf was one of the most productive authors of her century. She wrote in her diary, "More than anything, I want beautiful prose."

Woolf's working title for this novel was "The Hours." Michael Cunningham adopted that title for his modern adaptation of the book.

"Mrs. Dalloway, *with its irony-laden 'triumphs of civilisation,' its insistently bright march through the 'pageant of the universe,' was no mere place of pears or pudding. It was a world where the indomitable life that Clarissa loved was nonetheless shadowed by Septimus and his siren song—a place where dead soldiers washed up on the rocks, or on the streets of London.*"

—GAIL CALDWELL, *BOSTON GLOBE*

THE HOURS

BY MICHAEL CUNNINGHAM

There are still the flowers to buy.

THIS HOMAGE TO *Mrs. Dalloway* takes Virginia Woolf's story and inserts the author herself into it. It begins in 1941 with Woolf wading into the water, her pockets filled with stones. The note she leaves behind for her husband Leonard begins, "I feel certain I am going mad again." Her suicide casts a shadow over a novel composed of the interwoven narratives of three women.

Clarissa Vaughan (like Clarissa Dalloway) is fifty-two. A book editor in present-day Greenwich Village, she leaves her house to buy flowers for a party planned for that evening. The party will honor her friend Richard, a poet, who is dying of AIDS and hearing the same kinds of voices Septimus Warren Smith heard in *Mrs. Dalloway*.

Laura Brown is an unhappy housewife in postwar California. She yearns for quiet time, away from her family, and to escape into the novel *Mrs. Dalloway*. But it is her war hero husband's birthday and she must bake a cake. She closes the book and resolves to "rise and be cheerful."

And finally, Virginia Woolf is at work writing *Mrs. Dalloway*. She considers whether she will have Clarissa Dalloway take her own life.

This work is widely acknowledged as a tour de force. It won the Pulitzer Prize and PEN/Faulkner Award in 1991. For added insight, read it after *Mrs. Dalloway*.

"Mrs. Dalloway *is the first great book I ever read. I read it almost by accident when I was in high school, when I was 15 years old. . . . It felt like something for me to write about very much the way you might write a novel based on the first time you fell in love.*"

—MICHAEL CUNNINGHAM, INTERVIEW
BY ELIZABETH FARNSWORTH, *NEWSHOUR*, PBS

A SUMMER BIRD-CAGE

BY MARGARET DRABBLE

I had come home for my sister's wedding.

OLDER SISTER LOUISE Bennett is glamorous, sophisticated, and cold. Her plain younger sister Sarah has come home from Paris to be in Louise's wedding. Sarah has been alternately attracted and irritated by Louise, whose greatly anticipated arrivals home invariably end with disappointment.

The reader sees the match through Sarah's critical eyes. Louise is marrying a mildly successful novelist for his social position while she intends to continue her relationship with the man she loves. Sarah has made her own compromises. Despite a brilliant undergraduate record at Oxford, she has rejected a university career as incompatible for a woman who also wants to be attractive and desirable.

Laced with humor and cutting insights, the novel explores the choices women make. Sarah and Louise, very much creatures of their time, reflect the rising consciousness of women struggling with their identity in the early '60s. The naming of these "Bennett" sisters invites comparisons to the Bennet sisters of *Pride and Prejudice*.

This was the British author's stunning 1963 debut novel, written in her twenties when she was an aspiring actress and understudy to Vanessa Redgrave in the Royal Shakespeare Company. It proclaimed the arrival of a promising young novelist and provides a great place to start reading her work.

Drabble had her own form of sibling rivalry to deal with—her older sister is novelist A. S. Byatt.

"Just as Flaubert proclaimed, 'Madame Bovary, c'est moi,' I'd have said the same about Drabble, even though she was a much smarter and more accomplished moi."

—MAMEVE MEDWED, *BOSTON GLOBE*

THE SOURCE

BY JAMES MICHENER

On Tuesday the freighter steamed through the Straits of Gibraltar and for five days plowed eastward through the Mediterranean, past islands and peninsulas rich in history, so that on Saturday night the steward advised Dr. Cullinane, "If you wish an early sight of the Holy Land you must be up at dawn."

THIS 1965 HISTORICAL novel takes the reader through 12,000 years of history, back to the beginning of the Jewish faith, while tagging along on a fictitious modern archaeological dig in northern Israel at Tell Makor (based on the great tell of Hazor).

The protagonist in the framing story is John Cullinane, an Irish American archaeologist. He works with a close-knit group of men and women from neighboring kibbutzim to uncover artifacts and bones. With each layer uncovered, Michener writes another story, imagining life as it might have been.

The novel's sixteen stories span the ages, following the family of Ur from the Stone Age to modern times. It dramatizes the advent of monotheism, the Davidic kingdom, and on to Hellenistic and Roman times, and traces the history of the Jewish faith from early persecution through the founding of modern Israel and the contemporary conflict in the Middle East.

Weighing in at over a thousand pages, this was the prolific Michener's eighth novel.

"The Source *is a weird, wonderful rampage through history—with a time span even more ambitious than the author's* Hawaii."

—ROBERT PAYNE, *NEW YORK TIMES*

DEATH IN VENICE

BY THOMAS MANN

Gustav Aschenbach or von Aschenbach, as he had officially been known since his fiftieth birthday, set out alone from his residence in Munich's Prinzregentenstrasse on a spring afternoon in 19.. — a year that for months had shown so ominous a countenance to our continent — with the intention of taking an extended walk.

THIS NOVELLA, ORIGINALLY written in German, tells of Gustav von Aschenbach, a renowned poet who "longed to grow old, for he had always held an artist's talent to be fulfilled only if it could bear fruit at all stages of life." Well into middle age and seeking to recapture the sensual life he sacrificed for his work, he journeys south to Venice.

From his window at the Grand Hotel des Bains, he watches young Tadzio, a beautiful Polish boy, playing on the sands of Lido beach. He becomes obsessed with the youth, and the emotions he has long suppressed destroy the orderly fortress he has built around his life. His shattered inner world is mirrored by the decay and epidemic disaster spreading across the city.

Like his fictional hero, Mann went to Venice in 1911 with his wife and brother and was fascinated by a handsome Polish boy he saw on the beach. In a letter, Mann confessed that the experience inspired him to write this novella, first published in 1912 ("Nothing in *Death in Venice* is invented . . . ," he wrote).

"Mann seemed to be saying that yes, we all fade, we're all going to the same place, and so we might as well go down in a blaze of love, however we may degrade ourselves in the process, however ill-advised our taste in clothes and makeup."

—MICHAEL CUNNINGHAM, INTRODUCTION
TO THE 2004 (HARPERCOLLINS) EDITION

THE GOOD EARTH

BY PEARL S. BUCK

It was Wang Lung's marriage day.

THIS 1931 NOVEL tells the story of Wang Lung, a farmer with an enduring belief that the foundation of his family's security lies in the land.

In the beginning, he is a humble farmer with a small farm. He cannot afford a pretty wife, and weds O-lan, a slave girl from the neighboring House of Hwang manor. A good worker and loyal wife, O-lan bears him sons. Their harvests are bountiful, and through thrift and discipline, Wang Lung saves enough to buy more land from the Hwangs. But a year of drought and famine drives him to the city to beg for alms and pull a ricksha for meager pay. He refuses to sell his land.

At last, his fortunes change again. During an outburst of civil unrest, he joins in the looting of a wealthy home. He uses the money to return and restock his farm. As his fortune multiplies, at last he can take a second wife—this time a pretty one. His final triumph comes when he takes over the House of Hwang. With this comes the sad realization that his sons await his death so they can sell the land and become the kind of rich, idle city dwellers he detests. Foreshadowed is the coming clash between traditional China in the waning days of imperial rule and its revolutionary future.

Buck spent much of her life in China, and this book is free of the stereotypes and clichés that riddle earlier literature set in China. This story resonated in America where, during the Depression, millions of families lost their farms. It won the 1932 Pulitzer Prize.

"[The Good Earth] was a great book, but there were people who said, Well, because of this one book, and because Pearl Buck won the Nobel Prize, now people think that all Chinese people wore these coolie hats and gave birth to babies in the field."

—AMY TAN, *NEW YORK TIMES* INTERVIEW
BY DEBORAH SOLOMON

SENTIMENTAL EDUCATION

BY GUSTAVE FLAUBERT

On the morning of 15 September 1840 the Ville de Montereau *was lying alongside the quai Saint-Bernard belching clouds of smoke, all ready to sail.*

PASSION FOR AN older woman drives this novel, the last published in the great French author's lifetime. Set in Paris in the 1840s, the protagonist is Frédéric Moreau. Just eighteen years old, he is naive in the ways of the world. On a steamboat carrying him from Paris to his hometown of Nogent-sur-Seine, he becomes fatally enthralled with elegant, beautiful Madame Arnoux ("He loved her without reservation, without hope, unconditionally"). He befriends her husband just so he can be near her.

Three decades later, Moreau remains infatuated with the unattainable Madame Arnoux. Passive and indifferent to the inequities of the world around him, he has become a conformist, Flaubert suggests, like the privileged bourgeoisie of France who have accepted the social order and their own protected status within it.

Written with Flaubert's signature irony and pessimism, this work first appeared in 1869 and is considered the most influential French novel of the nineteenth century. Flaubert famously agonized over every detail and each word, struggling to select precisely the right word (*le mot juste*) to express each idea.

"Novelists should thank Gustave Flaubert the way poets thank spring. . . . He is the originator of the modern novel; indeed, you could say that he is the originator of modern narrative—that the war reporter and the thriller writer owe as much to him as the avant-garde fictionist."

—JAMES WOOD, *NEW YORK TIMES*

THE SOT-WEED FACTOR

BY JOHN BARTH

In the last years of the Seventeenth Century there was to be found among the fops and fools of the London coffee-houses one rangy, gangling flitch called Ebenezer Cooke, more ambitious than talented, and yet more talented than prudent, who, like his friends-in-folly, all of whom were supposed to be educating at Oxford or Cambridge, had found the sound of Mother English more fun to game with than her sense to labor over, and so rather than applying himself to the pains of scholarship, had learned the knack of versifying, and ground out quires of couplets after the fashion of the day, afroth with Joves and Jupiters, aclang with jarring rhymes, and string-taut with similes stretched to the snapping-point.

AND THAT'S JUST the first really long sentence in this bawdy costume drama set in late seventeenth-century England. A labyrinthine plot winds intrigue with counter-intrigue, mistaken identity with romance and adventure. The huge cast includes Ebenezer Cooke; his twin sister, Anna; and tutor-turned-suitor to both, Henry Burlingame. Ebenezer is a virginal poet who dubs himself "Poet and Laureate" of Maryland. He believes he's been commissioned by the third Lord Baltimore to write an epic poem for Maryland. But the third Lord B is at war with Protestants and runs a network of spies and saboteurs, so Ebenezer finds himself embroiled, instead, in political turmoil.

This monstrously long (800-plus pages), no-holds-barred satire of humanity is raucous, outrageous, and loaded with scatological humor. A highlight is a supposedly secret journal of Captain John Smith. Told in fake seventeenth-century English prose, it gives a warped version of the Pocahontas story.

"Unlike Pynchon, who accepts basic historical facts as true, John Barth doubts our standard versions of the past; and in The Sot-Weed Factor *he systematically distorts, mostly debunks, traditional accounts of history to create versions that are just as probable as those in textbooks."*

—RICHARD KOSTELANETZ, *NEW YORK TIMES*

THE RED TENT

BY ANITA DIAMANT

We have been lost to each other for so long.

DIAMANT TELLS THE story of Dinah, a silent female character in Genesis. She is the only daughter of the patriarch Jacob, sister to the twelve brothers whose descendants became the tribes of Israel. In Genesis, the son of a neighboring king rapes Dinah.

In Diamant's tale, Dinah's mother shared her husband Jacob with three other women, and Diamant imagines a warm, loving relationship among Dinah, her mother, and her three "aunties." Like the women of biblical times, they gathered in the red tent, sequestered during menses and childbirth. In that private place they shared their secrets with Dinah and passed along a heritage. Each had something special to impart—Leah's excellent recipes, Zilpah's legends and songs, Bilhah's kindheartedness, and Rachel's midwifery. Dinah says, "They held my face between their hands and made me swear to remember."

The novel takes the reader from Mesopotamia and Canaan down into Egypt, where Dinah finds a refuge. One reviewer suggested that this inventive revisionist history is what the Bible might have been like, had it been written by women.

Published without fanfare in 1997, this novel was not reviewed by a single major publication. It became a word-of-mouth bestseller, largely through Diamant's efforts to market the book to rabbis.

"The biblical text doesn't really talk too much about the women. They are hidden, they're silent. You never know what they are thinking; you don't know about their pain, let alone their joys."

—RABBI TAMARA MILLER, *WASHINGTON POST*

MIDDLESEX

BY JEFFREY EUGENIDES

I was born twice: first, as a baby girl, on a remarkably smogless Detroit day in January of 1960; and then again, as a teenage boy in an emergency room near Petoskey, Michigan, in August of 1974.

THE NOVEL'S OPENING continues, "But now, at the age of forty-one, I feel another birth coming on." That voice belongs to hermaphrodite Calliope/Cal Stephanides, the endearing, funny, incisive narrator of this 2002 Pulitzer Prize–winning novel.

The whole first half of this unique coming of age story takes place before Cal is born, and it tells the story of the "roller-coaster ride of a single gene through time," shifting effortlessly back and forth in time across three generations. The story begins in 1922 in Greece with grandparents, siblings Lefty and Desdemona. They escape the Turkish invasion and bribe their way onto a boat to America. Defying taboo, they arrive in America as husband and wife. The story continues against a historical backdrop of upheavals and social changes. In Detroit, Cal's father, Milton, a fast-food entrepreneur, becomes a hot-dog mogul. In San Francisco, Cal works as an erotic dancer, and then moves on to present-day Berlin.

Eugenides was taken with the idea of writing a novel about a hermaphrodite after reading Michel Foucault's *Herculine Barbin: Being the Recently Discovered Memoirs of a Nineteenth-Century French Hermaphrodite*. Eugenides turned to scientific research to understand the genetics of hermaphroditism and the establishment of sexual identity.

"Middlesex *wears its tragedy on one arm and its comedy on the other, and its gender assumptions inevitably serve as metaphors of constraint as well as liberation.*"

—GAIL CALDWELL, *BOSTON GLOBE*

EVERYTHING IS ILLUMINATED

BY JONATHAN SAFRAN FOER

*My legal name is Alexander Perchov. But all of my many friends
dub me Alex, because that is a more flaccid-to-utter version of
my legal name.*

THE NOVEL'S OPENING line is a twist on "Call me Ishmael,"
and from then on the prose is startling and funny with a story
that caroms into unexpected places. The narrator, Perchov, is a
young Russian. His tortured English is good enough for his job
as translator for Heritage Touring, his father's travel agency,
which arranges trips back to the "homeland" for American
Jews.

Perchov accompanies a tourist whose name is "Jonathan
Safran Foer" (Perchov calls him "Jon-fen") who seeks the
Ukrainian town of Trachimbrod. There he hopes to track down
Augustine, the beautiful woman who saved his grandfather
from the Nazis. They are accompanied by a driver, Perchov's
grandfather, who suffers psychosomatic blindness, and a particularly stinky dog named Sammy Davis Junior, Junior.

Like a nest of Russian dolls, the novel is composed of stories within stories. Perchov writes of the trip to the Ukraine in
retrospect, sending chapters to Jonathan who then makes corrections (for instance, he changes a description of himself from
"severely short" to "like me, he was not tall"). Meanwhile, Jonathan sends Perchov chapters of a novel he's writing, an epic
magical realist fable about Trachimbrod.

"Everything Is Complicated" might be a more appropriate
title, but complexity reveals itself in layers that surprise and
delight. From laughter, profound themes emerge. This extraordinary first novel was published in 2002.

"Not since Anthony Burgess's novel A Clockwork Orange *has the English language been simultaneously mauled and energized with such
brilliance and such brio."*

—FRANCINE PROSE, *NEW YORK TIMES*

The Poisonwood Bible

BY BARBARA KINGSOLVER

We came from Bethlehem, Georgia, bearing Betty Crocker cake mixes into the jungle.

JUN.
30

NATIONAL
INDEPENDENCE
DAY, REPUBLIC
OF CONGO/
BRAZZAVILLE

IN THIS MASSIVE, hugely successful novel set in 1959, zealous evangelical Baptist minister Nathan Price drags his wife and four daughters to the Congo village of Kilanga. Blindly self-righteous, Price is obsessed with proving himself by baptizing unwilling villagers.

Meanwhile his wife, Orleanna, struggles to keep the family alive, fed, and safe from animal and human predators. "I had washed up there on the riptide of my husband's confidence and the undertow of my children's needs," she says. Their marriage, as much as the place, become a "heart of darkness" as the story unravels through their daughters' eyes.

The struggles within the family provide a window on four young women coming of age. In a wholly unfamiliar setting, even their most basic beliefs are challenged by the Congolese.

The novel goes far beyond telling a family saga. It dramatizes the tragic legacy of colonialism and the ensuing political unrest. It also raises fundamental questions about what religion is and should be. Kingsolver brings her biologist's eye to the fascinating environment and the jungle itself becomes a character.

Kingsolver's fourth novel, this book was a 1998 Pulitzer finalist.

"I read [Doris Lessing's] the Children of Violence *novels and began to understand how a person could write about the problems of the world in a compelling and beautiful way. And it seemed to me that was the most important thing I could ever do, if I could ever do that."*

—BARBARA KINGSOLVER

July

GIFT FROM THE SEA

BY ANNE MORROW LINDBERGH

The beach is not the place to work; to read, write or think.

ONCE UPON A time, Anne Morrow Lindbergh spent a quiet summer at the beach. She wrote this book of lyrical meditations on life, love, peace, and solitude, drawing inspiration from shells she found.

A favorite for many, this book is poetic and quotable, as in: "One should lie empty, open, choiceless as a beach—waiting for a gift from the sea." On the role of a woman raising a family and keeping house and maintaining some sense of personal identity, she wrote, "What a circus act we women perform every day of our lives. It puts the trapeze artist to shame."

She argued that women should take the time to nourish their own "inner springs," and lamented the modern world's intolerance for a person's "need to be alone."

The book remained on the bestseller list for eighty weeks. In 1955, it was given the National Council of Women's first award for the "outstanding book about women by a woman." Ms. Lindbergh begged off attending the awards luncheon: "I am unable to give the time I want and feel I should give to my children and also give sufficient attention to the writing."

"Gift from the Sea *became a source of inspiration for a whole generation of wives and mothers—'the great vacationless class,' she called them— who, like herself, were beginning to search for more fulfilling lives once their children had grown and moved away.*"

—GEOFFREY C. WARD, QUOTED IN LINDBERGH'S
OBITUARY IN THE *NEW YORK TIMES*

Inheritance of Loss

BY KIRAN DESAI

All day, the colors had been those of dusk, mist moving like a water creature across the great flanks of mountains possessed of ocean shadows and depths.

THE INDIAN SOCIETY of this novel is caught between the fading ideals of a British civilization and the allure of Western capitalism.

Jemubhai Patel, despite his humble origins, becomes a judge in post-colonial India. An Anglophile, his success leaves him estranged from his Indian heritage. In retirement, he lives in a decaying house, bitter and contemptuous of his compatriots. His orphaned teenaged granddaughter Sai falls in love with her mathematics tutor, a young man embroiled in the Nepalese insurgency that turns into a violent rebellion against the colonialism and privilege that Patel embodies.

Meanwhile, the judge's cook has sent his son Biju to America to make a better life, but there he belongs to the "shadow class" of illegal immigrants and can find work only as a kitchen helper.

Desai takes a profoundly pessimistic view, showing that in both of these worlds—one a remote corner of India during growing Nepalese unrest, the other Manhattan's tough streets—privilege is self-perpetuating.

Published in 2006, this was Desai's second novel. At the age of thirty-five, she became the youngest woman to win the Man Booker Prize. She and her mother, Anita Desai, who had been a finalist for the award three times, were the first ever mother/daughter nominees.

"Although it focuses on the fate of a few powerless individuals, Kiran Desai's extraordinary new novel manages to explore, with intimacy and insight, just about every contemporary international issue: globalization, multiculturalism, economic inequality, fundamentalism and terrorist violence."

—PANKAJ MISHRA, *NEW YORK TIMES*

THE OLD MAN AND THE SEA

BY ERNEST HEMINGWAY

He was an old man who fished alone in a skiff in the Gulf Stream and he had gone eighty-four days now without taking a fish.

THIS NOVELLA WAS the last major work of fiction written by Hemingway. It tells the simple, moving story of Santiago, an aging Cuban fisherman. On his eighty-fifth day at sea, he struggles to land a gigantic marlin. After an epic battle, he emerges victorious against "brother" marlin. He lashes his catch to the side of the boat for the trip back, only to lose the fish to sharks that follow behind, waiting for an easy feed.

In this deeply symbolic novel, Hemingway portrays Santiago as a classic tragic hero. There are echoes of Christ in the way Santiago's hands are wounded and in the way that he falters as he carries the mast of his boat uphill. Unlike Hemingway's earlier protagonists, Santiago is not only courageous but also humble and gently proud. He feels a profound brotherhood with nature. This courageous warrior is defeated by stubborn pride.

Hemingway wrote this work in a two-month burst when he was fifty-one years old. It had been eleven years since he'd had a successful novel. The novella was first published in *Life* magazine in 1952. Within two days, more than 5 million copies had been sold. The *New York Times* proclaimed it his "big comeback." The novella won the Pulitzer in 1953. A year later, Hemingway was awarded the Nobel Prize for literature.

"Within the sharp restrictions imposed by the very nature of his story Mr. Hemingway has written with sure skill. Here is the master technician once more at the top of his form, doing superbly what he can do better than anyone else."

—ORVILLE PRESCOTT, *NEW YORK TIMES*

INDEPENDENCE DAY

BY RICHARD FORD

In Haddam, summer floats over tree-softened streets like a sweet lotion balm from a careless, languorous god, and the world falls in tune with its own mysterious anthems.

FORTY-FOUR-YEAR-OLD FRANK BASCOMBE finds his life at a "turning or at least a curving point" in this novel. The former sportswriter is divorced and sells real estate in suburban New Jersey. Work can be frustrating, and he's just shown a couple their forty-sixth potential home.

Bascombe has children with whom he can't quite connect, and a relationship to which he won't commit. He tries to find emotional and physical shelter in the house he bought from his ex-wife, but having reached his "existence period," he's become numb to life, cut off from the world by his own dreams.

On July 4, he picks up his troubled son and sets out on a trip to a sports hall of fame. At a baseball field, he's struck by a lightning bolt and everything changes. When he comes to, he once again trusts his feelings.

This tour de force novel was the first to win both the Pulitzer and the PEN/Faulkner awards (1996). Critics put Bascombe in the pantheon of great American fictional characters with Fitzgerald's Nick Carraway, Bellow's Augie March, and Updike's Rabbit Angstrom.

Ford introduced Frank Bascombe to the world in the 1986 novel, *The Sportswriter.*

"Richard Ford is the creator of 'dirty realism' and sad happiness; the dedicated chronicler of American suburbia and the burden of male anxiety. Like the painter Edward Hopper, he casts light on hitherto invisible lives."

—NICCI GERRARD, *OBSERVER*

THE BRIGHT FOREVER

BY LEE MARTIN

On the night it happened — July 5 — the sun didn't set until 8:33.

IN SMALL-TOWN INDIANA in the middle of summer, when residents might sit out on the porch and sip lemonade or stop by for a beer at the Top Hat Inn, the unthinkable happens. Gilley Mackey has threatened to tattle on his nine-year-old sister Katie for having overdue books, so just before sunset she piles the books into her bike basket and rides off to the library. She never comes back.

Katie's family owns the local glassworks. To outsiders they seem to have everything—wealth, good looks, community status. But things are not as they seem as tragedy peels away the veneer.

The first suspects are men, odd outsiders. One of them is Henry Dees, a lonely math teacher who has been tutoring Katie and has become obsessed with her. But the real killer is a predator who takes advantage of both Mr. Dees's and little Katie's vulnerabilities. As each character tells his or her part of the story and the pieces of the tragedy fall together, the reader realizes how each of them is in some way complicit in Katie's murder.

This was Martin's second novel and a surprise pick as a finalist for the 2006 Pulitzer.

"With what consummate skill Lee Martin conjures up a small town in the grip of tragedy and how deftly he explores the way in which a casual remark, a brief kiss, a white lie can have the most terrible consequences."

—MARGOT LIVESEY

JUBILEE

BY MARGARET WALKER

"May Liza, how come you so restless and uneasy? You must be restless in your mind."

WALKER IMAGINES THE life of her great-grandmother, Margaret Duggans Ware Brown, the daughter of a "house slave" and a white plantation owner in Georgia. At the age of seven, Vyry is delivered to serve as a slave in her father's house. Big Missy Salina knows why Vyry looks so much like her own daughter and takes it out on the girl. But little Vyry has a strong will of her own and hidden resources to draw upon.

Vyry finds hope and freedom by marrying Randall Ware, a free Negro blacksmith, and gives birth to a daughter and son. The Civil War breaks out, and Randall leaves her to join the Union forces. Word comes of his death, and Vyry finds refuge with a former field hand. The aftermath of the war brings flood, famine, and violence as the Ku Klux Klan rises from the war's ashes.

This 1966 novel is the saga of a strong, brave black woman, and of a family torn by the Civil War, Reconstruction, and violence. The voice is authentic and the story steeped in folk tradition.

A poet and novelist, Walker was born in Birmingham, Alabama, in 1915. Her father gave her her first writer's journal at the age of twelve. Poet Langston Hughes encouraged her writing. For more insight into Margaret Walker's legacy, read her essays in *How I Wrote* Jubilee.

"What [Margaret Walker] tells us in her books, with that voice of sun and sky, moon and stars, of lightning and thunder, is in that oldest voice of that first ancestor, who will always be with us."

—AMIRI BARAKA, *NATION*

THE SUN ALSO RISES

BY ERNEST HEMINGWAY

Robert Cohn was once middleweight boxing champion of Princeton. Do not think that I am very much impressed by that as a boxing title, but it meant a lot to Cohn.

JAKE BARNES, A thirty-four-year-old American newspaper correspondent in Paris, is one of the war-weary "lost generation." He survived the First World War, but wounds he suffered on the Italian front left him impotent. In a military hospital, he falls hopelessly in love with an Englishwoman, Lady Brett Ashley. Awaiting a divorce from her current husband and engaged to another, Brett is tormented because Barnes cannot consummate his love for her. Convinced that she could never live with Brett because she could not remain faithful, she takes off for Spain.

The pair are reunited when Jake and two friends go to Spain to fish and attend the running of the bulls at Pamplona. Both of his friends are also in love with Brett. Brett confides in Jake, telling him of her affairs with other men and of her unhappiness, even as she's obsessed with Pedro Romero, a spectacular nineteen-year-old matador. Jake becomes her procurer, introducing her to Romero. Friendships crumble and, at long last, so does Jake's infatuation with Brett.

This was Hemingway's first novel, written in his midtwenties. It turned him into an instant international celebrity. His lean, hard, athletic narrative prose style, informal colloquial dialogue, and quick scene changes were revolutionary when the novel was first published in 1926.

"The sun also ariseth, and the sun goeth down, and hasteth to his place where he arose."

—ECCLESIASTES 1:5

Foreign Affairs

BY ALISON LURIE

On a cold blowy February day a woman is boarding the ten A.M. flight to London, followed by an invisible dog.

OPPOSITES ATTRACT, AND in this satirical novel a pair of lonely expat academics in London find love in unlikely places. One is fifty-four-year-old spinster Vinnie Miner. She's an Ivy League professor on her way to study in England for six months. The other is Chuck Mumpson, a recently laid-off, folksy sewer supplier from Oklahoma in a cowboy hat whom Vinnie meets on the plane and dismisses him as a "large stupid semiliterate man." But she keeps running into him. Before long, against her better judgment, she's fallen in love.

Their relationship keeps Vinnie from becoming what she's always dreaded, "a minor character in her own life." In typical Lurie fashion, it's at the London Zoo while watching polar bears that Vinnie realizes she is at last free of literature's constraints and can express her physical being. The end of their affair is bittersweet.

On a parallel trajectory is her young colleague, Fred Turner, also doing research in England. He sees himself as a character in a Henry James novel. He, too, falls in love—with a beautiful and aristocratic English television actress.

This was Lurie's seventh work of fiction and a comic masterpiece. It won the Pulitzer Prize for Fiction in 1985.

"One can read Lurie as one might read Jane Austen, with continual delight."

—JOYCE CAROL OATES

HIGH FIDELITY

BY NICK HORNBY

Now . . . Laura leaves first thing Monday morning with a hold-all and a carrier bag.

WHO SAYS YOU can't turn back the clock? In this edgy, wildly funny 1995 novel, British pop-music maven Rob Fleming has just been dumped by Laura, his latest girlfriend. In his record store, Championship Vinyl, where he hangs out with a pair of fellow slackers, he licks his wounds. For hours he rearranges his record collection and makes top-five lists—top-five songs to play at a funeral, top-five films, top-five most memorable split-ups. Among his top authors are Raymond Chandler, Thomas Harris, William Gibson, and Kurt Vonnegut.

Fleming has this midlife crisis in his thirties. He revisits each of his failed relationships, trying to convince himself that it was never his fault. When he was just thirteen, there was Alison Ashworth. Their brief relationship: "First night: park, fag, snog. Second night: ditto. Third night: ditto. Fourth night: chucked." Then there was Charlie Nicholson who left him for Marco. And so it goes, as each of these pathetic and laugh-out-loud funny, disastrous relationships parade across the pages.

Critics compared Hornby's writing to Martin Amis, but Hornby says he feels a stronger kinship to the funny, less edgy work of Martin's father Kingsley Amis.

"It would be too easy to call Hornby's hapless North Londoners 'everymen'; in fact, he demands more of his characters than that. He presses them on toward remarkable things: they must learn to be honest, to communicate with their lovers, to be heroic, to be good."

—ZADIE SMITH, *TIME* MAGAZINE

Love in the Time of Cholera

BY GABRIEL GARCÍA MÁRQUEZ

It was inevitable: the scent of bitter almonds always reminded him of the fate of unrequited love.

THIS 1988 NOVEL tells a tale of thwarted love that flourishes after fifty-one years, nine months, and four days. It takes place in an unnamed Caribbean seaport—perhaps Cartagena or Barranquilla—and tells of a young telegrapher, Florentino Ariza, who falls profoundly in love with the beautiful, haughty Fermina Daza. Through letters they carry on a passionate affair. Fermina's father objects to their liaison, and eventually she rejects Florentino and instead marries wealthy physician Dr. Urbino, leaving Florentino in paroxysms of agony. He will always love her, he proclaims, and settles in to what turns into a lifelong wait.

Decades later, at Fermina's husband's funeral (he dies chasing a parrot up a mango tree), Florentino steps forward and once again declares his love. Furious, Fermina orders him out of the house. Flashbacks reveal what happened in the lives of the three characters—Florentino, Fermina, and Dr. Urbino—returning to Fermina's final rejection and Florentino's determination to continue courting and win her love.

Second in a trilogy of autobiographical novels by a great Colombian writer and Nobel laureate, the book seethes with unrequited, youthful passions that turn to deep love, seasoned by experience and grief in old age.

"He writes with impassioned control, out of a maniacal serenity: the Garcimarquesian voice we have come to recognize from the other fiction has matured, found and developed new resources, been brought to a level where it can at once be classical and familiar, opalescent and pure, able to praise and curse, laugh and cry, fabulate and sing and when called upon, take off and soar."

—THOMAS PYNCHON, *NEW YORK TIMES*

Sophie's Choice

BY WILLIAM STYRON

In those days cheap apartments were almost impossible to find in Manhattan, so I had to move to Brooklyn.

SET IN 1947 Brooklyn and told from the point of view of a struggling, twenty-two-year-old southern writer named Stingo (based on Styron himself), this is the tragic story of his friendship with a pair of doomed lovers who live in the apartment upstairs. One is a paranoid, mercurial, drug-addicted Jewish madman, Nathan Landau. The other is the beautiful Sophie Zawistowska. She is a Roman Catholic Polish immigrant and granddaughter of a rabid anti-Semite. Sophie survived the Nazi concentration camp at Auschwitz in body but not in spirit.

Sophie confides in Stingo her abiding self-hatred and suicidal thoughts as Nathan becomes increasingly violent and unpredictable. Stingo can't help falling in love with her.

These characters are ridden with guilt. Stingo over his casual treatment of his mother when she was dying of cancer, and for the tainted source of the money that finances his writing; Sophie for having been forced to make an unbearable choice.

Confronting the tragic end of Sophie and Nathan, Stingo says, "Someday I will write about Sophie's life and death, and thereby help demonstrate how evil is never extinguished from the world." This won the National Book Award in 1980.

"I think for years to come [Styron's] work will be seen for its unique power. No other American writer of my generation has had so omnipresent and exquisite a sense of the elegiac."

—NORMAN MAILER, *NEW YORK TIMES*

Madame Bovary

BY GUSTAVE FLAUBERT

We were in study hall when the headmaster walked in, followed by a new boy not wearing a school uniform, and by a janitor carrying a large desk.

EMMA ROUAULT YEARNS for romance and for the finer things in life. She's a beautiful, convent-educated farmer's daughter. When physician Charles Bovary's wife dies, he courts Emma. She sees this man, with his well-cut clothing and education, as her ticket out of the provincial life she abhors. But once married, she grows increasingly disillusioned. Charles is boring and clumsy, not at all her romantic ideal. Though they move to a livelier town and she gives birth to a daughter, neither motherhood nor her social life shake her from melancholy.

Her downfall comes at the hands of Rodolphe Boulanger, who sees her for what she is—venal and ripe for seduction. During a tempestuous three-year affair that sweeps Emma away in its romantic fantasy, she writes letters and visits her lover with indiscretion. She thinks he will carry her off to a new, exciting life. She's mistaken. Crushing debts come due and yet another failed affair leads to the ultimate despair.

The novel is now considered a poetic masterpiece, but that wasn't always so. The first installment appeared in 1856 in the *Revue de Paris* (the editor was an old friend from Flaubert's student days) when the author was thirty-five years old. Pages were cut from his manuscript and words like *concubine*, *concupiscence*, and *adultery* were deleted. The magazine's editors and Flaubert were put on trial for "outraging public morals and religion."

"Stylistically [Madame Bovary] *is prose doing what poetry is supposed to do."*

—VLADIMIR NABOKOV, *LECTURES ON LITERATURE*

Look Homeward, Angel

BY THOMAS C. WOLFE

A destiny that leads the English to the Dutch is strange enough; but one that leads from Epsom into Pennsylvania, and thence into the hills that shut in Altamont over the proud coral cry of the cock, and the soft stone smile of an angel, is touched by that dark miracle of chance which makes new magic in a dusty world.

THIS AUTOBIOGRAPHICAL COMING-OF-AGE story takes Eugene Gant from birth through nineteen years of age. Like Thomas C. Wolfe, he grows up in a small town in North Carolina, attends a state university and then Harvard. At last, he sets out for Europe to fulfill his destiny as a writer.

This is a romantic 1929 novel about Gant's education, his family life, and the world that surrounds him as he develops a writer's voice that rivals Walt Whitman's. To read it is to revel in sensations and in a rich and pungent sense of time and place as Gant experiences his world in moments. A first taste of whiskey. A first kiss. The death of a loved one. In short, the novel delivers a vivid sense of what it means to be alive.

Wolfe grew up in a home steeped in rhetoric. His father (William Oliver Wolfe), like Gant's fictional father, W. O. Gant, went about declaiming Shakespeare.

A legendary writer, Wolfe sometimes wrote ten thousand words a day. He credits his editor at Scribner, Maxwell Perkins, for transforming this first novel into a classic. Wolfe fell ill and died at just 37.

"There are young Americans today who are doing such passionate and authentic work that it makes me sick to see that I am a little too old to be one of them. There is . . . Thomas Wolfe, a child of, I believe thirty or younger, whose . . . novel, Look Homeward, Angel, *is worthy to be compared with the best in our literary production, a Gargantuan creature with great gusto of life. . . ."*

—SINCLAIR LEWIS, *NOBEL WRITERS ON WRITING*

LES MISÉRABLES

BY VICTOR HUGO

*In 1815, M. Charles-Francois-Bienvenu Myriel was Bishop of
D——. He was an old man of about seventy-five years of age; he
had occupied the see of D—— since 1806.*

PLAYED OUT AGAINST the backdrop of the Napoleonic wars, this novel tells the story of Jean Valjean, a starving orphan who steals a loaf of bread and gets caught. He's sentenced to five years of hard labor. He tries to escape, only to have fourteen years added to his sentence. Released at last, in middle age, he is shunned and denied shelter. He is bent on wreaking revenge until he is taken in by the saintly Bishop of Digne (Monsieur Bienvenu). But one further act of petty theft puts the police back on his trail, and though he assumes a respectable life, he remains a fugitive.

Javert is the relentless policeman (Hugo compares him to a wolf cub that devours its siblings) who finally catches up with Valjean. But in a wonderful plot twist, Valjean saves Javert's life and Javert, in return, surprises himself by saving Valjean's. Javert's soul is virtually derailed by this unfathomable act and he throws himself into the Seine.

This 1,200-page (in its original, unabridged version) morality play of revenge turned to redemption has captivated generations.

*"[Victor Hugo] had the powers of a great genius and the soul of an
ordinary man. . . . It was not as a mere technician that he wished to be
judged; he wrote with a very different intention; it was as a philosopher,
as a moralist, as a prophet, as a sublime thinker, as a profound historian,
as a sensitive and refined human being."*

—GILES LYTTON STRACHEY,
LANDMARKS IN FRENCH LITERATURE

NO ORDINARY TIME

BY DORIS KEARNS GOODWIN

On nights filled with tension and concern, Franklin Roosevelt performed a ritual that helped him to fall asleep.

IN JULY OF 1940, Eleanor Roosevelt told the Democratic Convention, "This is no ordinary time." Only Britain was engaged in the war with Hitler, but the United States was being drawn in. In this Pulitzer Prize–winning book, Goodwin tells the story of the home front, what went on inside the White House and in the nation, and of the couple, Franklin and Eleanor, who despite their flaws and weaknesses, were also far from ordinary.

Goodwin argues that two social developments—the New Deal and World War II—conspired to create "the most profound social revolution in the country since the Civil War—nothing less than the creation of modern America." But she tells that story through the prism of the personal lives of the Roosevelts and the friends and associates who lived with them during the war. In particular, she shows how Eleanor Roosevelt's voice emerged as the social conscience of the nation. No longer his lover but very much his partner, she hectored the more pragmatic Franklin, championing the causes of Jews fleeing the Holocaust, of laborers, of women, and of African Americans. Eleanor wrote in her autobiography, "I sometimes acted as a spur even though the spurring was not always wanted or welcome."

"The book takes you to war, to the White House, into a difficult marriage and a turbulent time. In an age when a lot of people foolishly rely on popcorn served up by so many media outlets as their sole source of information, when TV too often gives in to the tendency to be merely talking wallpaper, something like No Ordinary Time *reminds you there is no substitute for good writing and a great story."*

—MIKE BARNICLE

CHARMING BILLY

BY ALICE MCDERMOTT

Somewhere in the Bronx, only twenty minutes or so from the cemetery, Maeve found a small bar-and-grill in a wooded alcove set well off the street that was willing to serve the funeral party of forty-seven medium-rare roast beef and boiled potatoes and green beans amandine, with fruit salad to begin and vanilla ice cream to go with the coffee.

YOUNG BILLY LYNCH was charming; that was an accepted fact. That his weakness was drink was a given, too. The novel opens at his 1982 funeral in the Bronx and goes on to examine what happened to this gifted young man after he first met Eva from County Wicklow.

In flashbacks, we learn that Billy was a gregarious bloke who instantly turned strangers he met at the pub into pals. He was also a dreamer, a romantic who wrote a poem on a napkin and sent it off to his beloved Eva. He hung onto the delusion that Eva died, for the truth was far too humiliating and sad. Billy's cousin Dennis, his best friend, enabler, and frustrated savior, would even dump Eva's sister Mary and marry another in order to spare Billy pain.

This is anything but the usual sodden saga of an alcoholic Irishman and his extended family. The writer's elegant, evocative, tightly crafted character studies examine the power of lies, the devastation of alcoholism, and the redeeming force of family and friendship.

McDermott says that this "ultimately is a novel about faith, and what we believe in, and above all, what we choose to believe in." It took top literary prizes, including the 1998 National Book Award.

"What you get [from Alice McDermott's novels] is Irish-American angst—straight up, no chaser. You get probing family archeology, burnished prose and minimalist, backward-arching plots as her characters sift through battered memories for faint signs of redemption."

—DAN CRYER, SALON.COM

HOLES

BY LOUIS SACHAR

There is no lake at Camp Green Lake.

POOR STANLEY YELNATS. Unfairly accused of stealing the smelly used sneakers of baseball great Clyde "Sweet Feet" Livingston (actually they fell from the sky and landed on his head), he's sentenced to serve out an eighteen-month sentence at Camp Green Lake Juvenile Correctional Facility where nothing is green and there's no water, just a lakebed and a "dry, flat wasteland."

It's nothing like a "camp," either, as Stanley and his fellow inmates are roused before dawn each day to dig five-by-five-by-five holes in the desert. Only the treacherous Warden (she mixes rattlesnake venom into her nail polish), who insists digging holes builds character, seems to know what they're looking for.

Sounds grim but it's very funny, and particularly satisfying when the plot's jigsaw pieces fall together. Stinky smells figure prominently (for instance, Stanley's father made a fortune by inventing a cure for foot odor; one of Warden's ancestors was nicknamed Trout because his feet smelled like dead fish; and the imprisoned boys take refuge in onion fields).

Sachar came up with *Yelnats* by reversing the letters in *Stanley*. This 1998 book won the National Book Award and the Newbery Medal.

"Imagine a game where you know enough to make the next move exciting but not enough to know what that move is going to be. That's Holes, as deep as its title."

—BETSY HEARNE, *NEW YORK TIMES*

THE GRAPES OF WRATH

BY JOHN STEINBECK

To the red country and part of the gray country of Oklahoma, the last rains came gently, and they did not cut the scarred earth.

THE ANGER AND outrage Steinbeck felt when he visited migrant labor camps in northern California in the late 1930s inspired him to write this, considered his best novel. It opens with Tom Joad, the son of an Oklahoma family, returning home to what is rapidly becoming the Dust Bowl. Just released from jail, he picks up the preacher who baptized him. When he arrives home he finds his family dispossessed, the land he grew up on taken over by the bank and the house destroyed by a tractor. The family packs up a secondhand truck and sets out, eager to start over in California, where an orange handbill promises well-paid work picking fruit.

It's a long trek. Grandpa and Grandma die along the way. At a river, one son decides he's gone far enough. The people they meet who are headed back the other way are embittered and broken. They tell of penurious wages, dreadful working conditions, and labor trouble.

The Joads discover for themselves that the beauty and fertility of California mask fear, hatred, and violence.

This portrait of the Joad family's struggle to survive in the face of ruthless agricultural economics struck a chord. Detractors accused Steinbeck of being a communist and exaggerating the conditions. Eleanor Roosevelt came to his defense, and the controversy led to changes in the labor laws. The novel was awarded the Pulitzer Prize in 1940.

"It is a very long novel, the longest that Steinbeck has written, and yet it reads as if it had been composed in a flash, ripped off the typewriter and delivered to the public as an ultimatum."

—PETER MONRO JACK, *NEW YORK TIMES*

THE SCARLET LETTER

BY NATHANIEL HAWTHORNE

A throng of bearded men, in sad-coloured garments and grey steeple-crowned hats, inter-mixed with women, some wearing hoods, and others bareheaded, was assembled in front of a wooden edifice, the door of which was heavily timbered with oak, and studded with iron spikes.

THOUGH THE WORD is never used in the novel, this is a morality tale about the consequences of adultery. Hester Prynne has given birth to a child from an adulterous affair. Though she's publicly harangued and forced to wear the scarlet letter *A*, she refuses to name her lover. She raises her daughter, does good works, but still she's shunned by the community, while her former lover suffers a living hell.

Hester is independent and proud; she believes that she and her lover Dimmesdale have somehow triumphed. Her wronged husband, Roger Chillingworth, whom Hester believed lost at sea, settles nearby intent on revenge.

First published in 1850 and one of America's first psychological novels, it pits rigid seventeenth-century Puritan morality against passion and individualism. It was an instant bestseller.

Hawthorne was of Puritan descent. In a diary entry five years before this book was published, he speculated on what life would be like for a woman condemned for adultery who, under the "dismal severity of the Puritan code of law," was forced to wear the letter *A* stitched to her clothing.

"The Scarlet Letter *isn't a pleasant, pretty romance. It is a sort of parable, an earthly story with a hellish meaning.*"

—D. H. LAWRENCE, *STUDIES IN CLASSIC LITERATURE*

THE BRIDGE OF SAN LUIS REY

BY THORNTON WILDER

*On Friday noon, July the twentieth, 1714, the finest bridge in all
Peru broke and precipitated five travelers into the gulf below.*

ON THE SURFACE, this novel is the story of the collapse of a
rope suspension bridge, and of the five people crossing it who
met their death. They include a lonely Marquesa, estranged
from her beloved daughter, and the Marquesa's companion, an
orphan who was reared by a great abbess. Another orphan the
abbess had cared for is also killed—a young man who had been
grieving over his twin's death and had, at just that fatal moment,
decided to move on with his life. The last two victims are a man
who had devoted himself to the career of Peru's greatest actress
and the actress's young son.

Franciscan missionary Brother Juniper happens to be there
and witnesses the collapse. He takes on the quest of discovering
"Why did this happen to those five?" Was it "God's will" or
simply bad luck and pure chance that led to the tragedy? His
quest ultimately leads to his own death.

Published in 1927, this was Wilder's second novel and it
went on to win the Pulitzer Prize. Prime Minister Tony Blair
read this novel's closing sentences at a memorial service for
British victims of the 9/11 attack on the World Trade Center:
"There is a land of the living and a land of the dead and the
bridge is love, the only survival, the only meaning."

"Thornton Wilder's Bridge of San Luis Rey *is as close to perfect a moral
fable as we are ever likely to get in American literature."*

—RUSSELL BANKS, FOREWORD TO THE
2004 (HARPERCOLLINS) EDITION

FANNY HILL, OR THE MEMOIRS OF A WOMAN OF PLEASURE

BY JOHN CLELAND

Madam, I sit down to write you an undeniable proof of my considering your desires as indispensable orders. Ungracious then as the task may be, I shall recall to view those scandalous stages of my life.

FANNY MAY LOVE many, but she gives her heart to one. In this novel, she writes of her adventures—coming to London with a friend at fifteen, working at a brothel where she is introduced to the world of eroticism, and falling in love with Charles. When Charles's father sends him packing rather than endure such an inappropriate match, Fanny is thrown back on her considerable resources. Many episodes build up to the loss of her virginity—she gives it up to the man who will eventually be her husband.

Contemporaries had never seen anything like *Fanny Hill*. Cleland wrote it in debtor's prison. It received its first reading in 1737 at Beggars' Benison, a sex club in Scotland, but didn't find its way into print until ten years later. Its author, publisher, and printer were promptly incarcerated.

The book was a huge success. By 1800, there had been twenty editions published in English and another fourteen in French. Until 1966, this porn classic couldn't be sold in the United States.

"Fanny Hill doesn't have . . . weight or ambition. It is a rather fabulous alchemical experiment that throws the early realist novel and straight-up erotical into an alembic and ends up accidentally creating the Pornographer's Stone."

—SEAN WALSH, INTRODUCTION TO THE
2007 (BOOKKAKE) EDITION

Exodus

BY LEON URIS

The airplane plip-plopped down the runway to a halt at a big sign: WELCOME TO CYPRUS.

THIS 600-PAGE NOVEL interweaves historical facts with fictional events to tell the story of the birth of Israel as a modern nation. Its characters take part in the drama of Jewish history.

Most of the book's first segment concerns the Holocaust—first told from the viewpoint of a young girl who escapes to Poland, then told from the viewpoint of an Auschwitz survivor.

Next, Uris tells of two brothers, Jossi and Yakov Rabinsky, whose father is killed in a Russian pogrom. The pair slay their father's killer, flee, and go on to help establish the first Jewish settlements in Palestine. Over time, one becomes a moderate citizen; the other evolves into a full-fledged terrorist.

Finally, the novel tells of Israel's struggles under the British and a miraculous victory over Arab states seeking to "push Israel into the sea."

When the book was published in 1957, it was an instant bestseller in America and banned in the Soviet Union. It has been criticized for oversimplifying the dynamics of the Middle East and for stereotyped portrayals.

A high-school dropout and son of Russian-Polish Jews, Uris became a war correspondent. In 1956, he covered the Arab-Israeli fighting. In preparing to write this book, he read hundreds of books and underwent a grueling training program to prepare himself to travel 50,000 miles (12,000 in Israel alone) and interview hundreds of people.

"Leon Uris is a storyteller, in a direct line from those men who sat around fires in the days before history and made the tribe more human."

—PETE HAMILL, *NEW YORK TIMES*

AROUND THE WORLD IN EIGHTY DAYS

BY JULES VERNE

Mr. Phileas Fogg lived, in 1872, at No. 7, Saville Row, Burlington Gardens, the house in which Sheridan died in 1814.

THIS NOVEL WAS published in 1873, a century before the Concorde made it possible to travel at twice the speed of sound. The story begins with a wager. Banker Andrew Stuart bets 20,000 pounds that Phileas Fogg can't journey around the world in "eighty days or less; in nineteen hundred and twenty hours, or a hundred and fifteen thousand two hundred minutes." The phlegmatic, meticulous Fogg takes the bet. He has his astonished manservant, Passepartout, pack nothing but a "carpet bag, with two shirts and three pairs of stockings."

Traveling by balloon, train, steamship, sledge, and elephant, the pair encounter natural disasters and an attack by Sioux Indians. Through a combination of resourcefulness, determination, pluck, lavish spending, and a bit of blind luck, they scrape in just under the wire. Along the way, Fogg wins the heart of Aouda, a beautiful young widow he meets in India.

This wonderful, old-timey classic was the first major commercial success from a writer who looked into the future. Verne went on to publish nearly seventy novels and coined the term *scientific romance*. In this book, he foresaw the mile-a-minute train. In *Twenty Thousand Leagues Under the Sea* he prophesied submarine travel.

"Deep in these fascinating tales one forgot everything save the adventures so graphically related, and after reading them one looked with different eyes on the wonders of the earth, air, and water which the novelist had made so familiar."

—*TIMES* (LONDON) OBITUARY FOR JULES VERNE

BILLY BUDD

BY HERMAN MELVILLE

In the time before steamships, or then more frequently than now, a stroller along the docks of any considerable sea-port would occasionally have his attention arrested by a group of bronzed mariners, man-of-war's men or merchant-sailors in holiday attire ashore on liberty.

GOOD AND EVIL clash in this novella. Good is embodied in Billy Budd, a sailor pressed into service on a British warship. He's strong, loyal, and brave, adored by his shipmates and admired by officers. The brutal Master-at-Arms of the lower deck, Claggart, is evil incarnate. He hates Billy with an irrational passion and engineers his downfall by making it seem as if Billy participates in an attempted mutiny.

The two face off before Captain Vere, and Billy is unable to speak to refute the charges. In a flash of anger, Billy strikes Claggart dead. In so doing, he seals his own doom: He has killed his officer in a time of war and is condemned to hang. Though Captain Vere has acted as witness, prosecutor, judge, and executioner, at the moment of his death, Billy cries out "God bless Captain Vere."

Melville wrote this late in life, and it was unpublished at the time of his death in 1891. A revival of interest in Melville's work resulted in the discovery of the manuscript among his papers. Publication came at last in 1924.

"[Billy Budd] was Melville's final word, worthy of him, indisputably a passing beyond the tremendous nihilism of Moby Dick, to what may seem to some simple and childish, but to others will be wonderful and divine."

—JOHN MIDDLETON MURRY,
JOHN CLARE AND OTHER STUDIES

THE PILGRIM'S PROGRESS

BY JOHN BUNYAN

As I walk'd through the wilderness of this world, I lighted on a certain place, where was a Denn, And I laid me down in that place to sleep; And, as I slept I dreamed a Dream.

THIS STORY, NARRATED by a dreamer, tells of a man's epic pilgrimage from the City of Destruction to the Celestial City. Ragged Christian leaves his house, convinced that it will soon be burned down—the prophecy is foretold in the book he carries. He is in great distress ("he burst out, as he had done before, crying, 'What shall I do to be saved?'"). His family thinks he's gone mad.

He journeys on, with stops at allegorical places like the Slough of Despond, the House Beautiful, the Valley of Humiliation, Vanity Fair, Doubting Castle, and the Valley of the Shadow of Death. Like the places, the characters he meets along the way have telling names: Hopeful, Faithful, my Lord Fairspeech, my Lord Time-server, Mr. Facingbothways, and Mr. Anything. In the story's second part, Christian's wife, Christiana, is inspired to follow on a similar pilgrimage.

Bunyan felt that this allegory contained nothing but "sound and honest Gospel strains." Bible references and verses are on nearly every page. It may have been partly written at a desk in a jail cell where the passionately religious Bunyan was imprisoned for preaching without a license. The first edition of this book appeared in 1678. Its popularity was once second only to the Bible. The unheroic hero character Billy Pilgrim takes a parallel journey in Kurt Vonnegut's *Slaughterhouse-Five*.

"In no book do we see more clearly than in The Pilgrim's Progress *the new imaginative force which had been given to the common life of Englishmen by their study of the Bible."*

—J. R. GREEN

THE RED BADGE OF COURAGE

BY STEPHEN CRANE

The cold passed reluctantly from the earth, and the retiring fogs revealed an army stretched out on the hills, resting. As the landscape changed from brown to green, the army awakened, and began to tremble with eagerness at the noise of rumors.

HENRY FLEMING IS a volunteer Union soldier, a lowly private and farm boy who goes to war with dreams of glory and patriotic pride. Typical of the tens of thousands of green recruits who went to the front between Fort Sumter and the fall of Richmond, he's no hero.

Weary after months in drill camp, he yearns to show his valor. But war turns out to be anything but a glorious battlefront. It's a mean and nasty affair. Triumphs are accidental or arise out of blind courage fueled by the will to survive.

During the first battle, Fleming acquits himself creditably. He's breathing easier and feeling some pride when the shooting breaks out again. He drops his musket and runs. Exhausted, he later returns to his regiment. They assume his head wound was earned in battle with the enemy when in fact it came from the musket of a retreating soldier.

His regiment is assigned to what feels like a suicide mission, and Fleming gets to prove himself ("He had been touched with the great death, and found that, after all, it was but the great death. He was a man.").

Crane was barely twenty-five when he wrote this Civil War novel. Published in 1895, part of its staying power derives from its vivid language and unflinching look at war as armies confront each other and men "punched by bullets, f[a]ll in grotesque agonies."

"It is not at all difficult to point out in Crane's own words that he was acutely aware of the great farce and irony and absurdity that make up what he, and better we, know as war."

—HERMAN J. MANKIEWICZ

FEAR AND TREMBLING

BY SÖREN KIERKEGAARD

Not only in the commercial world but in the realm of ideas as well, our age is holding a veritable clearance sale.

THIS "DIALECTICAL LYRIC" takes as its starting point the story from Genesis of Abraham's journey up a mountain in "the land of Moriah" to sacrifice his beloved son, Isaac, as God has commanded him in order to demonstrate his faith. Danish philosopher and theologian Kierkegaard explores Abraham's suffering in this ultimate test of his faith. He presents his readers with four different versions in which Abraham fails the test.

The familiar story is used to frame larger philosophical questions. Can there be a theological suspension of ethics? Is there an absolute duty toward God? What is the role of faith? Part of Kierkegaard's answer: "faith begins precisely where thinking leaves off." In other words, if we rely on mere words to understand, we fail.

What we fear, suggests Kierkegaard, is truth, and what makes us tremble is the thought of the kind of greatness that Abraham exhibited.

The novel was first published in Copenhagen in 1843 under the pseudonym "Johannes de silentio" (John of silence) and earned the author the title "father of existentialism."

"Eagerly I took from Kierkegaard the idea that subjectivity too has its rightful claims, amid all the desolating objective evidence of our insignificance and futility and final non-existence; faith is not a deduction but an act of will, a heroism."

—JOHN UPDIKE

THE TRIAL

BY FRANZ KAFKA

Someone must have been telling lies about Joseph K., for without having done anything wrong he was arrested one fine morning.

MOVING ON TO the surreal, this novel tells the story of Joseph K., a young banker in Prague who confronts faceless power. He awakes one day to find that he has been arrested. No charges are revealed, and he knows of no crime he has committed. He is permitted to go free but must keep returning to court, a sort of purgatory populated by accused citizens and petty bureaucrats. Repeatedly he argues his case but no resolution is ever reached. Along the way, Kafka reveals details of Joseph's life—his job, his landlady, the woman who inhabits the room next to his—and his attendant anxiety and inability to quite fathom any of it.

This suffocating, claustrophobic story of utter helplessness is, of course, a parable. Joseph K. expresses every man's helplessness in the face of the unknowable, and through him Kafka explores the nuance of good and evil in ethics and in the law. It sounds grim, but Kafka is a satirist. His friends convulsed with laughter when he read aloud from this book.

Kafka was born in 1883, lived most of his life in Prague. When the Communists seized power in 1948, he was branded a decadent. His works were again denounced and suppressed following the brief political and artistic flowering that came to be known as the Prague Spring. Twenty years later, his work was published once again in his native land.

"Manipulator of characters, scenes, dialogue and plot; painstaking emulator of Dickens and Flaubert; and self-taunting blocked writer, Kafka is as accessible to readers as he is esoteric to interpreters."

—JONATHAN LETHEM, *NEW YORK TIMES*

THE WASTE LAND

BY T. S. ELIOT

April is the cruellest month, breeding
Lilacs out of the dead land, mixing
Memory and desire, stirring
Dull roots with spring rain.

THIS 422-LINE, FIVE-PART poem, written when T. S. Eliot was thirty-four and published in 1922 (the same year as James Joyce's *Ulysses*), takes the human soul on a journey in search of redemption. The poem reflects Eliot's personal angst, as well as his disillusionment with the moral decay of post–World War I Europe. His characters, if there are any, are the passive people of "Unreal city" (aka, London).

The journey ends in a desert with a "damp gust" and much-hoped-for rain bringing with it the possibility of change—for the poet and for the world.

Most of the poem was written in 1921 when Eliot, trying to cope with his wife's health problems, was himself on the verge of a breakdown. The text is obscure and difficult, rife with footnoted quotations and references to history and other cultures. It includes quotations in Sanskrit and words invented to express sounds, meant to be read aloud for the rhythm and richness of the language.

Eliot entrusted the 1,000-line draft of this poem to the poet Ezra Pound for editing, and dedicated it to him. Its revolutionary style—one could say without rhyme or reason—set a new direction for modern poetry. While some early critics recognized it as a masterpiece, others proclaimed it a hoax.

"Unlike the satirist, Eliot does not criticize an actual world but creates a 'phantasmal' world of lust, filth, boredom and malice on which he gazes in fascinated horror."

—LYNDAL GORDON, ELIOT'S BIOGRAPHER

A Good Man Is Hard to Find

BY FLANNERY O'CONNOR

The grandmother didn't want to go to Florida.

THROUGH HER SHORT stories, Flannery O'Connor earned a reputation as one of America's most brutal and talented writers of the twentieth century. A master of the short story, in this collection of ten stories she explores the dark side of human nature—greed, malice, fear, hypocrisy, cruelty, and jealousy, all fostered in a bed of ignorance.

In the title story, a family on a car trip meets an escaped convict (the Misfit) who casually murders all of them. Near the end of the story, the grandmother reaches out to touch the Misfit with compassion. He "sprang back as if a snake had bitten him and shot her three times through the chest." Later he comments, "She would have been a good woman . . . if it had been somebody there to shoot her every minute of her life."

Another story tells of the nineteen-year-old Bible salesman phallically named Manley Pointer. Pointer steals a young woman's artificial leg and leaves her marooned in a hayloft. O'Connor never read this one aloud in public because she said, like many of her stories, she couldn't get through it and not "bust out laughing."

Written with O'Connor's trademark sardonic humor, the miscreants in her stories never lose their credibility. Squarely in the Southern gothic tradition, shelve this one alongside Erskine Caldwell's *Tobacco Road*.

O'Connor published thirty-one short stories and two novels in her lifetime. As a young woman, she was diagnosed with lupus and died at the age of thirty-nine.

"*[R]ereading Flannery O'Connor's short stories, out loud, once again turned me upside-down. Bang went Mrs. Turpin. Bang went Parker. Bang went I.*"

—STUDS TERKEL, QUOTED IN THE *NEW YORK TIMES*

APPOINTMENT IN SAMARRA

BY JOHN O'HARA

*Our story opens in the mind of Luther L. (L for LeRoy) Fliegler,
who is lying in his bed, not thinking of anything, but just aware of
sounds, conscious of his own breathing, and sensitive to his own
heartbeats.*

IN A STORY set in the coal-mining town of Gibbsville, Pennsylvania, just after the stock market crash, Julian English is a
spoiled, well-to-do WASP and president of the Gibbsville Cadillac Motor Car Company. One Christmas, he throws a drink in
the face of Harry Reilly, a loud, intemperate Irish Catholic who
will soon take over his company.

What ensues is a three-day slide to self-destruction. Julian
humiliates his wife and hits a disabled friend. Alcoholism,
weakness, and self-hatred—the same demons that plagued
O'Hara—fuel his decline. Or perhaps it's the inevitability of
fate, as suggested by the title taken from an Arab folktale.

O'Hara shows us Julian's life and life in Gibbsville from
the inside—in bedrooms, breakfast rooms, offices, and speak-
easies—and through the eyes of his family members, mob
errand boys, and car salesmen.

This 1934 novel was O'Hara's first. He wrote it in a Manhattan hotel room using the bed as a desk and often working
through the night. Gibbsville is a thinly disguised version of
Pottsville, where O'Hara grew up. Though some critics dismiss
O'Hara's novels as mere potboilers, he has been called the biographer of the post-Fitzgerald generation.

*"[O'Hara] gave people like me a sense of a larger America. He got inside
the political back rooms and the parlors and told us what Americans
said, how they lived, the details of the clothing, the shoes, the cars."*

—GAY TALESE, QUOTED IN WILLIAM GRIMES,
"THE JOHN O'HARA CULT, AT LEAST, FAITHFUL,"
NEW YORK TIMES

August

THE GUNS OF AUGUST

BY BARBARA W. TUCHMAN

So gorgeous was the spectacle on the May morning of 1910 when nine kings rode in the funeral of Edward VII of England that the crowd, waiting in hushed and black-clad awe, could not keep back gasps of admiration.

THEY CALLED IT the Great War. The "guns of august" were those that opened fire in 1914. Military historian Tuchman details the hours during the years leading up to the bloody carnage of the first month of fighting.

She begins with the colorful, pompous funeral of England's Edward VII, which would mark the end of the old European order. She recounts the growing competitive situation between England and Germany, and how the assassination of Archduke Ferdinand at Sarajevo in 1914 set the stage for war. For Tuchman, those events created "the chasm between our world and a world that has died forever."

She tells a meticulously researched, utterly absorbing tale of arms and men, aspirations and ideals. Battle scenes and strategic problems are part of her story, but her focus on the human qualities and powerful personalities of the leaders makes this an utterly absorbing must-read for anyone interested in World War I.

Tuchman sprang to prominence with this work. Published in 1962, it won the Pulitzer Prize and made its author America's best-known contemporary historian. She would win a second Pulitzer in 1971 with *Stilwell and the American Experience in China.*

"President John Kennedy ordered the top people at the Pentagon to read Barbara Tuchman's The Guns of August *so they would understand how a series of escalations and miscalculations on all sides led to World War I."*

—STEVEN R. WEISMAN, *NEW YORK TIMES*

LIGHT IN AUGUST

BY WILLIAM FAULKNER

Sitting beside the road, watching the wagon mount the hill toward her, Lena thinks, "I have come from Alabama: a fur piece."

THIS NOVEL SPINS three loosely connected narratives with three main characters—Lena Grove, Joe Christmas, and Gail Hightower—their stories driven by lust, violence, racial prejudice, and repression.

The very pregnant Lena Grove walks away from her Alabama home to search for Lucas Burch, the father of her unborn child, secure in her faith that he will marry her. Into Mississippi she trudges, serene and Madonna-like. She tracks him to Jefferson where he works in a sawmill. Luckily for her, she's mistakenly taken instead to the stalwart Byron Bunch, who will fall in love with her and take care of her and her child.

Meanwhile, the swaggering Burch, who has hidden misdeeds of his past from Lena, has adopted a new identity as Joe Brown. He's taken up with violent bootlegger Joe Christmas. Christmas is a man tortured by a tragedy in his family's past and by the knowledge that he may be half-black. His tempestuous affair with religious spinster Joanna Burden releases his inner demons, driving him to murder her. Hoping to hide the crime, Brown/Burch sets fire to Miss Burden's house with her corpse inside.

The town's wraith-like former minister, Gail Hightower, is an outcast who lives by the Bible. Stuck in the past, he spends his time revisiting his own grandfather's death. In his house, Christmas meets a grisly end.

Faulkner's seventh novel, written in the depths of the Depression, this was published in 1932.

"[T]he stories of Lena Grove and Hightower appear to form concentric circles around a horrific center, the murder of Joanna Burden, as if the dark narrative at the novel's core needed somehow to be contained."

—DOREEN FOWLER, *FAULKNER*

DANGEROUS LIAISONS (LES LIAISONS DANGEREUSES)

BY PIERRE CHODERLOS DE LACLOS

Cecile Volanges to Sophie Carnay at the Ursuline Convent of Paris—, 3 August 17—

Well, Sophie dear, as you see, I'm keeping my word and not spending all my time on bonnets and bows, I'll always have time to spare for you!

THIS INFAMOUS FRENCH epistolary novel set in prerevolutionary France is rife with love affairs, infidelities, and power struggles. First published in 1782, it tells of the sexual rivalry between a pair of former lovers, the Marquise de Merteuil and the Vicomte de Valmont. Mme. Merteuil challenges Valmont to seduce Sophie Carnay, a beautiful, naive girl who has just come out of a convent and is betrothed to Mme. Merteuil's former lover, on whom she wishes to wreak her own vicious form of revenge.

Meanwhile, Valmont also sets his sights on seducing Madame de Tourvel, a virtuous married woman. He succeeds all too well, only to find that, to his dismay, he's fallen in love with her. For Mme. Merteuil, Valmont has crossed a line and she is, as the title suggest, dangerous when betrayed.

Lives are toyed with, destroyed, and lost as wealth and boredom combine. In the end, Merteuil and Valmont are destroyed by their own decadence. You'll have to decide if it's a morality tale or pure entertainment.

This was Laclos's one and only novel, written when he was an officer in the French military. It reflects libertine attitudes common at the time and foreshadows the outrage that would spark the French Revolution.

"If this book burns, it can be only as ice burns."

—BAUDELAIRE, AFTER READING
LES LIAISONS DANGEREUSES

THE ADVENTURES OF AUGIE MARCH

BY SAUL BELLOW

I am an American, Chicago born—Chicago, that somber city— and go at things as I have taught myself, free-style, and will make the record in my own way: first to knock, first admitted; some-times an innocent knock, sometimes not so innocent.

HANDSOME, INTELLIGENT YOUNG Augie March admits that he has "a weak sense of consequence." His strong-willed, wealthy mistresses would call him needy and easily seduced by flattery. A sucker for other people's schemes, he lets con men, salesmen, and wheeler-dealers talk him into handling prize-fighters, stealing books, smuggling immigrants, organizing unions, guarding Trotsky in Mexico, and training a recalcitrant eagle to hunt giant lizards. Some of his adventures are more successful than others.

If this darkly comic novel sounds like a picaresque tale, it is. Set in the Depression in gangster-ruled West Side Chicago, the story begins in Augie's impoverished childhood when his nearly blind mother entrusts Augie and his brothers to the care of a boarder, Mrs. Lausch, whose child-rearing methods come direct from czarist Russia. Augie's first job gets him into a crooked real-estate deal and a love affair, followed by the first of a string of broken engagements, setting a pattern for Augie to be manipulated by others and then manage to slip away.

Though Augie never finds himself, his humanity and love for his family redeem him.

Nobel laureate Bellow set many of his works, like this one, in the Chicago where he grew up. Published in 1953, this was his breakthrough book.

"There is a narcissistic enthusiasm for life in all its hybrid forms propelling Augie March, and there is an inexhaustible passion for a teeming-ness of dazzling specifics driving Saul Bellow."

—PHILIP ROTH, *NEW YORKER*

THE BOYS OF SUMMER

BY ROGER KAHN

That morning began with wind and hairy clouds.

THE BROOKLYN DODGERS, what a team! Jackie Robinson and Pee Wee Reese and Roy Campanella and Duke Snider. . . .

Author Roger Kahn grew up in the '30s and '40s within throwing distance of Ebbets Field, home of the Brooklyn Dodgers. As a boy, he was a passionate fan. As a young sports reporter for the *New York Herald Tribune*, he covered the team during their exhilarating and maddening 1952 and 1953 seasons when they lost the World Series to the New York Yankees.

Kahn tells the inspiring story of how, in 1947, the team broke baseball's color line and won the pennant. In the ten years from 1947 through 1956, the Dodgers won the pennant six times. When the team moved to Los Angeles in 1958, many felt it had left its soul in Brooklyn.

This novelistic true story is by turns tragic and comic, an always-fascinating tale of the team, their memorable games, and their let-downs in the clutch that made their perennial motto "wait until next year." Kahn portrays the mythic players who were in their prime and reveals the not-so-pretty picture of what happened decades later as they aged.

Its first printing of 12,000 copies in 1972 sold out in days. Decades later, *Sports Illustrated* rated it number two among the best sports books of all time. Kahn said that Jackie Robinson told him that his phone rang off the hook when the book was published. "Now they're finding out I wasn't an Uncle Tom after all because of your damn book." Kahn took that as a compliment.

"[The Boys of Summer *is a*] baseball book the same way Moby Dick *is a fishing book. . . . No book is better at showing how sports is not just games."*

—SPORTS ILLUSTRATED

HIROSHIMA

BY JOHN HERSEY

At exactly fifteen minutes past eight in the morning, on August 6, 1945, Japanese time, at the moment when the atomic bomb flashed above Hiroshima, Miss Toshiko Sasaki, a clerk in the personnel department of the East Asia Tin Works, had just sat down at her place in the plant office and was turning her head to speak to the girl at the next desk.

FAR MORE MOVING and horrifying than any postapocalyptic fiction, this book tells the true stories of six survivors of the atomic bomb dropped on Hiroshima. Most of the city was destroyed in an instant. The rest was rubble and in flames. The heat propelled flames from one neighborhood to the next and streets filled with building debris, felled power lines, and smoldering corpses. In shock and agony, those who lived through it tried to flee.

American journalist Hersey interviewed survivors. His flat, detached narrative with its clinical restraint brought home to Americans the hell unleashed by nuclear attack.

It was first published in the *New Yorker* a year after the attack, taking over an entire cartoonless issue. Its impact was electrifying. The issue quickly sold out and within days became a collector's item. The entire text was broadcast over ABC radio. When it was published as a book, it was an instant bestseller.

Hersey was just thirty-one when he wrote this book. He had already won the Pulitzer for his novel *A Bell for Adano*.

"*The* New Yorker *this week devotes its entire editorial space to an article on the almost complete obliteration of a city by one atomic bomb, and what happened to the people of that city. It does so in the conviction that few of us have yet comprehended the all-but-incredible destructive power of this weapon, and that everyone might well take time to consider the terrible implications of its use.*"

—*NEW YORKER*, AUGUST 31, 1946

CAT'S CRADLE

BY KURT VONNEGUT

Call me Jonah. My parents did, or nearly did. They called me John.

THIS DARKLY COMIC, autobiographical 1963 novel catapulted Vonnegut from writer to literary icon. The story's narrator is working on a book about what certain Americans were up to at the very moment when Hiroshima was bombed. Dr. Felix Hoenikker, for instance, the "father of the atomic bomb," was playing with string making a "cat's cradle" which he foisted upon his terrified son to whom he'd never previously spoken.

Years later, when Hoenikker is playing around with water and ice, he invents something even more deadly: Ice-9. This "seed of doom" turns water to ice, upon contact. Hoenikker touches it and is promptly frozen stiff. Serves him right.

The narrator, a practitioner of the fictional religion of Bokonism which espouses living *fomas* ("harmless untruths" that make one better able to face reality), tells what happens after that. Fomas are of little help as he witnesses the inevitable destruction of the world by Ice-9.

Vonnegut uses humor and satire to examine basic questions of human existence. In his autobiography, Vonnegut observed, "Mark Twain finally stopped laughing at his own agony and that of those around him. He denounced life on this planet as a crock. He died." One could say the same of Vonnegut and of this novel's narrator.

Vonnegut's fourth novel, this won the 1964 Hugo Award for best fantasy or science fiction novel.

"Two messages recur through all of Vonnegut's writing. The first is Be Kind; the second is God doesn't care whether you are or not."

—C. D. B. BRYAN, *NEW YORK TIMES*

THE CHOSEN

BY CHAIM POTOK

For the first fifteen years of our lives, Danny and I lived within five blocks of each other and neither of us knew of the other's existence.

IN THIS NOVEL set in Brooklyn as World War II nears its end, two boys—religious Jew Reuven Malter and Orthodox Hasidic Danny Saunders—meet during a baseball "holy war" between their school teams. Danny is the son of a zaddik, a dynastic rabbi with a loyal following. As his father's oldest son, he is obligated to become a rabbi. Secretly Danny reads forbidden secular books and yearns to be a psychologist. Reuven is the son of a widower, a gentle scholar who approaches the study of sacred text as a rationalist.

Danny hits a ball that smashes into Reuven's face, shattering his eyeglasses. Reuven undergoes eye surgery and Danny visits him in the hospital, determined to become friends. Their worlds can't mix, but their friendship endures, and in the background the state of Israel rises from the ashes of World War II.

Potok, who grew up in a community of deeply traditional Hasidic Jews, is known for drawing his readers into the world of Hasids with their beards and dark caftans and fur-trimmed hats. In his books, he explores what was, for him, simultaneously a joyous and oppressive world.

Published in 1967 and an immediate bestseller, this was Potok's first novel.

"[Chaim Potok] wrote directly from the interior of the Jewish theological experience, rather than from the social experience. And they were bestsellers. . . . Here's somebody who wrote Jewish theological fiction that everybody read."

—CYNTHIA OZICK, QUOTED IN POTOK'S OBITUARIES

THE MOVIEGOER

BY WALKER PERCY

This morning I got a note from my aunt asking me to come for lunch. I know what this means.

THIS NOVEL PRESENTS a week in the life of John "Binx" Bolling, a stockbroker from New Orleans. He spends his thirtieth birthday adrift, fooling around with his secretaries and going to the movies, and then embarks on a harebrained search for authenticity that ends up alienating everyone around him. His goal is to avoid being "Anybody from Anywhere."

For Binx, in a world drained of meaning there is nothing to do but go to the movies. There, according to his neighborhood movie theater marquee, "Happiness Costs So Little." Loaded with existential angst, the novel opens with this quote from Kierkegaard: "the specific character of despair is precisely this: it is unaware of being despair."

This was Percy's first novel, published when he was forty-five years old. Though not enthusiastically promoted by its publisher, it came to national attention after journalist A. J. Liebling bought a copy. He liked it and gave it to his wife, fiction writer Jean Stafford, who happened to be judging the 1962 National Book Award. The book won, earning this unique voice in American fiction a lasting reputation as a major southern novelist.

"More than any, [Walker Percy's] six novels are responsible for taking the focus of Southern letters off the front porch of the country store and putting it on the golf course and in the subdivisions that characterize the modern South."

—MALCOLM JONES, *NEW YORK TIMES*

THE HEART IS
A LONELY HUNTER

BY CARSON McCULLERS

In the town there were two mutes, and they were always together.

IN THIS NOVEL set in a town in the Deep South, probably Columbus, Georgia, in the depths of the Great Depression, poor folks like twelve-year-old tomboy and aspiring pianist Mick Kelly, nervous unbalanced drunkard Jake Blount, and black doctor Benedict Mady Copeland yearn for love. They unload their woes into the ear of a deaf-mute who, like a Christ without a voice (and aptly named "Singer"), radiates a kind of peace and understanding. These characters try to reach out from their isolation but find only despair.

When Singer kills himself after his friend, another deaf-mute, dies in an insane asylum, he deprives his congregation of its confessional. Each of its members are doomed—to loneliness, death, accidents, insanity, fear, or mob violence.

This novel is remarkable for the powerful emotions it stirs and for its utterly convincing and sympathetic portrayal of African Americans at a time when no southern white authors except perhaps Faulkner had done this. Humane, powerful, bleak, but ultimately hopeful, the novel was published in 1940 when McCullers, who once hoped to study music at Juilliard, was just twenty-three. Since a childhood bout of rheumatic fever, she had suffered ill health and depression.

"To me the most impressive aspect of The Heart Is a Lonely Hunter *is the astonishing humanity that enables a white writer, for the first time in Southern fiction, to handle Negro characters with as much ease and justice as those of her own race."*

—RICHARD WRIGHT, *NEW REPUBLIC*

THE UNBEARABLE LIGHTNESS OF BEING

BY MILAN KUNDERA

The idea of eternal return is a mysterious one, and Nietzsche has often perplexed other philosophers with it: to think that everything recurs as we once experienced it, and that the recurrence itself recurs ad infinitum!

THIS NOVEL OF existential angst is set in Prague on the eve of the "velvet revolution." Physician Tomas is a skilled surgeon who speaks out against the Czech regime and ends up working as a window washer. His wife, Tereza, is a barmaid who photographs the Russian invasion, only to have her photos used as evidence against dissidents. The pair escape to Zurich after Russian tanks roll in.

Tomas loves Tereza, a small-town girl who adores animals and the quiet of the countryside. But he also loves making love to other women, including his favorite mistress, Sabina. Sabina, in turn, is adored by the faithful Franz.

Fed up with Tomas's philandering, Tereza leaves him. Tomas follows her to Prague, knowing he'll be punished for his vocal stance against Communism. The book's unforgettable ending concerns the death of a pet dog.

A philosophical writer, Kundera laces his narrative with commentary on his characters, essays, and arguments. The novel asks the big questions: What is the nature of love? Is it better to live silently under oppression or protest? What is a life well lived?

"Kundera is a man of the Enlightenment, and is not loath to champion reason over emotion, pointing out, as he has frequently done in his essays as well as his fiction, that many of the worst disasters mankind has suffered were spawned by those who attended most passionately to the dictates of the heart."

—JOHN BANVILLE, *GUARDIAN*

Of Human Bondage

BY W. SOMERSET MAUGHAM

The day broke gray and dull.

FIRST PUBLISHED ON August 12, 1915, this autobiographical novel tells the coming-of-age story of orphan Philip Carey, a young man born with a clubfoot. Carey grows up with a religious aunt and uncle. A loner, tormented through school, he discards plans to become a minister after a trip to Heidelberg during which he's seduced by the world of ideas.

Flawed and utterly human, Carey struggles to find freedom and to express himself. He returns home at nineteen and enjoys a romantic fling with a worldly older woman but breaks off the relationship. He moves to London to practice accounting, then to Paris to try his hand at being an artist, then back to London to pursue medicine. There he meets Mildred, a beautiful, vulgar waitress who torments him (Bette Davis played her brilliantly in the movie). She makes love to him, leaves him, returns to live off him, drains him of his money and meager self-respect, and finally returns to the street. Carey's obsessive love for this woman, who stands for everything he detests, is a fascinating counterpoint to Maugham's own closeted homosexuality.

Originally titled "Beauty from Ashes," this is considered one of the best of the realistic novels published during the decades surrounding the turn of the century.

"You take that book Of Human Bondage, *by Somerset Maugham. I read it last summer. It's a pretty good book and all, but I wouldn't want to call Somerset Maugham up. I don't know. He just isn't the kind of guy I'd like to call up, that's all. I'd rather call Thomas Hardy up."*

—HOLDEN CAULFIELD, IN J. D. SALINGER'S
CATCHER IN THE RYE

WAITING

BY HA JIN

Lin Kong graduated from the military medical school toward the end of 1963 and came to Muji to work as a doctor.

IN A STORY set in China, army doctor Lin Kong grows tired after seventeen years of waiting for his wife Shuyu, a traditional country woman, to grant him a divorce. Each year, he begs her to set him free, and each year she has agreed, only to renege before the judge. Under the army's moral code, a contested divorce is granted only after eighteen years of living separately.

Meanwhile, Lin Kong is secretly and passionately in love with Manna Wu. He finally gets his wish, but by that time he and his beloved are old and profoundly changed. He reflects on his disappointment: "You were misled by your own frustration and passivity, believing that what you were not allowed to have was what your heart was destined to embrace."

China's *Dr. Zhivago*, this novel captures the reader and reveals a fascinating portrait of Chinese society during and since the Cultural Revolution.

Ha Jin grew up in China and was once an officer of the People's Liberation Army. He had been writing in English for only a decade when he wrote this book. When he accepted the 1991 National Book Award, he said, "Above all, I thank the English language, which has embraced me as an author."

"If Beckett's waiting reflects on the absurdity of life, then Ha Jin's take on passing time is that life's smaller pleasures are often worth the wait."

—DAREN SHIAU, *STRAITS TIMES* (SINGAPORE)

A Dance to the Music of Time

BY ANTHONY POWELL

The men at work at the corner of the street had made a kind of camp for themselves, where, marked out by tripods hung with red hurricane-lamps, an abyss in the road led down to a network of subterranean drain-pipes.

ANTHONY POWELL'S TWELVE-VOLUME series of books published from 1951 to 1975, *A Dance to the Music of Time*, tells the story of an English aristocratic family from World War I to the 1970s. Weighing in at over a million words, it follows several *hundred* characters across two world wars and the collapse of the British Empire. The central character is the ruthless, ambitious Kenneth Widmerpool.

The saga, told with dry humor, begins at a tony prep school (probably Eton). Teenaged narrator Nicholas Jenkins, a character based on Powell himself, shares rooms with two friends. Through them, he meets the movers and shakers of London. At school with them is Widmerpool, a boy whose father peddles "liquid manure." His poor background makes him the laughingstock of the school. For lack of funds, he takes an office job to attend university. He becomes an opportunistic businessman, then a left-wing politician, and by the seventh volume he controls the livelihoods of his former classmates. "That boy will be the death of me," says one of the well-heeled classmates. The remark turns out to be prescient.

One anonymous critic described *Dance*: "Proust translated by Wodehouse."

"I would rather read Mr. Powell than any English novelist now writing."
—KINGSLEY AMIS

Midnight's Children

BY SALMAN RUSHDIE

*A film screen dominates the stage and shows us the infinite
crowd that is India today—a present-day, carnivalesque Independence Day celebration which bleeds into other aspects of modern India, the potent contrasts and diversity of religious and
secular, urban and rural, north and south.*

TWO CHILDREN, BORN in Bombay at midnight at the very
moment when India and Pakistan become independent nations,
are switched at the hospital. Saleem is raised by a wealthy Muslim family. Shiva is raised Hindu by an impoverished street
singer. The pair are destined to become mortal enemies.

Like each of the 1,001 children born on India's day of
independence, Saleem and Shiva have special powers. Shiva's
gift is great strength. He becomes a street fighter and India's
most honored war hero. Saleem's gift is telepathy and an enormous nose with an extraordinary power of smell. He becomes
the manager of a Bombay pickle factory devoted to what he
calls "the chutnification of history . . . the pickling of time!"

In vain, "midnight's children" await Saleem's convening of
a "midnight parliament." But Saleem knows if he does, he'll
have to reveal Shiva as the rightful heir to all his privileges. And
so, the great promise of midnight's children and their gifts goes
unfulfilled. Magical realism serves to protest the fragmentation
of the nation.

Published in 1981, this book won the Booker Prize as well
as a special Booker Prize as the best British novel of a quarter-
century.

*"Rushdie, with his godly gift of the gab, is a garrulous story-teller who
single-handedly returns the English language to the tradition of magic
realism: that charmed line extended from Cervantes through Sterne to,
most recently, Milan Kundera and Gabriel Márquez."*

—BILL BUFORD, *NEW STATESMAN*

A SUITABLE BOY

BY VIKRAM SETH

*"You too will marry a boy I choose," said Mrs. Rupa Mehra firmly
to her younger daughter.*

THIS NOVEL, ONE of the longest ever written in the English
language (over 1,300 pages), is framed by two weddings. At the
first, Lata's older sister enters an arranged marriage. Their traditional mother, Rupa Mehra, tells Lata that she, too, will marry
the boy her mother chooses for her. A year later, modern, well-
educated Lata marries a "suitable boy" whom she has chosen
with her mother's approval.

Through the lives of the members of four extended families—the Mehras, Kapoors, Khans, and Chatterjis—Vikram
Seth tells the story of a newly independent India as religious
intolerance shakes the partitioned nation. He paints a broad
canvas, and stories of many are brought to the page, including
characters as diverse as illiterate peasants and Nehru himself.
Much of the pleasure of the book is in the extraordinary texture
of daily life, rendered in loving detail.

This was Seth's first novel. He told an interviewer that he
wrote the first hundred pages and then stopped cold, realizing
he had to research the period he was trying to re-create. For
more than a year he pored over old newspapers, records of
legislative proceedings, and old maps. He interviewed freedom
fighters and musicians. It took him six years in all to complete
the book, which was published in 1993.

*"The plot, as in Jane Austen, revolves around Lata and her suitors, but
the richness of the book comes from the hundreds of interactions
between families and friends, brought together as passing strangers or
made enemies by legal, religious, musical, literary, economic and social
institutions."*

—RICHARD B. WOODWARD, *NEW YORK TIMES*

THE GOD OF SMALL THINGS

BY ARUNDHATI ROY

May in Ayemenem is a hot, brooding month.

IN 1960s KERALA, India, small things have marked Rahel Ipes, her twin brother Estha, and their colorful extended family with tragedy. The novel opens with Rahel returning from living overseas. She hopes to reconnect with Estha. Once they were so close, "like a rare breed of Siamese twins, physically separate but with joint identities." But the trauma of the past has caused Estha to stop speaking and withdraw from the world.

Why has Estha stopped speaking? Why was Rahel sent away? To answer these questions, the novel steps back in time, revealing what happened in 1969 when their English cousin, Sophie Mol, came to India for a Christmas vacation. While she was there, she died. The story unfolds in lush, evocative prose and dreamlike storytelling laced with ruminations on life, love, death, and human nature.

A heretofore unknown writer, Arundhati Roy received a whopping million-dollar advance for this novel. She faced obscenity charges in India for its graphic depiction of intercaste lovemaking. It won the 1997 Booker Prize. With its publication, Roy took her place alongside celebrated Indian novelists Salman Rushdie and Vikram Seth.

"Roy manages to catch, in the skein of the Ipes' haunted history, a sense of India's deep past, the mingling of dark inhabitants and light invaders going back to the Aryan authors of the Vedas, the roots of Hinduism."

—JOHN UPDIKE, *NEW YORKER*

On the Road

BY JACK KEROUAC

I first met Dean not long after my wife and I split up.

SUPPOSEDLY KEROUAC WROTE this, his second novel, in a three-week-long burst of coffee and Benzedrine–fueled inspiration. It tells of a cross-country road trip, like Prozac on wheels, in search of affirmation. In the process, young college student Sal Paradise finds beatitude. The trip takes him to Denver and San Francisco, Los Angeles, Texas, and Mexico. Sometimes with Dean Moriarty who drifts through life as if it were one long joyride, sometimes with other decadents in hot pursuit of pleasure, his journeys in search of "kicks" often end in death or derangement.

Kerouac considered manuscript revision a form of lying, and to achieve his goal of spontaneity he threaded a roll of Teletype paper into his typewriter and wrote this story straight through on a single continuous sheet. The result was a loose writing style that felt more like jazz than prose narrative.

Published in 1957, ten years after it was written, this book became the holy grail for disaffected American youth of the postwar generation. The *New York Times* proclaimed it "the most beautifully executed, the clearest and the most important utterance yet made by the generation Kerouac himself named years ago as 'beat,' and whose principal avatar he is."

In 1991, the original manuscript, a single-spaced, 120-foot-long scroll, sold at a Christie's auction for a cool $2.4 million.

"To Jack Kerouac, a new Buddha of American prose, who spit forth intelligence into eleven books written in half the number of years . . . creating a spontaneous bop prosody and original classic literature."

—ALLEN GINSBERG'S DEDICATION IN
HOWL AND OTHER POEMS

HERZOG

BY SAUL BELLOW

*If I am out of my mind, it's all right with me, thought
Moses Herzog.*

MOSES HERZOG IS a middle-aged, intellectual historian of
the Romantic movement who carries around a paperback volume of Blake's poems and contemplates suicide. Failed as a
father, lover, and academic, he wonders if he's going off the deep
end. He decides there's nothing else to do but go shopping for
clothes on Madison Avenue.

An absurd antihero, he believes brotherhood is "what
makes a man human," but his wife has left him for his best
friend and he came of age at a time when 6 million fellow Jews
were being killed. Like other surviving Jews of his generation,
he feels compelled to affirm the values of a people that Hitler
tried to incinerate.

In an extended journey of self-discovery, Herzog revisits his
past in brief episodes, fleeting memories, and extended flashbacks as he churns out unsent letters to friends and enemies
and famous people, living and dead.

Ian McEwan called Moses Herzog the most vivid of all
Bellow's characters, his "most achieved dreamer, the least practical of men in an America of vigorous, material pursuits."

In 1965, this won the National Book Award and was the
first novel by an American to win the International Literary
Prize. In 1976 Bellow was awarded the Nobel Prize in
Literature.

*"Herzog is Bellow's grandest creation, American literature's Leopold
Bloom."*

—PHILIP ROTH, *NEW YORKER*

MYSTIC RIVER

BY DENNIS LEHANE

When Sean Devine and Jimmy Marcus were kids, their fathers worked together at the Coleman Candy plant and carried the stench of warm chocolate back home with them.

TRAGEDY STALKS YOUNG Dave Boyle, Jimmy Marcus, and Sean Devine, friends who grow up together in a tough Boston neighborhood. A defining moment comes when the three are playing ball on the street and two men pull up in a car. They threaten to arrest the boys, but only Dave gets abducted. Four days later, he escapes but returns changed, the friendship among them forever tainted.

Years later the boys have drifted apart. Jimmy is a reformed thief who's done years of hard time. When Jimmy's nineteen-year-old daughter Katie is murdered, his grief and despair transform into rage and lust for revenge. Sean, now a homicide cop, gets assigned to the case and tries to keep Jimmy from acting on his conviction that Dave is the one responsible.

The title refers to a local spot where weapons and bodies are dumped. As one character says, it's where "we bury our sins."

This is a dark, brutal, compelling read in which no one comes out a winner. Lehane wrote this literary novel against his publisher's wishes—they wanted him to continue his successful PI novel series. Published in 2001, it turned into a blockbuster and was a finalist for numerous literary awards.

"Like Bruce Springsteen's song 'The River,' Lehane's Mystic River *looks back at what might have been, the ways in which the past impinges on the present. And like the song, you can't get it out of your head."*

—DEBORAH WILKER, *SUN SENTINEL*

THE DEATH OF THE HEART

BY ELIZABETH BOWEN

The morning's ice, no more than a brittle film, had cracked and was now floating in segments.

INNOCENT SIXTEEN-YEAR-OLD PORTIA Quayne, who has been dragged across Europe through a series of shabby hotels by her parents, has the fragile order in her life shattered when her father and mother die. Grieving and bereft, she's sent to the London home of her half-brother, Thomas Quayne, and his wife, Anna. Distracted and distant, Thomas gives Portia the run of the handsome but cold house. There she learns "to be lonely," her only friend the reticent but kindly housekeeper, her only confidante her diary.

Eddie, a twenty-three-year-old "bright little cracker that, pulled hard enough, goes off with a loud bang" works with Thomas. A slick opportunist, he makes advances to Anna, but it's Portia who falls madly in love with him.

In a tale of disillusionment and loss of innocence, Portia discovers that Anna has been reading her diary. Humiliated, she runs off and throws herself at Eddie's feet with inevitable results.

Bowen's own life story is reflected in this novel, considered her masterpiece and published in 1938. She grew up in a handsome, somewhat down-at-the-heels family mansion in the Irish countryside. Both of her parents had died by the time she was thirteen. By twenty-five she was married and had published her first book of stories.

"[Elizabeth Bowen] belongs to the great tradition of English moral comedy going back to Jane Austen, stopping off at Henry James, with some of the aromas of Proust, a writer she greatly admired."

—HOWARD MOSS, *NEW YORK TIMES*

Dog Soldiers

BY ROBERT STONE

*There was only one bench in the shade and Converse went for it,
although it was already occupied.*

THIS POIGNANT TALE of rejection begins in Saigon and ends
in the California desert near the Mexican border south of Death
Valley. Its story revolves around three kilograms of pure
heroin.

A confused and traumatized hack journalist, John Converse,
buys the heroin in Vietnam. He packs it up in a briefcase and
gives it to his Marine buddy Raymond Hicks, a self-styled
samurai and Zen psychopath. Hicks is supposed to smuggle the
drugs to Converse's wife, Marge, in Berkeley, where it will clear
a cool thirty grand. But in California, some sketchy, brutal
"regulatory agents" show up and things go awry.

Marge and Hicks flee with the drugs to a hippie retreat and
the Feds take Converse hostage, demanding the drugs as ran-
som for his release. Meanwhile, Converse is tortured. And tortured some more. The finale is a Vietnam-style firefight on a
California mountainside and a trek across the salt flats.

In 1971, Stone got press credentials and went to Vietnam.
He didn't find his subject on the battlefield but in Saigon's drug
scene. Published in 1974, this novel won the National Book
Award.

*"Bare bones this is a powerful crime story. The real thing. Real criminals.
Real cops. Real streets. Nothing tarted up for effect. But it is also, for
me, the truest portrait of that time I've ever read."*

—ED GORMAN

FALCONER

BY JOHN CHEEVER

*The main entrance to Falconer—the only entrance for convicts,
their visitors and the staff—was crowned by an escutcheon rep-
resenting Liberty, Justice and, between the two, the sovereign
power of government.*

IN THIS DARK novel with a surprise, uplifting ending, convicted murderer Ezekiel Farragut ("fratricide, zip to ten, #734-
508-32"), once a second-rate college professor and closeted
homosexual, goes to a prison called Falconer for killing his
brother Ebenezer. There, Ezekiel struggles to hang onto his
humanity.

The novel's narrative evokes prison life in a surreal and
disjointed riot of partial and disconnected episodes. Ezekiel's
fellow prisoners tell their stories. In prison, he experiences a
kind of spiritual and carnal rebirth. He escapes and finds
redemption ("Rejoice, he thought, rejoice").

This 1977 novel, which showcases Cheever at the peak of
his literary powers and addressing his own demons, came late
in Cheever's career. By the time it was published, the author was
in his sixties and most of his books were no longer in print.

Regarded by critics as a kind of American Chekhov, Cheever
found spiritual resonance in the quotidian details of the everyday. "The constants that I look for are a love of light and a
determination to trace some moral chain of being," he once
wrote. He published three other novels and more than a hundred short stories and was awarded the Pulitzer Prize.

*"[John Cheever] is a magician. He can take a watch chain or something
and tell you the whole man."*

—RALPH ELLISON, QUOTED IN *TIME* MAGAZINE

THE PAINTED BIRD

BY JERZY KOSINSKI

In the first weeks of World War II, in the fall of 1939, a six-year-old boy from a large city in Eastern Europe was sent by his parents, like thousands of other children, to the shelter of a distant village.

THIS FIRST-PERSON ACCOUNT vividly conveys the impact of the Nazi era on a little boy. He is only six when his Christian parents, who have been involved in anti-Nazi activity before the war, send him to wait out the German occupation in safety in a remote Eastern European village. But the old woman who was to take care of him dies before he arrives and the little boy is left to fend for himself.

Dark-eyed and dark-haired, he is doomed to stand out among the fair villagers who hound him from place to place. They call him the Gypsy, and wherever he goes he is tortured and tormented. Over and over he faces primitive brutality, inflicted by ordinary men and women in a sort of horrifying Boschian landscape.

Liberation finds him transformed, bitter, and vengeful. Only hatred has enabled him to survive.

Published in 1965 when the author was thirty-two, this work was long believed to be autobiographical. Its title is taken from an episode in which the deranged man paints the wing of one of the birds he has ensnared, releases it, and then watches as it's attacked by its own flock.

"*Since the artistic truth of* The Painted Bird—*its portrayal of man's endless capacity for cruelty toward men in whom they do not recognize their brothers, which is the motive and theme of the Holocaust—is unimpeachable and entire, it turns out that Kosinski did not bear false witness, after all, and need not have worried about his fabulations.*"

—LOUIS BEGLEY, *NEW YORK TIMES*

NAKED LUNCH

BY WILLIAM S. BURROUGHS

I can feel the heat closing in, feel them out there making their moves, setting up their devil doll stool pigeons, crooning over my spoon and dropper I throw away at Washington Square Station, vault a turnstile and two flights down the iron stairs, catch an uptown A train . . .

MORE A COLLECTION of loosely related anecdotes and hallucinations than a novel, this work chronicles a narcotic addict's descent into hell by way of the United States, Mexico, and Tangier. The nonlinear narrative mostly concerns drugs—buying them, taking them, sex acts and perversions performed while on them, the paranoia of getting caught with them, and medical interventions that attempt to control addiction.

Burroughs was a member of the Beat Generation. When this novel came out in 1959, a *Newsweek* reviewer allowed that it was a masterpiece, "but a totally insane and anarchic one, and it can only be diminished by attempts to give it a social purpose or value whatever." Burroughs's explanation of what he was up to only adds to the confusion. He described the book as "a frozen moment when everyone sees what is on the end of every fork."

This book was the subject of the last major literary censorship battle in the United States and banned in Boston in 1962 (obscenities include child murder and pedophilia). That ruling was reversed in 1966. Not recommended for readers with delicate sensibilities, this is still an intriguing trip for readers made of stronger stuff.

"Burroughs must be the greatest writer of graffiti who ever lived. His style has the snap of a whip, and it never relents. Every paragraph is quotable."

—NORMAN MAILER, *THE SPOOKY ART: SOME THOUGHTS ON WRITING*

THE GOLDEN NOTEBOOK

BY DORIS LESSING

The two women were alone in a London flat.

LIKE MULTIPLE NARRATORS, divorced writer Anna Wulf reveals different aspects of her life in separate notebooks. In a black one she writes of an experience in Africa that led her to write her first novel. In a blue one she examines her problems with men. In a red one, she writes of her political life and disappointment with the Communist Party. The yellow one contains bits of her professional writing.

Entangled in an unhappy affair and losing her sanity, she attempts to pull the four narratives (and herself) together in the eponymous golden notebook. In it she reflects on her own—and women's—multiple, often conflicting identities and responsibilities, and therein she traces a journey to emotional breakdown.

Published in 1962, this was Lessing's twelfth book. Born in Persia (now Iran), raised in Rhodesia (now Zimbabwe), and living in London, she was then virtually unknown in the United States. At eighty-eight, she was awarded the 2007 Nobel Prize in Literature. In its citation, the Swedish Academy said, "The burgeoning feminist movement saw [*The Golden Notebook*] as a pioneering work and it belongs to the handful of books that inform the twentieth century view of the male-female relationship."

Appropriately, we celebrate this book on the anniversary of the day in 1920 when the Nineteenth Amendment to the Constitution was signed, giving women the right to vote.

". . . it is natural, I suppose, for her not to know or to guess how much The Golden Notebook (predating and superseding even the most sophisticated of all the "women's liberation" works) meant to young women of my generation."

—JOYCE CAROL OATES, *SOUTHERN REVIEW*

THE NEEDLE'S EYE

BY MARGARET DRABBLE

He stood there and waited. He was good at that. There was no hurry. There was plenty of time. He always had time. He was a punctual and polite person, and that was why he was standing there, buying a gift for his hostess.

ROSE VASSILIOU IS a divorced mother of three children, in the midst of a tawdry custody battle with her abusive ex. Though she is a wealthy heiress, she chooses to live in a working-class section of London where she and her family can go unrecognized.

Simon Camish is the inverse of Rose. He's a successful lawyer with a wealthy wife who has cut himself off from his working-class roots in Northam. Initially attracted to his wife for her outward gaiety, warmth, and easy affection, he finds that beneath the veneer she is cold and artificial.

Rose and Simon are drawn together. When Rose needs help to protect her children, Simon is there for her.

Despite her ordinary virtue, Rose emerges as heroic when she sacrifices her soul and surrenders to her marriage "for the sake of the children." She finds a kind of peace in submission.

Like all Drabble's novels, this 1972 masterpiece is rich with psychological insight and dry wit. Her first literary success came at age twenty-three with *A Summer Bird Cage*.

"Like Doris Lessing, that genius of the forcefully 'creating' work of fiction, Miss Drabble presents characters who are not passively witnessing their lives (and ours) . . . but one who has taken upon herself the task, largely ignored today, of attempting the active, vital, energetic, mysterious re-creation of a set of values by which human beings can live."

—JOYCE CAROL OATES, *NEW YORK TIMES*

THE LITTLE DISTURBANCES OF MAN

BY GRACE PALEY

I was popular in certain circles, says Aunt Rose. I wasn't no thinner, only more stationary in the flesh.

GRACE PALEY TELLS stories, but mostly she writes about people. Like Aunt Rose who, in the opening lines of this collection's first story, "Goodbye and Good Luck," reminisces about her long affair with a famous Yiddish theater actor.

This volume of ten stories, her first published collection from 1959, gives a taste of Paley's wildly funny but ultimately serious take on life. Most often she wrote about ordinary Jewish women, single mothers who muddled through ordinary lives in New York City.

In "The Loudest Voice," for instance, a Jewish immigrant wife announces to her husband in dismay that their child is to be in an elementary school Christmas pageant. "Listen," she says, "I'm surprised to see my neighbors making tra-la-la for Christmas." His reply: "You're in America! . . . In Palestine the Arabs would be eating you alive. Europe you had pogroms. Argentina is full of Indians. Here you got Christmas."

Paley, a much-beloved teacher and lifelong political activist who called herself a "somewhat combative pacifist and cooperative anarchist," produced four dozen stories in three volumes. Her 1994 volume *Collected Stories* was a finalist for both the Pulitzer Prize and the National Book Award. In 1993, she was awarded the Rea Award for her contribution to the short story as an art form.

"If certain kinds of novels are like supertankers, steadily carrying acres of crude energy from continent to continent, and certain kinds of lyric poems resemble spy planes bolting through the stratosphere, Ms. Paley's stories are like nimble skiffs, coursing from one engaging harbor to another."

—ROBERT PINSKY, *NEW YORK TIMES*

STONES FROM THE RIVER

BY URSULA HEGI

As a child Trudi Montag thought everyone knew what went on inside others.

TRUDI MONTAG LIVES in a small town in Germany in the tumultuous years between 1915 and 1952. One neighbor erects a statue of Hitler in his front yard and another is killed trying to tear it down as Trudi and her father sequester fleeing Jews in their cellar.

As the town's only dwarf, the unforgettable Trudi shares outcast status with the town's Jews. Her mother, Gertrud Montag, had an affair with another man while her husband was fighting in World War I. Guilt drove her mad and to an early death.

Trudi, who has been compared to Oskar, the dwarf in Günter Grass's *The Tin Drum*, longs for friendship, love, and acceptance. She finds rejection and brutality but resists the pull of hatred in response. She finds solace and renewal in the Rhine River. She becomes the town's storyteller and informal historian, hoarding the secrets of others.

Hegi grew up in Germany. When she came to the United States at eighteen years of age, she realized that her American friends knew more about the war than she did. By writing this novel, she said, she tried "to understand what happened in Germany." This was published in 1994.

"This moving elegiac novel commands our compassion and respect for the wisdom and courage to be found in unlikely places, in unlikely times."

—SUZANNE RUTA, *NEW YORK TIMES*

BRAVE NEW WORLD

BY ALDOUS HUXLEY

A squat grey building of only thirty-four stories.

FIRST PUBLISHED IN 1932, this classic sci-fi novel is set in London after World War III in the year A.D. 2540. In a stark, frightening vision of a new world order, its Utopia is one ruled by hedonism, populated by genetically engineered humans who indulge in *soma* (a sort of Prozac/LSD cocktail), and who conform to a rigidly defined social class system. "Community, Identity, Stability" is its motto.

Bernard Marx refuses to conform and be a happy, stable Alpha. He introduces a young man known as The Savage into this repressed society. The Savage battles with the World Controller as if he's channeling the complete works of Shakespeare.

It's hard to fathom how this prophetic fantasy could have been written before Stalin's rise to power, before psychotropic drugs became standard treatment for disorderly conduct, and before embryos could be nurtured in Petrie dishes and cells cloned. According to the American Library Association, this is one of the most frequently challenged books in print.

Huxley, whose mentor was D. H. Lawrence, was a vocal social critic as well as an author. Huxley died on the day John F. Kennedy was assassinated.

"Huxley's philosophy might be summed up as: the world can be made better, but only if we make ourselves better."

—NICHOLAS MURRAY, HUXLEY'S BIOGRAPHER

1984

BY GEORGE ORWELL

It was a bright cold day in April, and the clocks were striking thirteen.

FIRST PUBLISHED IN 1949 when 1984 seemed far in the future, this novel imagines a totalitarian society in which "big brother," conceptualized as a perpetually open eye, watches you and everyone else, and in which Thought Police read minds. The government's goal is nothing less than the destruction of individual identity.

The world has been divided into three super-states—Eastasia, Eurasia, and Oceania—and war is ongoing. England has become Airstrip One with London its capital. English is being transformed into "Newspeak," rife with bureaucratic jargon and limited to vocabulary that expresses concepts amenable to the state. The world's literary classics are being "translated" into this new language. Elite Party members are forbidden to love or engage in sexual relations.

Winston Smith, a minor Party member and worker at the Ministry of Truth, inhabits this gray, depressing world. Its "gritty dust" coats his skin and his life is never his own—he eats tasteless public meals and drinks Victory Gin. A rebellious hero, he and his girlfriend are arrested and brutally brainwashed.

This prescient, bitterly satirical book delivers a horrifying vision of a totalitarian Utopia in which privacy has been sacrificed on the altar of order. Original British and American editions were heavily censored and it was banned in the Soviet Union.

"What Orwell feared were those who would ban books. What Huxley feared was that there would be no reason to ban a book, for there would be no one who wanted to read one."

—NEIL POSTMAN, *AMUSING OURSELVES TO DEATH*

September

The Jungle

BY UPTON SINCLAIR

It was four o'clock when the ceremony was over and the carriages began to arrive.

BILLED AS "THE *Uncle Tom's Cabin* of wage slavery" and dedicated to "the workingmen of America," Sinclair intended this 1906 novel as an exposé of working conditions in the nation's meatpacking industry. In it, a young, eager Lithuanian immigrant takes a job as "shoveler of guts" at "Durham" (based on Armour & Co.). He witnesses dangerous working conditions and watches the company cheat its workers and speed up assembly lines.

But what sparked public outrage even more were the descriptions of dead rats shoveled into sausage-grinders, diseased cows slaughtered for beef, and workers falling into steaming vats of lard where they could be overlooked for days until only their bones remained.

President Theodore Roosevelt was deluged with letters. Foreign sales of American meat plummeted and the industry actually lobbied for the federal government to pass legislation to allay public fears about the food supply. The uproar led directly to passage of a landmark federal food safety law, which took effect in 1907. The book remains one of the most influential of the twentieth century.

Sinclair wrote nearly a hundred provocative books. His targets included ministers who scam the public (*The Profits of Religion*), book publishers (*Money Writes!*), and the prosecution of Sacco and Vanzetti (*Boston*). He won the 1943 Pulitzer Prize for the nearly forgotten *Dragon's Teeth*, one of a series of eleven novels about Hitler's rise to power.

"I aimed at the public's heart and by accident hit it in the stomach."

—SINCLAIR LEWIS

GONE WITH THE WIND

BY MARGARET MITCHELL

Scarlett O'Hara was not beautiful, but men seldom realized it when caught by her charm as the Tarleton twins were.

ON THIS DATE in 1864, Union troops occupied Atlanta, a focal point of *Gone with the Wind* and the place where Scarlett O'Hara finds redemption. Scarlett is one of literature's most spirited, flirtatious, greedy, and self-centered creatures. Dashing scoundrel Rhett Butler, a cynical realist, remains one of literature's great hunks. Theirs is a battle of wills.

The opening chapter is set in plantation country in northern Georgia, just before the war. Scarlett, who has convinced herself that she is in love with the pliant Ashley Wilkes, preens before her male admirers and petulantly declares, "There won't be any war and I'm tired of hearing about it." But of course there was a war, or there wouldn't have been any story.

Hailed by a *New York Times* reviewer upon its publication as "the best Civil War novel that has yet been written," this was Mitchell's one and only book. She was a housewife and former journalist living in Atlanta when she showed a scout for a publishing house the 1,000-plus-page manuscript, which she'd written over a seven-year period. Some of it was typewritten, some handwritten, some of it scribbled on the backs of laundry lists.

Mitchell said of her book: "I wrote about the people who had gumption and the people who didn't." It won the Pulitzer Prize in 1937.

"*I shall never forget the picture I have of Margaret Mitchell as I then saw her—a tiny woman sitting on a divan, and beside her the biggest manuscript I have ever seen, towering in two stacks almost up to her shoulders.*"

—H. L. LATHAM, EDITOR AT THE MACMILLAN COMPANY

THE SNOW LEOPARD

BY PETER MATTHIESSEN

At sunrise the small expedition meets beneath a giant fig beyond
Pokhara—two white sahibs, four sherpas, fourteen porters.

MATTHIESSEN TAKES THE reader on an arduous physical and spiritual journey in this meditative account of a seemingly fruitless odyssey. September 1973, a year after his wife died of cancer and soon after he converted to Zen Buddhism, Matthiessen set off on a five-week, 250-mile pilgrimage on foot across Tibet from Katmandu, Nepal. His companions were wildlife biologist George Schaller, Sherpa guides, and Buddha. Their goal: to find Himalayan blue sheep and the elusive snow leopard.

In lighter-than-air, mystic prose written in journal format, the book reveals the wonders of nature and occasionally makes us feel the presence of Buddha. On the journey, Matthiessen struggled to come to terms with his relationship with his wife and with her death.

Initially, Matthiessen was a fiction writer who wrote about life in New York. He said that his shift to nonfiction, travel, and nature writing was fueled by the need to support his family. His travels have taken him to some of the loneliest and most starkly glorious places on earth.

This book won the 1980 National Book Award.

"Mr. Matthiessen . . . is our greatest modern nature writer in the lyrical tradition that I have called Franciscan—to honor St. Francis' 'Canticle of the Creatures'—but extending through Thoreau, Fabre, W. H. Hudson and Loren Eiseley."

—STEPHEN JAY GOULD, *NEW YORK TIMES*

The Feast of Love

BY CHARLES BAXTER

The man—me, this pale being, no one else, it seems—wakes in fright, tangled up in the sheets.

ON THIS NOVEL'S first page, Charlie (the author) has insomnia. He's sitting on the front step of his house in Ann Arbor (where Baxter really lives) when his neighbor, Bradley (who looks to Charlie "like an exceptionally handsome toad"), comes by walking his dog, also named Bradley.

Bradley suggests Charlie call his book "The Feast of Love" and that he write about real people. Soon what's happening in the fictional present merges with the novel Baxter is writing, and we're off into a hall of mirrors that breaks just about every literary boundary.

Baxter brilliantly uses a "Rashomon"-style narrative, repeating scenes from the viewpoints of a rich array of characters. For instance, Bradley hears from Charlie about Kathryn, his ex. Then Bradley calls her up and we get her side of the story. Turns out Bradley hummed distractedly while making love to Kathryn, and was only dimly aware of her lesbian affair.

Interspersed between the stories of older characters is the story of Chloé, an adolescent girl with a stud in her tongue and torn jeans, who is passionately in love with a pierced and tattooed former drug addict.

In all its glorious complexity, this extraordinary novel explores the splendid, horrifying, and hilarious sides of love between ordinary people. It was nominated for the National Book Award in 2000.

"Charles Baxter's . . . Feast of Love is a rich symphony of interlocking stories about romantic love, parental love, and sexual connection."
—ELIZABETH BENEDICT, *THE JOY OF WRITING SEX*

THE ACCIDENTAL TOURIST

BY ANNE TYLER

They were supposed to stay at the beach a week, but neither of them had the heart for it and they decided to come back early.

NO ONE CREATES poignant, dysfunctional characters like Anne Tyler. Case in point: Macon Leary, the eponymous "accidental tourist" who likes his world orderly. His guidebooks for businessmen tell how to be on the road and feel as if you never left home. Not that he's fallen that far from the family tree—his relatives alphabetize the food in their kitchen cupboards, too.

Tragedy strikes. After Macon's son is killed in a senseless shooting at a fast-food restaurant and his wife, Sarah, who was once his high-school sweetheart, leaves him, Macon gives in to all those neuroses that have been circling about him like vultures. He pares his routine to bare essentials. He lives in sweatsuits and launders his clothes underfoot while sloshing around in his evening shower. He sleeps in tomorrow's underwear so he won't have to wash pajamas. Even Macon realizes that he's come "within an inch, within a hairsbreadth of turning into one of those pathetic creatures you see on the loose from time to time—unwashed, unshaven, shapeless, talking to themselves, padding along in their institutional garb."

Not a moment too soon, he meets dog trainer Muriel Pritchett at the Meow-Bow Animal Hospital.

The Accidental Tourist won the 1985 National Book Critics Circle Award for Fiction and was a finalist for the Pulitzer Prize.

"[Anne Tyler's] fiction has strength of vision, originality, freshness, unconquerable humor."

—EUDORA WELTY

THE ADVENTURES OF TOM SAWYER

BY MARK TWAIN

"Tom!"
No answer.
"Tom!"

THIS POPULAR 1876 story of a rapscallion orphan's summer adventures opens with his Aunt Polly hollering his name. She wants to discuss some missing jam. As usual, Tom eludes her.

In one of the book's famous episodes, Tom plays hooky from school and gets into a fight. Aunt Polly punishes him— Saturday he'll have to whitewash the fence instead of playing with his friends. But, Tom being Tom, when his friends show up he manages to feign so much enjoyment painting that fence that soon they're bribing him to let them help. Just like that, the fence is painted.

Tom's buddy, Huck Finn, the son of the town drunk, never goes to school at all. One night, Huck and Tom witness Injun Joe murdering Dr. Robinson. Terrified, they run away. They sail off, down the Mississippi River on a raft. On an island, they find refuge. There, they swim and fish and smoke to their heart's content until homesickness drives them back to Saint Petersburg, Missouri, just in time to attend their own funerals. Despite his blood oath never to reveal the murderer, Tom testifies in court to keep an innocent man from being convicted.

The novel's setting is based on Hannibal, Missouri, where Twain grew up. Its characters were "drawn from life." He was surprised to discover that this novel, which he wrote for adults, turned out to be a favorite with children.

"In that . . . rendition of a remembered past, Twain recalls Hannibal, Missouri, in the eighteen-forties as a perpetual summer in which distinct and sweetly irreconcilable life forms, the Child and the Adult, play out their comedic fates."

—E. L. DOCTOROW, *NEW YORKER*

RABBIT, RUN

BY JOHN UPDIKE

Boys are playing basketball around a telephone pole with a back-board bolted to it. Legs, shouts. The scrape and snap of Keds on the loose alley pebbles seems to catapult their voices into the moist March air blue above the wires.

IT'S 1960, AND hapless Harry "Rabbit" Angstrom is a twenty-six-year-old "beautiful brainless guy" whose life peaked at eighteen when he was a high-school basketball star. Now selling kitchen gadgets, he's on a downward spiral to mediocrity.

Rabbit runs away from his pregnant, alcoholic wife, their two-year-old son, and his suffocating life ("You get the feeling you're in your coffin before they've taken your blood out"), but he gets only as far as West Virginia before he gets lost. He returns home and begins an affair, ends an affair, returns to his wife, takes a job at his father-in-law's car dealership. But nothing gets better.

Desperate for something he can't name, Rabbit keeps running away . . . and coming back . . . and running away . . . never able to commit to himself or anyone else. Along the way, the writing soars.

This book, published in 1960 and the first of four Rabbit novels and a novella, established Updike as a major literary talent.

"*One thinks of Flaubert and his doomed fantasist Emma Bovary, for John Updike with his precisian's prose and his intimately attentive yet cold eye is a master, like Flaubert, of mesmerizing us with his narrative voice even as he might repel us with the vanities of human desire his scalpel exposes.*"

—JOYCE CAROL OATES, *NEW YORK TIMES*

Snow Crash

BY NEAL STEPHENSON

The Deliverator belongs to an elite order, a hallowed subcategory. He's got esprit up to here.

THE HERO OF this swashbuckling, cyberpunk classic, set in the future ruins of Southern California, is named Hiro Protagonist (he chose his own name). His business card announces to the world: "Last of the freelance hackers" and "Greatest sword fighter in the world."

In the real world, Hiro delivers pizza for a service that is run with military precision by high-tech thugs. He lives in a U-Stor-It in L.A. with two swords and a Ukrainian grunge metal guitarist. He helped program a virtual world called Metaverse. In Metaverse, he's a cyber-warrior out to conquer "snow crash," a computer virus that can leap the species boundary and infect hackers' brains, "mess[ing] with binary code for a living."

Raven, the novel's villain, is out to destroy America. Then there's Y. T., a fifteen-year-old skateboarder who zips along the highways by magnetically attaching herself to vehicles.

Stephenson's first novel, an academic satire called *The Big U*, came out in 1984, the same year that William Gibson's *Neuromancer* invented the term *cyberspace*. He found his calling in sci-fi with this 1992 book, which grew out of an abortive attempt to develop a live action CD-ROM (hardware wasn't yet up to it). The *Village Voice* called him "The Quentin Tarentino of post-cyberpunk science fiction."

"Snow Crash *certainly painted a compelling picture of what such a virtual world could look like in the near future, and I found that inspiring.*"

—PHILIP ROSEDALE, CREATOR OF
THE VIRTUAL WORLD SECOND LIFE

EAST OF EDEN

BY JOHN STEINBECK

The Salinas Valley is in Northern California. It is a long narrow swale between two ranges of mountains, and the Salinas River winds and twists up the center until it falls at last into Monterey Bay.

STEINBECK CALLED THIS combination novel/memoir "a sort of autobiography of the Salinas Valley." It tells of two families, the Trasks and the Hamiltons. Their stories span three generations, from the Civil War to World War I. Steinbeck himself appears as a minor character.

Stories from the past and present are interwoven and often cast as allegorical retellings of Bible stories from Genesis. Adam Trask is the "Abel" of the novel, his brother Charles is "Cain." Noble Adam marries Cathy, a young woman he saves after finding her beaten half to death. This former prostitute who murdered her parents, like an intoxicating "Eve," tempts Adam into evil. She gives birth to twin boys, Caleb and Aron (Cain and Abel, again), and abandons them.

As narrator, Steinbeck is often philosophical ("I believe there are monsters in the world born to human parents"). And yet, good and evil are painted in shades of gray and lives are made meaningful by "the glory of choice."

This is the "big book" (600-plus pages) that Steinbeck promised himself he'd write after *Grapes of Wrath*. Published in 1952, it was the one he said he'd been "practicing" for thirty-five years. Lasting power? When Oprah relaunched her book club in 2004, this book was her first pick.

"In his writing there are no heroes or villains . . . not even the romanticized victims we call anti-heroes, just people caught in the web of nature."

—JACKSON J. BENSON, STEINBECK'S BIOGRAPHER

Pilgrim at Tinker Creek

BY ANNIE DILLARD

I used to have a cat, an old fighting tom, who would jump through the open window by my bed in the middle of the night and land on my chest.

A SELF-PROCLAIMED "POET and a walker," Annie Dillard was just twenty-seven when she spent a year exploring on foot Tinker Creek from Tinker Mountain to the Roanoke River. She'd completed a master's thesis on Thoreau. In this book, an extended meditation that was awarded the 1974 Pulitzer Prize, she uses extravagant language to draw word pictures of the glorious drama of that natural world.

Nature held Dillard in its thrall, as it holds us when we read: "I see some event that would otherwise be utterly missed and lost, or something sees me, some enormous power that brushes me with its clean wing, and I resound like a beaten bell." Like Thoreau, she writes a "meteorological journey of the mind."

Linking her observations to physics, literature, religious traditions, human history, medicine, and folklore, she's not talking just about nature but also about the human condition and our relationship with the Divine.

"A giant water bug in Tinker Creek *sucks the guts out of a frog and Dillard sees the whole bloody cosmos go down that arthropodal gullet. A huge polyphemus moth hatches in a bottle too small to contain its spread wings and she sees a biblical Behemoth straining against the glassy confines of creation."*

—CHET RAYMO

THE ECHO MAKER

BY RICHARD POWERS

Cranes keep landing as night falls. Ribbons of them roll down,
slack against the sky. They float in from all compass points, in
kettles of a dozen, dropping with the dusk.

AT THE START of this story of personal catastrophe set against
the national calamity of 9/11, Mark Schluter's truck overturns
on a lonely stretch of Nebraska highway. Though the only witnesses are thousands of migrating sandhill cranes, someone
calls the accident in to the police and leaves a handwritten note
at Mark's hospital bedside: "I am No One/but Tonight on
North Line Road/GOD led me to you/so You could Live/and
bring back someone else."

Mark, a twenty-seven-year-old meatpacker and video game
aficionado, emerges from a coma with Capgras syndrome,
amnesia that erases emotional connections and makes him
believe his sister Karin has been replaced by an impostor. Soon
he thinks that his dog, his favorite radio station, and even his
house are all fakes set up in a government conspiracy. Karin
turns for help to a renowned neuropsychologist who is a dead
ringer for Oliver Sacks. Karin, who is attracted to two men—a
conservationist and a land developer—comes to realize that all
of us, like her brother, fail to recognize that birds like the sandhill crane are our kin.

You'll emerge from this novel embracing the pedestrian,
recognizable, everyday-ness of your own existence, and wondering how you know who you really are. Powers's ninth novel,
this won the 2006 National Book Award.

"The Echo Maker *probes the boundaries of the human, asking questions*
about the way we understand ourselves and those around us, and about
the nature of our connection to the web of life which surrounds us."

—JAMES BRADLEY, *SYDNEY MORNING HERALD*

THE ROAD

BY CORMAC McCARTHY

When he woke in the woods in the dark and the cold of the night he'd reach out to touch the child sleeping beside him.

THE WORLD, TEN years after man-made disaster, is filled with "creedless shells of men tottering down the causeways like migrants in a feverland." Two of the last survivors—a man and his son, who was born shortly after disaster struck—roll an old shopping cart piled with a meager hoard of canned goods and blankets as they forage along a melted interstate in a charred wasteland strewn with ash and corpses. They hide from gangs that have turned to cannibalism for survival. A pall of pollution hides the sun and stars, and all vegetation and virtually all forms of wildlife have been killed.

A reason for the apocalypse is never given, and the book suggests that it's not a result of military strife. A man notes, "On this road there are no godspoke men. . . . They are gone and I am left and they have taken with them the world."

Though his wife ended her life rather than continue on with her family, and clearly there is nothing to live for, still the man is driven to protect his son, a last bit of goodness in a tainted world. "Are we still the good guys?" the little boy asks.

A novel of love and despair with surprisingly funny moments, this won the 2007 Pulitzer.

"The eventual safety of a character in a McCarthy novel is always in doubt, but the reader's usual sense that a disembowelment or clean shot to the brainpan lies only a paragraph away has never been so excruciating as in The Road, *where the life of a child whose innocence is literally singular is threatened from the first paragraph of the novel."*

—MICHAEL CHABON, *NEW YORK REVIEW OF BOOKS*

BLINDNESS

BY JOSÉ SARAMAGO

*The amber light came on. Two of the cars ahead accelerated
before the red light appeared.*

IN THIS PROFOUND allegorical novel from a Portuguese
writer and Nobel laureate, a car sits at a traffic light that's
turned green. The driver shouts, "I am blind." A "good" Samari-
tan helps the driver get home, then steals his car, only to go
blind himself.

Soon there's an epidemic of "the white evil," a contagious
form of blindness. The blind, who have no memory of their lives
before blindness, are quarantined in an asylum. Those who've
had contact with them are interned in an adjoining wing.

A doctor's wife seems miraculously immune. When her husband goes blind, she fakes the symptoms in order to remain
with him. In the internment camp she bears witness to the
breakdown of civilization.

Saramago says he was sitting in a restaurant waiting to be
served when the idea for this novel came to him. "The question
suddenly came into my head, 'And if we were all blind?' And
then immediately, as if answering myself, 'But we are all
blind.'"

Saramago was born in 1922 but didn't start writing full-
time until 1979. This novel was published in 1998. In 2004 he
wrote a sequel, *Seeing.*

*"More frightening than Stephen King, as unrelenting as a bad dream,
José Saramago's* Blindness *politely rubs our faces in apocalypse."*

—JESSE BERRETT, SALON.COM

JULIAN

BY GORE VIDAL

Yesterday morning as I was about to enter the lecture hall, I was stopped by a Christian student who asked me in a voice eager with malice, "Have you heard about the Emperor Theodosius?"

THIS ENTERTAINING, FICTIONAL first-person "memoir" of the fourth-century emperor Constantine's nephew, Emperor Julian "the Apostate," was supposedly dictated during the campaign against the Persians where he met his death. Julian was a ruler with a philosophic bent and a passion for the Hellenistic deities. He was famous for his failed attempts to halt the spread of Christianity.

The novel hews close to the historical facts. Julian's father was murdered by his cousin, the reigning emperor, Constantius Augustus. He spent his childhood held prisoner. He believed fervently in pagan ideas. A man of contrasts, he was a worldly sensualist as well as a nearly compulsive ascetic. He was also a military genius who refused to be Constantine's puppet ruler. He died in battle, a month after his thirty-first birthday and after only sixteen months as a humane and compassionate ruler.

Vidal conveys Julian's exuberant vitality and Rome's glorious pageantry, replete with elephants, dancing girls, bejeweled eunuchs, and debauched orgies. This 1964 work is considered one of the prolific Vidal's best and richest historical fictions.

"Unfortunately, I never achieved the high office that Julian did as Emperor of Rome, but I certainly was an apostate."

—GORE VIDAL, INTERVIEW IN
CONVERSATIONS WITH GORE VIDAL

THE FIRE NEXT TIME

BY JAMES BALDWIN

Dear James: I have begun this letter five times and torn it up five times.

THIS COLLECTION OF essays was published in 1963, in the midst of the civil rights movement's run through the South. Writing with a religious fervor and an apocalyptic tone, Baldwin remembers his own evangelical upbringing. He was born in poverty, the illegitimate son of a woman who cleaned houses to make a living in 1924 Harlem. His stepfather was a righteous, angry Baptist preacher.

Baldwin saw Christianity as another form of slavery forced on blacks. Oppression was the basic condition of their lives. He likened the book's title, taken from biblical prophecy, to urban violence. In these essays, he captures African Americans' rising impatience at the slow pace of change.

Soon after this book's publication, Baldwin was on the cover of *Time*. Although he played the role of political activist and spokesperson, he saw his role as "bear[ing] witness to the truth." But many of his contemporary civil rights leaders were wary of being associated with an openly gay man.

In 1948, Baldwin moved to France to find refuge from oppressive racial and homophobic bigotry.

"In 1959, when he was thirty-five, [Baldwin] wrote from his self-imposed exile in Europe that he had left America because he wanted to prevent himself from becoming merely 'a Negro writer.' He went on to become exactly that: the greatest Negro writer of his generation."

—HILTON ALS, *NEW YORKER*

IRONWEED

BY WILLIAM J. KENNEDY

Riding up the winding road of St. Agnes Cemetery in the back of a rattling old truck, Frances Phelan became aware that the dead, even more than the living, settled down in neighborhoods.

FRANCIS PHELAN IS a prodigiously unlucky man. The novel tells how he threw a stone that fatally cracked a strikebreaker's skull during a rally at an Albany trolley company. So he ran from Albany. Years later, he picked up his thirteen-day-old son by his diaper. When the safety snap opened and the baby dropped and was killed, he ran again.

He becomes a tragic figure, adrift for twenty years, a bum fleeing from his own guilty memories. In 1938 and "inching toward death," he makes a final effort to reconcile with his past. He returns to Albany and roams familiar streets with his buddy Rudy (a character who makes Eeyore look upbeat). Over a few days of drinking and fighting, his hallucinations merge past with present. Apparitions of victims of his past violence rise up to taunt him. He conjures excuses and alibis, and points to others who were at fault, only to dismiss them all and stand as his own accuser.

In this fierce and unforgiving exploration of a hapless Everyman, Kennedy unearths breathtaking truths. The third novel in Kennedy's "Albany" cycle, it won the 1983 National Book Critics Circle Award and the Pulitzer Prize. In so doing, it put Albany on the literary map.

"[William Kennedy] could take material from skid row and write about these people as [if they were as] fully human as anyone else. The people he wrote about didn't know they had become pariahs."

—SAUL BELLOW

My Antonia

BY WILLA CATHER

I first heard of Antonia on what seemed to me an interminable journey across the great midland plain of North America.

MIDDLE-AGED JIM BURDEN looks back with nostalgia at his youth. As an orphan boy of ten in the late nineteenth century, he moved to rural Black Hawk, Nebraska, to live with his grandparents. On the train, he met Antonia Shimerdas, an immigrant girl of fourteen from Bohemia, another about-to-be transplanted newcomer.

Initially disoriented and profoundly shaken by his first glimpse of the featureless void of the prairie, Burden soon finds its vastness uplifting and exhilarating. He's equally taken with Antonia, who becomes his best friend.

The novel takes us through Antonia's childhood, the hardship of working on a farm, her father's death, and her move into town as a young woman. There she is seduced by a glamorous railroad man who reneges on his promise to marry her, leaving her pregnant and alone with their child. Spirit unbroken, Antonia takes her baby and returns to the serenity of the prairie.

First published in 1918 when Cather was forty-five and written in spare, simple prose that expresses a profound reverence for the natural world, this was Cather's fourth novel and the second of her trilogy of prairie novels. Cather's childhood hometown of Red Cloud was the model for Black Hawk. One critic called Cather poet laureate of the American prairie.

"In the world of Willa Cather novels, history lives in its persistence in the memory, and in lost hidden places that wait to be found and to be known for what they are."

—EUDORA WELTY, *NEW YORK TIMES*

The Good Terrorist

BY DORIS LESSING

The house was set back from the noisy main road in what seemed to be a rubbish tip.

LESSING BRINGS TO these pages a pessimist's view of society's moral decay. She asks: What leads a person to participate in an act of domestic terrorism? She takes the reader step by step along the way with Alice Mellings, a thirty-six-year-old college graduate and daughter of upper-middle-class lefties. She's also a member of a splinter group of revolutionaries with a vague plan to join the IRA and zeal to end the injuries and injustice suffered by ordinary people at the hands of that amorphous entity, society.

Alice lives in a house condemned by the authorities who tried to make it uninhabitable. She hates the middle class, but she cooks and cleans and shops, creating an aura of respectable, middle-class domesticity, playing housewife to a homosexual named Jasper who barely tolerates her. She and her fellow radicals depend on the state's welfare system, which they also hate. When explosives find their way into her hands and those of her fellow muddled mercenaries, the result seems inevitable.

Published in 1985, the book's scenario echoes the 1983 bombing of Harrods department store and feels chillingly real.

"The terrorist act with which the book ends is no more an outgrowth of ideology and alienation than it is of the dissociation that allows such victimization to occur, among professional alleviators of need on the one hand and committed enemies of social injustice on the other."

—MARILYNNE ROBINSON

A ROOM OF ONE'S OWN

BY VIRGINIA WOOLF

But, you may say, we asked you to speak about women and fiction—what has that got to do with a room of one's own?

IN THIS EXTENDED essay, which was adapted from a lecture delivered to women at Cambridge, Virginia Woolf addresses the question of whether a woman could produce work to match the quality of Shakespeare's. In a response laced with irony and wit, she enumerates what such a woman would need (a place to write, an income, the fullest worldly experiences, and intellectual freedom) and what she would have to overcome (family, children, insufficient education, and a lack of privacy).

What would have happened, she imagines, to a hypothetical sister of Shakespeare, who possessed all the talent and genius of her sibling? She argues that, despite her gifts, no woman in that age of wife beating could have written the plays. Even Jane Austen had to write in the common sitting room and hide her work under blotting paper. Woolf traces the position of the woman writer through history and finishes with a witty contrast of contemporary men's lives and women's lives.

In 1929 when this was published, Woolf did not expect her words to be taken seriously: "I forecast, then, that I shall get no criticism, except of the evasive jocular kind."

"She says little that has not been said before; indeed, she sets out to prove a point that most intelligent people accept as truistic; but seldom has the point been driven home more cogently or embellished with wittier comment."

—LOUIS KRONENBERGER, IN THE
1929 *NEW YORK TIMES* REVIEW OF THE BOOK

Fahrenheit 451

BY RAY BRADBURY

It was a pleasure to burn.

GUY MONTAG IS a fireman in a dystopian future. His job is not to put out fires but to burn books and the houses of those who conceal them. Books, according to the powers-that-be, are false, useless, and only serve to make people unhappy. The minimum punishment for anyone caught reading one is incarceration in a mental hospital. "Normal" people anesthetize themselves with television and drugs.

One night, Montag meets Clarisse McClellan, a liberated idealist who makes him question his actions and beliefs. She's killed in a car accident, but she gets him thinking. Soon after, while ransacking a house filled with books, he inadvertently reads a line: "Time has fallen asleep in the afternoon sunshine." It's a line from a poem by the mid-nineteenth-century poet Alexander Smith. Intrigued, Montag steals the book and reads it. And steals more, increasingly alienating his wife as he begins to burn televisions instead of books, trying to stop the mindlessness.

Soon, they really are out to get him.

This was Bradbury's fifth book. By the time it was published in 1953, he was already acclaimed the uncrowned king of science fiction. This book was written during the paranoia of the early 1950s, but its government-promoting anti-intellectualism has a frightening resonance today. The title refers to the temperature at which paper burns.

"When Hitler burned a book, I felt it as keenly, please forgive me, as his killing a human, for in the long sum of history they are one and the same flesh."

—BRADBURY, IN THE INTRODUCTION TO
THE 1966 (SIMON AND SCHUSTER) EDITION

DUNE

BY FRANK HERBERT

In the week before their departure to Arrakis, when all the final
scurrying about had reached a near unbearable frenzy, an old
crone came to visit the mother of the boy, Paul.

SET 10,000 YEARS in the future, this iconic sci-fi work imagines a quest for Melange, a "spice of spices." The priceless,
addictive, hallucinogenic substance found only on the harsh
desert planet of Arrakis (Dune) is required for space travel and
grants prescience and longevity.

During a battle for control of Arrakis, Duke Paul Atreides
is cast into the desert to die. He joins forces with Fremen, a tribe
of desert dwellers who worship and ride giant sandworms. Fremen become Atreides's army to reclaim the planet.

First published in 1965, this was the first of Herbert's six
Dune novels. Way ahead of its time, this was the first sci-fi novel
to hinge on ecology. Also unique, this future world has no computers. In subsequent novels, the fictional Duniverse stretches
forward and back covering 16,000 years, exploring violence,
politics, religion, and the human condition.

Many consider this interstellar *Lord of the Rings*, which
won the first Nebula Award, the best sci-fi novel ever written.
It sold more than 12 million copies worldwide after initially
being rejected by sixteen publishers.

"[Mr. Herbert's] adroit mix of religion, ecology, space opera, Arabs, giant
worms, longevity drugs, politics, dynastic wars, extrasensory power
and sex showed just how exhilarating the science fiction romance of
conceptual breakthrough could be."

—JOHN CLUTE

Uncle Tom's Cabin

BY HARRIET BEECHER STOWE

Late in the afternoon of a chilly day in February, two gentlemen were sitting alone over their wine, in a well-furnished dining parlor, in the town of P——, in Kentucky.

ON THIS DATE in 1863 as the Civil War raged on, President Lincoln signed the first of two executive orders that comprised the Emancipation Proclamation. A year earlier, allegedly he'd greeted the author Harriet Beecher Stowe, "So you're the little woman who wrote the book that started this great war."

This was America's first social protest novel, and it took as its subject matter the cruelty and dehumanization of slavery. Rich in melodrama, its scenes have become iconic—the slave Eliza, holding her son in her arms and leaping from one cake of ice to the next across the Ohio River with bloodhounds and slavers hot on her heels; Simon Legree's boastful villainy; lovely little Eva's tragic death; and black orphan Topsy's reluctant reformation.

With her story, Stowe, a white teacher who lived in Connecticut, delivered a searing indictment of slavery, a system that robbed human beings of the most basic human rights. Their families and belongings could be destroyed and they could be sexually exploited at whim by their masters. The novel presents Christianity as the antidote.

Published in 1852, the novel took the world by storm. Within a year, 300,000 copies had been sold in the United States and more than 2 million worldwide.

"I finished Uncle Tom's Cabin, *a powerful and disagreeable book; too dark and Spagnoletto-like for my taste when considered as a work of art. But, on the whole, it is the most valuable addition that America has made to English literature."*

—LORD MACAULEY, DIARY, 1852

SLAUGHTERHOUSE-FIVE

BY KURT VONNEGUT

All this happened, more or less. The war parts, anyway, are pretty much true.

BILLY PILGRIM, AN American chaplain's assistant during World War II, is "tall and weak, and shaped like a bottle of Coca-Cola." Captured by the Germans and sent to Dresden, a place that was not supposed to be a military target, he develops a problem. He becomes "unstuck in time." Interludes of schizophrenia have him living in a parallel dimension in which he's been kidnapped by aliens and taken to the planet Tralfamadore, "where everything was beautiful, and nothing hurt."

In his mind, Pilgrim becomes a time traveler, visiting different points in his life in a search for meaning. In the real world, he bears witness to the bombing of Dresden. His life ends with his assassination. The novel has two subtitles: "The Children's Crusade" and "A Duty-Dance with Death."

Vonnegut drew on experiences. He was held in Dresden as a prisoner of war and witnessed the 1945 firebombing. Afterward, he and the other surviving prisoners were assigned to remove the dead.

Absurd, hilarious, heartbreaking, and profound, acclaimed as one of the greatest antiwar novels ever written, this was published in 1969 against the backdrop of the Vietnam War.

"The drama of any air raid on a civilian population, a gesture in diplomacy to a man like Henry Kissinger, is about the inhumanity of man's inventions to man."

—KURT VONNEGUT, IN THE PREFACE TO A 1994 EDITION

ANGELA'S ASHES

BY FRANK McCOURT

My father and mother should have stayed in New York where they met and married and where I was born.

IN BROOKLYN, FRANKIE'S beloved father drank the family's money so his mother had to resort to begging. Three of his siblings died of illness in infancy. The family couldn't afford sheets or blankets. They returned to Limerick and things got even worse—the family was reduced to living in a ramshackle, rat- and fly-infested apartment with a flooded first floor and the reek of next door's public toilet. By age eleven, Frankie was the chief breadwinner, stealing food and dreaming of a better life for himself and his family. His hospital stay to get treatment for typhoid fever felt like a resort vacation.

Still, there's far more humor, honesty, and compassion than bitterness and resentment in this bestselling memoir of childhood. McCourt takes what his father bequeathed him—a childhood of illness and bone-chilling poverty and a magical gift for storytelling—and creates a remarkable work of literature.

Not all readers were enchanted with McCourt's version of an impoverished Irish childhood, and some accused him of "telling lies about Limerick." Newspapers reported that when the film based on the book was released, some Limerick businessmen organized a book burning.

Published in 1996, it nevertheless won both the Pulitzer and the National Book Critics Circle awards.

"Writing in prose that's pictorial and tactile, lyrical but streetwise, Mr. McCourt does for the town of Limerick what the young Joyce did for Dublin: he conjures the place for us with such intimacy that we feel we've walked its streets and crawled its pubs."

—MICHIKO KAKUTANI, *NEW YORK TIMES*

NEUROMANCER

BY WILLIAM GIBSON

The sky above the port was the color of television, tuned to a dead channel.

IN THIS FICTIONAL future, computer technology and bioengineering have created superhumans. Case, a computer hacker so intimately plugged into his machine that he can physically sense the flow of electronic data, lives with fellow "cowboys" in a "consensual hallucination" that Gibson dubbed *cyberspace* (coining the term for the first time). Case sells his talents to the world's giant corporations, which have evolved into powerful and virtually immortal beings.

When Case double-crosses his employer and gets caught, he's stripped of his ability to key into cyberspace. He winds up drug addicted, down and out on a futuristic skid row near Tokyo Bay. A mysterious special-forces vet comes to his rescue, restores his talents, and teams him with a beautiful, biologically engineered female assassin. Their mission: to crack a space colony's computer security.

Reviewers called it kaleidoscopic, picaresque, decadent, and streetwise. Published in 1984 (the same year Apple started to sell Macintosh computers), this was Gibson's debut novel and the first installment in a trilogy. Considered the definitive work of cyberpunk fiction, Gibson wrote the manuscript on a manual typewriter. It was the first ever to win the trifecta of sci-fi awards—Nebula, Hugo, and Philip K. Dick.

"The present is more frightening than any imaginable future I might dream up. If Marshall McLuhan were alive today, he'd have a nervous breakdown."

—WILLIAM GIBSON

THE RECOGNITIONS

BY WILLIAM GADDIS

Even Camilla had enjoyed masquerades, of the safe sort where the mask may be dropped at the critical moment it presumes itself as a reality.

MASQUERADES AND DECEIT of every sort permeate this novel, its characters a collection of phonies. Wyatt Gwyon is an artist who fakes Flemish and modern masterpieces. His father is a Calvinist minister who converts to Catholicism and then Mithraism, dragging his clueless congregation along with him. His friend is a playwright who steals other people's words and gives them to characters who represent himself.

Weighing in at over 900 pages, when first published in 1955 this first novel drew tepid reviews. The *New York Times Book Review* critic found the book difficult and unnecessarily cryptic (for instance, the hero's name isn't mentioned until hundreds of pages in). He dismissed it: "*The Recognitions*—or that part of it that is understandable—is no more than very talented or highly ingenious or, on another level, rather amusing."

Since then, Gaddis has been compared to literary greats like Joyce, Proust, and Melville, and ranked alongside contemporary author Thomas Pynchon. He published three other novels, including *JR*, which won the National Book Award in 1975. Critics speak of *The Recognitions* as the most overlooked work of the last century.

"The novel is like a huge landscape painting of modern New York, peopled with hundreds of doomed but energetic little figures, executed on wood panels by Brueghel or Bosch, and looking incongruously ancient beneath layers of yellowed lacquer. . . . Peel away the erudition and you have The Catcher in the Rye: *a grim winter sojourn in a seedy Manhattan, a quest for authenticity in a phony modern world."*

—JONATHAN FRANZEN, *HOW TO BE ALONE*

REVOLUTIONARY ROAD

BY RICHARD YATES

*The final dying sounds of their dress rehearsal left the Laurel
Players with nothing to do but stand there, silent and helpless,
blinking out over the footlights of an empty auditorium.*

THE SUBJECT OF this 1961 novel is self-deception. A dissatisfied couple—thirty-year-old Frank and April Wheeler—live in
a cozy, newish house in the bedroom community of Revolutionary Hill Estates in suburban Connecticut. Despite the patina of
a perfect middle-class life, they are unhappy with themselves
and with each other.

Frank's job in the city is dull. With little to do at home,
April wonders where are all those "marvelous golden people . . . who made their lives work out the way they wanted
without even trying, who never had to make the best of a bad
job because it never occurred to them to do anything less than
perfectly the first time?" A former actress, she tries getting
involved in community theater and fails miserably.

Frank consumes himself with work and an affair in the city.
April proposes they move to Paris to address their joint malaise.
Violent arguments ensue and plans to move are abandoned.
Finally a violent tragedy brings life in Revolutionary Hills
Estates to an unaccustomed juncture.

This scathing satire with its indictment of suburban mediocrity was Yates's first novel.

"We [writers] marvel at its consummate writerliness, its almost simple
durability as a purely made thing of words that defeats all attempts at
classification. Realism, naturalism, social satire—the standard critical
bracketry—all go begging before this splendid book."

—RICHARD FORD, INTRODUCTION
TO THE 2001 (METHUEN) EDITION

THE WIND-UP BIRD CHRONICLE

BY HARUKI MURAKAMI

When the phone rang I was in the kitchen, boiling a potful of spaghetti and whistling along with an FM broadcast of the overture to Rossini's The Thieving Magpie, *which has to be the perfect music for cooking pasta.*

IN THIS SWIRLING, dreamlike tale set in suburban Tokyo, Toru Okada is a laid-back young man, a World War II Japanese Army veteran. He's quit his boring job as a gofer in a law firm to become a house husband. His wife Kumiko supports them. His cat, which he named after his nasty, hyper-conservative brother-in-law, disappears. When Kumiko disappears, too, his brother-in-law informs him that she is having an affair and wants a divorce. But Toru has reason to distrust this particular messenger.

The laconic, likeable Okada's world shifts and morphs and fractures. Moving and magical scenes intertwine, and reality and dreams become indistinguishable. A woman whose voice he can't quite place keeps engaging him in erotic phone calls. By night he consults sister psychics who visit his dreams, and by day he obsesses over death. He descends to the bottom of a dry well, plumbing the depths of his subconscious and seeking his wife, ultimately having to face his own action and inaction during the war.

This is a mystery intertwined with a love story and a tale of redemption. It is also a satire of modern Japanese culture. Murakami is one of Japan's most celebrated novelists, and this was his third work, published in Japanese in 1994 and 1995 in three separate volumes.

"Murakami is that unusual creature, a metaphysical novelist with a warm, down-to-earth voice and a knack for creating credible characters and spinning a lively yarn."

—LAURA MILLER, SALON.COM

VANITY FAIR

BY WILLIAM MAKEPEACE THACKERAY

While the present century was in its teens, and on one sunshiny morning in June, there drove up to the great iron gate of Miss Pinkerton's academy for young ladies, on Chiswick Mall, a large family coach, with two fat horses in blazing harness, driven by a fat coachman in a three-cornered hat and wig, at the rate of four miles an hour.

THE NOVEL'S TITLE comes from an allegory in *The Pilgrim's Progress* in which John Bunyan wrote of a town fair held in a village called Vanity. Thackeray subtitled this "a novel without a hero," and none of the characters in this biting satire of nineteenth-century English greed and hypocrisy are even slightly heroic.

The novel opens with Becky Sharp and Amelia Sedley en route to Russell Square, having just finished their schooling. Becky is cold, smart, and calculating; Miss Amelia is good-natured and dull. They meet Amelia's betrothed, the dashing, feckless Captain George Osborne, and his loyal friend, Captain William Dobbin, and Amelia's brother, Joseph Sedley. The stage is set for a lifetime of romantic, financial, and familial entanglements as Becky, who never had financial security as a child, desires wealth above all else. Amelia marries Osborne, blind to his failings and oblivious to the true devotion Dobbin has for her.

First published in installments from 1847 to 1848, this enduring classic contains period social commentary laced with delicious melodrama.

"[Thackeray] had the superlative talent of making you intimate with his people. You took hold of the buttons on their coats, and you held fast."

—*NEW YORK TIMES* REVIEWER ON THE
PUBLICATION OF A NEW EDITION IN 1898

THE AUTOBIOGRAPHY OF MISS JANE PITTMAN

BY ERNEST J. GAINES

I have been trying to get Miss Jane Pittman to tell me the story of her life for several years now, but each time I asked her she told me there was no story to tell.

THIS 1971 NOVEL takes the form of eloquent tape-recorded recollections of 110-year-old Miss Jane, a woman whose life in rural southern Louisiana spanned slavery, the Civil War, Reconstruction, the civil rights movement, and '60s black militancy.

The story begins when Jane is ten and a slave, living on a plantation. Freed a year later, no sooner have she and a group of former slaves set off for Ohio when they are set upon by Klansmen and a gang of rebel soldiers. Big Laura, "tough as any man I ever seen," is killed. Jane and Laura's son Ned turn south again. In Louisiana, Jane finds work on a plantation and adopts Ned as her own. Jane marries a cowboy, and Ned grows up to be an educator and freedom fighter.

"The black man or white man who tell you to stay in a corner want you to keep your mind in a corner, too," Ned says. "For his outspokenness, he is assassinated and Jane turns to the church for solace. After the death of another martyr, years later, Jane joins the civil rights movement.

Gaines told a *New York Times* interviewer that in writing this book, he "tried to show the strength of black people. But I was criticized when I was writing *Miss Jane Pittman* because blacks were expected to write novels of protest. If you read the novel you'll see that there is protest in it." The book was turned into an award-winning television movie.

"Like the beautifully vivid sturdy and serviceable language of the black, white and Creole people of Louisiana, Gaines is mellow with historical reflection, supple with wit, relaxed and expansive because he does not equate his people with failure."

—ALICE WALKER, *NEW YORK TIMES*

October

THINGS FALL APART

BY CHINUA ACHEBE

Okonkwo was well known throughout the nine villages and even beyond.

THIS NOVEL TRACES Nigerian tribal leader Okonkwo's fall from grace to exile and ruin on the eve of colonialism. Achebe makes Okonkwo cruel and sympathetic, a classic tragic hero who falls victim to his own belief that he is in control as he resists the white missionaries' religion and burns their church. His son, Nwoye, converts without questioning and becomes alienated from his own Igbo village, its traditions and its people.

Achebe's first novel, published in 1958, the book provides a fascinating, unflinching look at life in precolonial Nigeria. It illuminates the complex realities of traditional life and the turmoil and no-win choices wrought by British domination. "This dark side is real," Achebe said in a 2007 interview, adding that there is often no good reason "why the righteous suffer" or "why a good cause fails."

Probably the most widely read contemporary African author, Achebe wrote numerous other novels, essays, and short stories. Called the father of modern African literature, in 2007 he was awarded the Booker International Prize.

"Writing with a beautiful economy, Achebe seized the basic African subject—the breakup, under colonialism, of tribal society—so firmly and fairly that the book's tragedy, like Greek tragedy, felt tonic; a space had been cleared, an understanding had been achieved, a new beginning was implied."

—JOHN UPDIKE, *NEW YORKER*

THE FAMISHED ROAD

BY BEN OKRI

In the beginning there was a river. The river became a road and branched out to the whole world. And because the road was once a river it was always hungry.

AZARO IS AN "abiku," a spirit child condemned to die and be reborn endlessly. On the eve of Nigerian independence, he's reborn, the only son of poor Yoruban parents living in an urban ghetto, probably Lagos. "Tired of coming and going," and unwilling to break his beloved mother's heart, he chooses to fight death. His fellow unborn spirits are more than a little reluctant to let him live.

Often possessed by "boiling hallucinations," Azaro maintains his ties to the spirit world. Other abiku try tricks to lure him back to their world, and he narrowly avoids death so often that his parents nickname him Lazaro (Lazarus).

Though life is painful and death would provide release, he is determined to survive. He yearns to become a wise politician though there are virtually no role models in a country where politicians bully and bribe their way into office.

Lauded for its poetic images and brilliant energy, this is a book in which magic and reality compete. Time and space are fluid and storylines meander. Azaro's struggles to stay alive are meant to mirror Africa's struggles for democracy, and the "famished road" of the title is Nigeria's independence, beset by hunger and often devouring its own people.

This novel was awarded the 1991 Booker Prize.

"As one startling image follows the next, The Famished Road *begins to read like an epic poem that happens to touch down just this side of prose."*

—LINDA GRANT, *INDEPENDENT*

THE BLUE FLOWER

BY PENELOPE FITZGERALD

Jacob Dietmahler was not such a fool that he could not see that they had arrived at his friend's home on the washday.

FRITZ VON HARDENBERG is a young man who will become a leading German Romantic poet of the eighteenth century. The eldest son in a lively, boisterous, affectionate household, the intense, dreamy young man first sets eyes on twelve-year-old Sophie von Kühn, the daughter of a former army captain, as she stands at a window "tapping idly on the glass as though she was trying to attract the attention of someone outside." One look and he's smitten. Not beautiful or aristocratic or worldly or wealthy, not all that bright, and much too young even by the standards of that time, Sophie is a spectacularly inappropriate choice. But Fritz is blind to her shortcomings and convinced of her "human perfection" and "moral grace." His family is shocked by his hopeless romanticism.

Their courtship takes a tragic turn when she contracts tuberculosis. She dies alone, Fritz having deserted her bedside to attend to his poetic meditations.

Set in Leipzig and Berlin after the French Revolution, this comedy of manners mocks its characters with their highfalutin' notions of philosophy and art. Fritz is based on an historical figure who lived from 1772 to 1801 and became a famous visionary poet using his family name, Novalis. Published in 1995, this won the National Book Critics Circle Award.

"Reading Penelope Fitzgerald's new novel, The Blue Flower, *you may feel as if you've walked inside a painting by Caspar David Friedrich— one of those luminous canvases of the German romantic period in which the golden light that bathes the landscape seems to be shining down not just from the sun, but from some other—and loftier— dimension."*

—FRANCINE PROSE

THE ENGLISH PATIENT

BY MICHAEL ONDAATJE

She stands up in the garden where she has been working and looks into the distance.

IN APRIL 1945, the eponymous English patient is pulled from the burned and blackened wreckage of a plane abandoned by retreating German troops. He's taken to the Villa San Girolamo, a partially destroyed Italian monastery near Florence, where he is nursed by Hana, a young Canadian who knows only that he's English. To her, he is a "despairing Saint" who jots quotations from Kipling and Stendahl in his copy of Herodotus's *Histories*.

As she pours calamine over his chest, his whispers drag "the listening heart of the young nurse beside him to wherever his mind is, into that well of memory he kept plunging into during the months before he died."

The pair is joined by David Caravaggio, a shadowy Canadian thief whose hands have been mutilated by the Germans, and Kirpal "Kip" Singh, a young Indian munitions expert who is clearing the area of German bombs and mines. Kip wonders if the mysterious patient might be his father.

If Hana is the heart of this novel, Kip is its soul. The novel's climactic moment is Kip's primal scream as he hears the news about Hiroshima. This won the Booker Prize in 1992.

"This book and its author have such a fine reputation that they verge on the overrated—until you reread the book and remember just how vivid and convincing it is."

—MICHAEL CHABON, SALON.COM

THE GREAT FIRE

BY SHIRLEY HAZZARD

Now they were starting. Finality ran through the train, an exhalation.

THE "GREAT FIRE" of the title is World War II, and like *The English Patient*, this story is set in its aftermath. It could be subtitled "Love in a Time of Chaos."

Thirty-two-year-old war hero and prison camp survivor Aldred Leith walks across Asia to discover the impact of the war. He comes to Japan and witnesses the effects of the atomic bomb. On an island off China's mainland he finds lodging with the Driscoll family. Mr. Driscoll is a medical administrator from Australia. Aldred is smitten by the Driscolls' beautiful seventeen-year-old daughter Helen, a "little mermaid" of a girl. She devotedly nurses her older brother, Benedict, who suffers from a degenerative disease.

This novel wanders back and forth in time. The lovers are separated, reunited, separated again, until finally united at last. Reviewers proclaim it a masterpiece, a "tapestry in clear and elegant prose."

Published more than two decades after Hazzard's blockbuster *The Transit of Venus*, this won the 2003 National Book Award. Hazzard told a journalist that the character Aldred Leith was inspired by a man she'd once loved: "He was the reason I began writing the book. I wanted to remember him."

"[Shirley Hazzard] is unique among moderns in that the irony is confined to her style and not to the work's content. She believes in love—indeed, she believes in Love—yet writes about it in such cool, subdued, finical prose that one might be forgiven at times for thinking her a cynic. But she is not."

—JOHN BANVILLE, *NEW YORK TIMES*

THE REMAINS OF THE DAY

BY KAZUO ISHIGURO

Tonight, I find myself here in a guest house in the city of Salisbury.

THE PROPRIETY-BOUND, EMOTIONALLY repressed narrator of this novel is Mr. Stevens, the venerable butler at Darlington Hall. Though he's an expert on all aspects of butlering, he's ignorant of affairs of his own heart and blind to his former employer Lord Darlington's imperfections—in particular, his actions on behalf of the Nazis.

As the book opens, Stevens is in service to the new American owners of Darlington Hall. He's borrowed their car to drive to Cornwall. He hasn't said as much, but he plans to find Miss Kenton, Darlington Hall's former housekeeper, and persuade her to return. It's revealed that Miss Kenton once loved Stevens but realized that his loyalty to Lord Darlington and the needs of Darlington Hall's tarnished silver would always come before her.

Though Stevens is stiff, upright, and humorless, he's thoroughly sympathetic and even endearing in his cluelessness (Anthony Hopkins immortalized the character in the movie version.) The writing is sublime. This 1989 novel, which was the Japanese-born British author's third, won the 1989 Booker Prize.

"As a political fable, [The Remains of the Day] is both subtle and humane. I can think of several club-footed polemical novelists, in fact, who would benefit from a careful reading of this book. The rest of us can simply read it for pleasure, and be richly rewarded."

—JONATHAN COE

PLAY IT AS IT LAYS

BY JOAN DIDION

What makes Iago evil? some people ask. I never ask.

THIS POWERFUL MASTERPIECE of bleak, 1960s-style existential angst opens in a psychiatric hospital. Maria Wyeth's all-caps reply to the novel's opening question is "NOTHING APPLIES."

Maria is from a Nevada town that a new highway was supposed to transform into a destination. But foreshadowing the coming disappointments in her life, the highway was built elsewhere. She has had a modest acting career, a failed affair, and a disastrous marriage. Now she lives in Movieville, California, another form of nowhere. She's given birth to a daughter with an "aberrant chemical in her brain" and gone through a horrific abortion. To stave off her own disintegration, she drives at top speed along the freeways in her yellow Corvette Sting Ray, on her way to nowhere in particular, shrouded in a fog of drugs. Her father taught her "life is a crap game." One in which she knows nothing is at stake. "I know what 'nothing' means," she says, "and keep on playing."

In a last-gasp effort to wrench herself from terminal physical and emotional nihilism, Maria tries to rescue her daughter from the home where she's been committed.

This completely terrifying view of the meaninglessness of what we call life was published in 1970. The story and characters appalled some critics and fascinated others. Virtually all were impressed by the spare, powerful, and what one critic called "surgical prose." Chapters are distilled to a single page, characters encapsulated in a single sentence.

"She writes with a razor, carving her characters out of her perceptions with strokes so swift and economical that each scene ends almost before the reader is aware of it; and yet the characters go on bleeding afterward."

—JOHN LEONARD, *NEW YORK TIMES*

THE MAMBO KINGS PLAY SONGS OF LOVE

BY OSCAR HIJUELOS

It was a Saturday afternoon on La Salle Street, years and years ago when I was a little kid, and around three o'clock Mrs. Shannon, the heavy Irish woman in her perpetually soup-stained dress, opened her back door and shouted out into the courtyard, "Hey, Cesar, yoo-hoo, I think you're on television, I swear it's you!"

TRIUMPHS AND TRAGEDIES play out against the backdrop of 1950s Cuban-émigré life. Cesar and Nestor Castillo, Cuban-born musicians, form a band in New York. At the height of the mambo boom, they play dance halls, nightclubs, and birthday parties (*fiestas de quince*). They have a hit record and appear on *I Love Lucy* as Ricky's singing cousins.

These colorful, flawed heroes are loaded with musical talent. Cesar, who has left his wife and family in Cuba, is a relentless hedonist and womanizer. His advice to Nestor: "If you want a woman, treat her good sometimes, but don't let her get too used to it." Nestor is introverted and somber, and when his relationship with Maria ends abruptly, he writes twenty-two versions of a song dedicated to her memory. The woman Nestor later marries can never match this lost love.

Nestor dies, leaving Cesar chastened. His return to Cuba is disappointing. His and his brother's fifteen minutes of fame turn out to be no more than that.

Hijuelos's second novel, published in 1990, this became the first by a Hispanic writer to win the Pulitzer for fiction.

"[T]he Mambo King is to be admired and envied as a man who squeezed the juice out of life before life squeezed the juice out of him."

—R. Z. SHEPPARD, *TIME* MAGAZINE

THE HOUSE OF THE SEVEN GABLES

BY NATHANIEL HAWTHORNE

Halfway down a by-street of one of our New England towns stands a rusty wooden house, with seven acutely peaked gables, facing towards various points of the compass, and a huge, clustered chimney in the midst.

THE EPONYMOUS HOUSE of this novel is a gloomy ancestral home in Salem, Massachusetts, with a legacy of dishonor. It belongs to Miss Hepzibah Pyncheon, a spinster with a near-sighted scowl and stiff joints. One of her prized possessions is a map of a great territory that ought to have belonged to her family.

Miss Pyncheon is reduced to opening a little shop on the first floor of the house and selling gingerbread and marbles in order to support her brother Clifford who has been released from prison after serving thirty years on charges of murdering his rich uncle. A cousin, Judge Pyncheon, who engineered Clifford's arrest and imprisonment, tries to get the depressed and unfo-cused Clifford consigned to an asylum. The judge, it turns out, has his own reasons for wanting to get his hands on the house.

Hawthorne subtitled the novel "A Romance," and there are bright notes when little country cousin Phoebe arrives, infusing a charming air of freshness and hope into the fusty house. "She was like a prayer offered up in the homeliest beauty of one's mother-tongue." Phoebe is wooed by Holgrave, a lodger. We root for Miss Pyncheon to reclaim her home and with it her family's honor, for Clifford to emerge from the shadow of false accusations, and for Phoebe to find happiness.

"[The House of the Seven Gables] is a large and generous production, pervaded with that vague hum, that indefinable echo, of the whole multitudinous life of man, which is the real sign of a great work of fiction."

—HENRY JAMES

THE CATCHER IN THE RYE

BY J. D. SALINGER

If you really want to hear about it, the first thing you'll probably want to know is where I was born and what my lousy childhood was like, and how my parents were occupied and all before they had me, and all that David Copperfield kind of crap, but I don't feel like going into it, if you want to know the truth. In the first place, that stuff bores me, and in the second place, my parents would have about two hemorrhages apiece if I told anything pretty personal about them.

NARRATED IN A cynical, jaded voice laced with informal slang, Holden Caulfield tells his story from a California psychiatric hospital. He's been kicked out of Pencey Prep, the last in a series of exclusive boys' schools that have thrown him out. Loathe to return home to face his parents' disapproval, he scrapes together some cash and spends a few days in New York. There he visits nightclubs and movie theaters and tries to bury himself in alcohol, cigarettes, and sex. His little sister Phoebe saves him.

This is the story of a painfully unhappy and disaffected seventeen-year-old boy whose little brother has died. Holden is prescient, observant, and spot-on at sizing up others. His reminiscence of prep-school life is a devastating indictment: "Pencey was full of crooks."

The novel is one of the most influential and most frequently banned books of the last century. It was published in 1951 after being turned down by the publisher who originally solicited it. The *New Yorker* declined to print an excerpt because the Caulfield children were not believable and the writing too showy. Fifty years later, it had sold 60 million copies.

"Each generation feels disappointed in its own way, though, and seems to require its own literature of disaffection. For many Americans who grew up in the 1950s, The Catcher in the Rye *is the purest extract of that mood. Holden Caulfield is their sorrow king."*

—LOUIS MENAND, *NEW YORKER*

BLACK BOY

BY RICHARD WRIGHT

*One winter morning in the long-ago, four-year-old days of my life
I found myself standing before a fireplace, warming my hands
over a mound of glowing coals, listening to the wind whistle past
the house outside.*

THIS IS NO sentimental tale of an idyllic childhood told in
retrospect by a sanguine adult. Wright wrote this harrowing, at
times poetic, autobiographical account of his southern childhood to "give tongue to voiceless Negro boys."

Wright's voice is feverish, angry, and bitter as he revisits this
youth. He grew up in the slums of Memphis and in the rural
slums of Arkansas and Mississippi. His father deserted his
mother. A sensitive youngster, his childhood was marked by
hunger and fear, poverty, abuse, and racism. His uncle's murder
by a white man was never even investigated. A boyhood friend
was lynched. He learned to survive contact with whites by looking down and assuming a mask of obsequious humility.

Published in 1945, five years after his acclaimed novel
Native Son, this is considered a classic of America autobiography. Poignant and deeply disturbing even today, this work was
denounced as obscene on the floor of the Senate in 1945 by
Senator Theodore Bilbo, a Mississippi Democrat.

*"Living in the South doomed me to look always through eyes which the
South had given me, and bewilderment and fear made me mute and
afraid. But after I had left the South, luck gave me other eyes, new eyes
with which to look at the meaning of what I'd lived through."*

—RICHARD WRIGHT, *LEXINGTON READER*

Goodbye, Columbus

BY PHILIP ROTH

The first time I saw Brenda she asked me to hold her glasses.

FIRST PUBLISHED IN 1959 in a volume with five short stories, this novella offered a thoroughly modern take on the old boy-gets-girl/boy-loses-girl story with a boy-finds-himself ending. The boy is Neil Klugman, a smart guy who's an undergraduate at Rutgers. He lives with his aunt and uncle in blue-collar Newark and works at the public library. She's Brenda Patimkin, a Radcliffe undergrad and beloved daughter of nouveau-riche parents living in Short Hills.

Neil and Brenda may live in the same state but their homes are worlds apart. Their passionate but ill-starred love affair lasts through one long summer and a meeting in a hotel room—after which he comes to his senses.

This book presents an unflattering portrait of middle-class American Jews. Alienated by social fakery, Neil Klugman might be Salinger's Holden Caulfield a few years later.

Like his character, Roth grew up in Newark. Roth was just twenty-six when this, his first published book, won the 1959 National Book Award. Fifty years and more than two dozen books later, he continues to affront, transgress, and provoke contemporary sensibilities.

"Roth is a serious writer who has never been somber in print; his narrative voice is unique, and so is the way he consistently wrings slapstick comedy out of the tics and obsessions of his characters."

—PAUL GRAY, *TIME* MAGAZINE

THE ADVENTURES OF OLIVER TWIST

BY CHARLES DICKENS

Among other public buildings in a certain town, which for many reasons it will be prudent to refrain from mentioning, and to which I will assign no fictitious name, there is one anciently common to most towns, great or small: to wit, a workhouse; and in this workhouse was born; on a day and date which I need not trouble myself to repeat, inasmuch as it can be of no possible consequence to the reader, in this stage of the business at all events; the item of mortality whose name is prefixed to the head of this chapter.

A FELICITOUS COMBINATION of melodrama and social and political satire, this timeless novel tells the story of an orphan born in a workhouse near London. At nine, he's put to work by the pompous beadle, Mr. Bumble, picking oakum. In a famous episode, the boys, all desperately hungry, draw lots and Oliver loses. He must ask, "Please sir, I want some more."

The workhouse board members, a well-fed bunch, are outraged at this and offer Oliver up for five pounds sterling to anyone who will take him away. Off he goes to apprentice to the local undertaker, Mr. Sowerberry. After a run-in with a bullying fellow apprentice, Oliver runs away.

On London's streets he meets the Artful Dodger and falls among thieves working for the cunning Fagin. Too late, Oliver realizes his new friends do not *make* wallets. He is arrested for pickpocketing. His victim, the kindly Mr. Brownlow, takes pity on Oliver and brings him home. Fagin's gang kidnaps him back. Finally, the thieves are brought to justice and Oliver is restored to his wealthy grandfather.

Dickens's second novel, published in 1838, this was the first well-known English novel to have a child as its protagonist.

"Oliver Twist turned the world upside down and offered a new view of things to Dickens's readers: life at the bottom of Victorian society as seen through the eyes of a child."

—JANE SMILEY, *CHARLES DICKENS*

AS I LAY DYING

BY WILLIAM FAULKNER

Jewel and I come up from the field, following the path in single file.

SEEMS LIKE EVERY novel with lyrical prose, stream-of-consciousness style, and multiple narrators is dubbed "Faulknerian." This 1930 novel shows why that's a good thing.

The epic narrative is told through fifty-nine interior monologues. Most are "spoken" by members of the Bundren family, a clan of poor southern white folks struggling to fulfill their mother Addie's wish, to be buried in the distant town of Jefferson beside her father. Her son, Cash, is a carpenter who builds a coffin and lays her in it. Through flood and fire, Cash and Addie's husband head to Jefferson, carrying the decomposing body. With them are Addie's other children.

Darl, the mad visionary son, insists that he has no mother. Dewey Dell, the only daughter, unmarried and pregnant and seeking a secret abortion, cannot mourn her mother. Jewel, the product of Addie's adulterous affair with Vardaman, is still a child and refuses to believe Addie is dead. Jewel bores holes in the coffin so Addie can breathe. His chapter is the shortest: "My mother is a fish."

In one section, Addie speaks: "I could just remember how my father used to say that the reason for living was to get ready to stay dead for a long time." This sadistic, disturbed woman is even more dangerous dead than alive.

Published in 1930 when Faulkner was working nights at a power plant, he proclaimed it a "tour de force." He was right, though many contemporary critics were not convinced.

"Of all Faulkner's novels, As I Lay Dying *is the warmest, the kindliest and most affectionate. In no other work is he so receptive to people, so ready to take and love them, to hear them out and record their turns of idiom, their melodies of speech."*

—IRVING HOWE, *WILLIAM FAULKNER: A CRITICAL STUDY*

SEPHARAD

BY ANTONIO MUÑOZ MOLINA

We have made our lives far away from our small city, but we just can't get used to being away from it, and we like to nurture our nostalgia when it has been a while since we've been back, so sometimes we exaggerate our accent when talking among ourselves, and use the common words and expressions that we've been storing up over the years and that our children can vaguely understand from having heard them so often.

SEPHARAD IS THE Hebrew word for Spain, and Sephardic Jews have their own language and traditions. Molina opens this book, written originally in Spanish, with a nostalgic journey back to his childhood growing up in a Sephardic community. Instead of Proust's madeleines, there are borrachuelos.

Seventeen meandering and interlocking stories of Sephardic Jews, dislocated from Spain, are narrated by a man who has been diagnosed with leukemia and regrets that his children will never know the world in which he grew up. Their stories crisscross Europe ("In our dry inland country, night trains are the great river that carries us to the world outside and then bring us back") and move forward and back in time. Subtitled "A Novel of Novels," most of its journeys are grim voyages of pain, displacement, tragedy, and horror related to the Holocaust, the gulag, or the Spanish Civil War.

A well known author in Spain, the publication of the much acclaimed English translation of this book brought Muñoz Molina's years of anonymity in the United States to an abrupt end. It won the 2004 PEN/Book-of-the-Month Club Translation Prize.

"[Sepharad] is a net of images and horrors, of lives seen at surprising angles, all bound to the subject of Spain—the land the rabbis identified with the biblical Sepharad—and the fearful business of leaving it."

—MICHAEL PYE, *NEW YORK TIMES*

CLOUDSPLITTER

BY RUSSELL BANKS

Upon waking this cold, gray morning from a troubled sleep, I realized for the hundredth time, but this time with deep conviction, that my words and behavior towards you were disrespectful, and rude and selfish as well.

ON THIS DATE in 1859, abolitionist John Brown raided the federal arsenal at Harpers Ferry, intending to incite a slave insurrection. Two days later, federal troops led by Robert E. Lee took back the arsenal. Five raiders, including Brown's son, Owen, escaped. Six weeks later, "Old Osawatomie," as Brown became known after his raids in the free state of Kansas, was executed for treason.

Banks reimagines the two decades of Brown's life leading up to the raid and the events immediately surrounding it. The novel is a series of long letters written by John Brown's son Owen long after Brown's execution. By then Owen is an old man, living in isolation as a shepherd in the California mountains where he escaped after his father's and brothers' deaths.

In this, his last "confession," Owen tells of a father, haunted by a vengeful God who demanded that he deliver the ultimate sacrifice in order to free the slaves. "Was my father mad?" Owen asks.

Published in 1998, this fascinating, complex amalgam of fact and fiction written in finely crafted prose sheds new light on one of history's flawed heroes and on a soon-to-be fractured American landscape in the run-up to the Civil War.

"Cloudsplitter *gnaws at the moral impossibilities of being white. For Owen and his father, being white was so difficult that in dreams they darken their skins to find tranquility."*

—SCOTT L. MALCOMSON

A THOUSAND ACRES

BY JANE SMILEY

At sixty miles per hour, you could pass our farm in a minute, on County Road 686, which ran due north into the T intersection at Cabot Street Road.

WITH SHADES OF *King Lear*, a domineering father decides to divide among his three daughters the thousand-acre Iowa farm that he spent a lifetime acquiring. Sister Caroline stands in for Cordelia, Ginny for Goneril, and Rose for Regan. After their mother died, Ginny and Rose raised Caroline. While Ginny and Rose and their husbands still live just down the road from their formidable, blustery father and have continued to cook and care for him, Caroline has moved away and become a lawyer.

Facing his own mortality, their father offers to deed the farm to his daughters. When Caroline hesitates to accept, her father peremptorily cuts her from the will: "You don't want it, my girl, you're out." In the aftermath, long simmering resentments and secrets boil to the surface.

A family tragedy, this novel is equally an exploration of the tragedy of America's disappearing family farm. This was Smiley's fifth novel. Published in 1991, it won the National Book Critics Circle Award and the Pulitzer.

"*[Jane Smiley] has beautifully and precisely catalogued the bitter intimacy of human relationships, the universality of misunderstanding and grief. Her Pulitzer prize–winning triumph,* A Thousand Acres, *adapted the greatest tragic narrative, reworking* Lear *in the sprawling, workaday landscape of the American prairie and granting, to the humble Cook family, the calamities of kings.*"

—CLAIRE MESSUD, *CONTEMPORARY LITERARY CRITICISM*

TREASURE ISLAND

BY ROBERT LOUIS STEVENSON

Squire Trelawney, Dr. Livesey, and the rest of these gentlemen having asked me to write down the whole particulars about Treasure Island, from the beginning to the end, keeping nothing back but the bearings of the island, and that only because there is still treasure not yet lifted. . . .

WITH ITS BUCCANEERS, treasure map, buried gold, mutiny at sea, and boy hero, *Treasure Island* set the standard for swashbuckling fiction. The boy is Jim Hawkins, an innkeeper's son. He meets hard-drinking seafarer Billy Bones, who's taken lodging at the inn. Literally frightened to death by a pair of former shipmates, before Bones dies he confides to Jim and Jim's mother that these men were after his sea chest.

In the chest, Jim finds money, a journal, and a map to an island where treasure is buried. Squire Trelawney proposes buying a ship, hiring a crew, and taking Jim and a local doctor along to find the treasure. Long John Silver, with his "timber leg," is engaged as cook for the voyage.

The ship sets sail, but soon Jim realizes many of the crew members are pirates who plan to mutiny. A battle for the treasure and for survival ensues. Ever since the novel's publication in England in 1883 readers have debated the moral ambiguity of Silver. The tall, powerful, wily figure turns out to be a former mate of the infamous Captain Flint.

Stevenson wrote this to entertain his stepson, Lloyd Osbourne. Though Stevenson was sickly through much of his life and was expected to die from tuberculosis in his twenties, he traveled widely and died at age forty-four of a stroke on his adopted island of Samoa.

"[Robert Louis Stevenson's] books are for the most part books without women, and it is not women who fall most in love with them."

—HENRY JAMES, *CENTURY MAGAZINE*

KING SOLOMON'S MINES

BY H. RIDER HAGGARD

*It is a curious thing that at my age—fifty-five last birthday—
I should find myself taking up a pen to write a history.*

ALLAN QUATERMAIN LEADS a group deep into Africa's unexplored regions, looking for a man (Captain Good) who disappeared after setting out to find the legendary King Solomon's diamond mines. Deeper and deeper into the jungle Quatermain treks with a pair of Zulu guides and an old friend whose false teeth will come in handy. They encounter enraged elephants, climb a mountain so cold that the centuries-old corpse of a Portuguese explorer is perfectly preserved in ice, and cross a vast dry desert. They find themselves captured by the fierce Kukuana tribesmen who, in an annual ritual, murder a beautiful young woman.

Can Quatermain and his men help the rightful king of the Kukuanas get back his throne from the one-eyed King Twala and the impish witch Gagool? Can they face the White Death and the White Dead? Find the diamond treasure? And, oh yeah, rescue the man they set out to find in the first place?

More realistic than anything that had come before it, this novel was inspired by Haggard's own experiences in Africa. When it was first published in 1885, posters put up in the dead of night greeted Londoners the next morning with the message "The Most Amazing Book Ever Written." It was the first of what came to be known as the "lost world" genre.

Supposedly Haggard wrote this because his brother bet him that he couldn't write a ripping yarn half as good as *Treasure Island*.

"In this narrative Mr. Haggard seems, as the French say, to have 'found himself.' He has added a new book to a scanty list, the list of good, manly, and stirring fictions of pure adventure."

—ANDREW LANG, *SATURDAY REVIEW*

DARKNESS VISIBLE:
A MEMOIR OF MADNESS

BY WILLIAM STYRON

In Paris on a chilly evening late in October of 1985 I first became fully aware that the struggle with the disorder in my mind—a struggle which had engaged me for several months—might have a fatal outcome.

IN THE WINTER of 1985 at the age of sixty, William Styron was on the verge of committing suicide. He'd returned from an agonizing trip to Europe where he was supposed to give a talk and receive an award. In its wake, he gave up drinking. He marks that moment as the start of his descent into despair. He'd made an appointment with his lawyer and rewritten his will when he had a change of heart and instead committed himself to a mental hospital.

In this memoir, he writes a vivid portrait of depression, a "howling tempest in the brain," and of intractable insomnia, self-loathing, forgetfulness, a zombielike stupor, and unfocused anxiety. He imagines his mind "being inundated by floodwaters: one by one the normal circuits began to drown." Tranquilizers only make him sicker. Psychotherapy is useless, and he detests group therapy, dismissing it as "organized infantilism."

He credits seclusion and time for what turns out to be a near-miraculous moment when he feels "no longer a husk but a body with some of the body's sweet juices stirring again."

Styron expresses a kinship with other artists, fellow sufferers like Virginia Woolf, Sylvia Plath, Anne Sexton, and Ernest Hemingway. The title echoes Styron's first novel, *Lie Down in Darkness*, published forty years earlier, which tells the story of a young woman's suicide. Styron captures the exquisite despair of depression and the arduous journey back.

"When we think of creative writers, we think of boldness, sensitivity, restlessness, discontent; this is the manic-depressive temperament."
—KAY REDFIELD JAMISON, *NEW YORK TIMES*

MARCH

BY GERALDINE BROOKS

October 21, 1861

This is what I write to her: The clouds tonight embossed the sky.
A dipping sun gilded and brazed each raveling edge as if the fir-
mament were threaded through with precious filaments.

IN THIS HISTORICAL novel about the heavy toll that war
demands and exacts, Geraldine Brooks imagines the absent
father of Louisa May Alcott's *Little Women*, an idealist to the
core, going off fight in the Civil War. In her version, young
Father March is a poor Yankee peddler who enjoys the luxury
of leisure as a guest on a plantation. Later, he's an idealistic
chaplain for the Union Army. His superiors find him too radical
and send him to Mississippi to organize a school for newly
freed slaves and their children. He ends up in a Washington
hospital, sick with fever and guilt. In the book's final section,
his wife, Marmee, takes up the tale, and her perspective of how
and why her husband entered the war shatters what the reader
has learned about him.

As the characters in *Little Women* were thinly disguised
versions of Alcott's mother and sisters, Father March in this
novel is based on Alcott's father, Bronson Alcott. Fictional characters mix with figures from history like Ralph Waldo Emerson,
Henry David Thoreau, and John Brown.

This book won the Pulitzer Prize for Literature in 2006.

"The Alcott book and characters have floated like ghosts all through
March. That story of scorched gowns, amateur theatricals, pickled
limes, balls and picnics and pianos provides a wonderfully effected,
unstated but understood contrast to this story of the war."

—KAREN JOY FOWLER, *WASHINGTON POST*

An American Childhood

BY ANNIE DILLARD

The story starts back in 1950, when I was five.

ANNIE DILLARD RECALLS her 1950s Pittsburgh childhood, a time when "Every woman stayed alone in her house . . . like a coin in a safe." She writes lovingly of her quirky and caring parents. Her father, who worked in the movie business, helped make the movie *Night of the Living Dead* and read Kerouac's *On the Road* "approximately a million" times, as did Dillard herself. Her mother reveled in words and gave Dillard "the freedom of the streets as soon I could say our telephone number."

This meditation on growing up and growing aware explores the author's rhapsodic discovery of the world around her—from the joy of shooting a slingshot, to floating Popsicle sticks in puddles, to throwing snowballs at cars, to watching a girl figure skate on an ice-coated street. Dillard's rapture came to an abrupt halt at fifteen when, filled with anger and perceiving hypocrisy everywhere, "I became a dark object I could not ignore."

This memoir came seven books and thirty years after Dillard's meditations on the natural world were published in *Pilgrim at Tinker Creek*. Reading it is like eating a favorite comfort food.

"The territory [Dillard] marks off lies at the edge of knowledge where philosophy is helpless and language, more often than not, fails—this is the world of meaning, love, thought, grace, pleasure and, most important in her autobiography, what it feels like to be awake and alive in the world."

—CAROL SHIELDS, *GLOBE AND MAIL*

ENDER'S GAME

BY ORSON SCOTT CARD

I've watched through his eyes, I've listened through his ears, and I tell you he's the one. Or at least as close as we're going to get.

THIS "GAME" TAKES place on Earth in a violent future. Buggers, an aptly named alien species, have almost annihilated the human race. Preparing for the next battle, youngsters like six-year-old Andrew "Ender" Wiggin are being trained at Battle School.

Ender is a whiz kid, a genius whose prowess at pinball brings him to the attention of the military. His training takes the form of good-versus-bad games like "buggers and astronauts." At ten, he's been promoted to Command School. There, children make war on children. Thinking he's zapping computer simulations, he annihilates the race of alien insects and saves humanity.

From a predictable story line, Card launches a complex and unpredictable character who eventually asks, "Why are we fighting buggers?" By the end, he realizes that he's guilty of committing genocide.

This novel won science fiction's Hugo and Nebula awards in 1986. With virtual reality, game simulations, and genetically enhanced children, Card was ahead of his time. The Ender series has developed a cult-like following.

"[Orson Scott Card] may well be considered Heinlein's true heir—not because his fiction recirculates the Master's mannerisms and ideology . . . but because of his knack for attack-dog narrative, his fertile invention, and the moral conviction he brings to his work."

—THOMAS M. DISCH,
THE DREAMS OUR STUFF IS MADE OF

ALL THE KING'S MEN

BY ROBERT PENN WARREN

To get there you follow Highway 58, going northeast out of the city, and it is a good highway and new. Or was new, that day we went up it.

BASED ON THE life of Louisiana's larger-than-life governor Huey P. Long, this novel dramatizes the rise of populist southern politician Willie Stark, a redneck who gains power through leadership and dirty politics. We see his transformation from idealistic attorney to ruthless manipulator of people.

Willie is used to being able to "fix" things. When he runs up against an honest judge, he orders the novel's narrator, Jack Burden, to dig up a few facts to besmirch the judge's reputation: "It's dirt makes the grass grow," Willie says. But what if there's no dirt to dig, Jack asks? Willie sets him straight: "There's always something."

Willie knows a thing or two about dirt. His tools are bribery, blackmail, and sheer force. As official henchman, Burden becomes as sullied and corrupt as his boss.

Born in Kentucky, Warren dishes up the corruption of southern politics with eloquence and rage. Upon its publication, critics rated this novel head and shoulders over works about Huey Long by other contemporaries such as John Dos Passos. It was awarded the Pulitzer in 1947. This provocative treatment of overweening power from the man who became America's first poet laureate has lost none of its punch.

"In Willie, Warren created not only a zesty campaigner but a figure who combined earnest populism with unscrupulous tactics, high-minded aspirations with tough-minded calculation, an irresistible appeal with appalling cynicism. He is a big figure, an American original."

—WALTER GOODMAN, *NEW YORK TIMES*

ADVERTISEMENTS FOR MYSELF

BY NORMAN MAILER

*Like many another vain, empty, and bullying body of our time,
I have been running for President these last ten years in the
privacy of my mind, and it occurs to me that I am less close than
when I began.*

THIS COLLECTION, FIRST published in 1959, is a compendium of stories, essays, reviews, interviews, novel excerpts, plays, and poems (including one called "The Drunk's Bebop and Chowder"). Each is kicked off by an "advertisement"—an autobiographical comment. In the first one, Mailer muses, "Perhaps I should hire a public relations man to grease my career, but I do not know if I can afford him (not with the size of the job he would have to do for me), and moreover I would be obliged sooner or later to spoil his work."

This book was published when Mailer was thirty-six years old at a time when the accolades heaped on his 1948 debut novel *Naked and the Dead* had not been matched by the two novels that followed. Excerpts from those novels and unpublished earlier works are included in this compendium, along with vigorous, witty, astringent essays on topics like Picasso, the virtues of marijuana, and the dichotomy of Hip versus Square (Ted Williams is Hip; Mickey Mantle is Square).

Taken together, the pieces are a potent reminder of the brilliance of this self-obsessed, angry agent provocateur whose feuding, misogynism, drinking, drug-taking, and womanizing often overshadowed his writing.

"Norman Mailer, Towering Writer with Matching Ego, Dies at 84"
—*NEW YORK TIMES* OBITUARY HEADLINE,
NOVEMBER 10, 2007

SOMETHING WICKED THIS WAY COMES

BY RAY BRADBURY

The seller of lightning rods arrived just ahead of the storm.

THIS FANTASY CLASSIC opens with a pair of thirteen-year-old lads, Will Halloway and Jim Nightshade, sitting on the front lawn of Will's house in Green Town a week before Halloween, waiting for something to happen. Lightning-rod salesman Tom Fury approaches them. He prophesies that a storm is coming.

At 3 A.M., a train rumbles through Green Town. In its wake, "Cooger & Dark's Pandemonium Shadow Show" springs up. There, the boys meet Mr. Dark, the tattooed carnival leader ("His picture crowds flooded raw upon his flesh") and his partner, the flame-haired Mr. Cooger. Among other things, the mysterious carnival has a merry-go-round that runs backward, playing Chopin's funeral march backward, too. Those who ride it grow a year younger with each revolution.

The carnival casts a spell over many townspeople. Jim is sucked in by its sinister allure. When his buddy tries to save him, both are held captive. The boys learn that each of Mr. Dark's tattoos represents a person who traded his soul for a chance to live out a secret fantasy. Only Will's philosophical, taciturn father, a janitor in the town library, can prevent the boys from becoming eternal performers in the Pandemonium Shadow Show.

"Ray Bradbury is Edgar Allan Poe for optimists. Creepy without being terrifying, cynical without being despairing, he's the author you read under the covers by flashlight, untroubled by the prospect of nightmares."

—MARY ELIZABETH WILLIAMS, *NEW YORK TIMES*

TENDER IS THE NIGHT

BY F. SCOTT FITZGERALD

On the pleasant shore of the French Riviera, about halfway between Marseilles and the Italian border, stands a large, proud, rose-colored hotel. Deferential palms cool its flushed façade . . .

THIS NOVEL BEARS witness to the disintegration of a marriage. The husband is a brilliant young psychiatrist, Dr. Richard Diver. The wife is wealthy Nicole whose split personality is the product of an abusive relationship with her father. She saves herself by marrying Dick, who becomes her husband as well as her healer. Due to the constant attention that she requires, he cuts back his practice and forfeits his professional life.

Circling the edges of the marriage is Rosemary Hoyt, a young ingénue movie star. She takes up with the Divers during a summer vacation on the Riviera. Dick falls in love with her and his marriage is threatened. Nicole responds by literally trying to steer their marriage off a cliff.

By the end, as a physician and as a human being, Dr. Diver has collapsed. His youth has vanished and he's reduced to a meaningless career as a general practitioner in upstate New York where he grew up.

This 1934 book was first published eight years after *The Great Gatsby*. The last novel Fitzgerald completed, it takes its title from John Keats's poem, "Ode to a Nightingale." The *New York Times* ran favorable and unfavorable reviews in tandem, two days apart.

"[F. Scott Fitzgerald's works] read so easily that perhaps you had to have some feeling for writing and perhaps the tiniest curiosity about it to be aware of the conscientiousness of it, the sweat and tears and, literally, in Scott's case, the blood."

—JOHN O'HARA, *AN ARTIST IS HIS OWN FAULT*

Scoop

BY EVELYN WAUGH

While still a young man John Courteney Boot had, as his publisher proclaimed, "achieved an assured and enviable position in contemporary letters."

THIS IS A scathingly funny send-up of the British tabloid press of the 1930s from one of the great satirists of the twentieth century. In it, the aptly named tabloid *The Beast* mistakenly sends columnist William Boot, an innocent nature lover, instead of his war-correspondent brother, John, to "Ishmaelia" to cover the supposedly civil-war-torn country. Bumbling and slapstick ensue.

Waugh had once been a Fleet Street reporter, and in this book he draws on his own experience in Addis Ababa where he found himself cooped up in a squalid hotel with a hoard of other reporters, all of them so desperate for some kind of news to write about that they were interviewing waiters, cab drivers, and passers-by. In *Scoop*, reporters file three- and four-word messages (early Tweets?) that are expanded by their editors into sensational accounts of events that didn't happen.

Corker, a wire reporter with whom Boot hooks up with on his travels, expresses Waugh's contempt for the press: "News is what a chap who doesn't care much about anything wants to read. And it's only news until he reads it. After that it's dead."

This prolific author produced twenty-eight books between 1928 and 1964. This one was published in 1938. In 1944, Edmund Wilson proclaimed Waugh "the only first-rate comic genius that has appeared in English since Bernard Shaw."

"Mr. Waugh writes with such mastery that the use of 321 pages of his prose—prose that in this generation is practically peerless—to bring off too obvious a farce seems rather wasteful, almost as wasteful as was Mussolini's use of his war machine to capture Abyssinia."

—ROBERT VAN GELDER, *NEW YORK TIMES*

THE TURN OF THE SCREW

BY HENRY JAMES

The story held us, round the fire, sufficiently breathless, but except the obvious remark that it was gruesome, as, on Christmas even in an old house, a strange tale should essentially be, I remember no comment uttered till somebody happened to say that it was the only case he had met in which such a visitation had fallen on a child.

FRIENDS SIT AROUND the fire at an old house on Christmas Eve sharing ghost stories. One tells of an impressionable young governess, hired by a disinterested uncle to care for his orphaned niece and nephew. The sweet young thing is left alone in the great house to tend to Flora and Miles. When things only the governess sees go bump in the night, she tumbles to the possibility that the former governess, Miss Jessel, and her lover are controlling the children from their graves.

Told largely through the governess's journal entries, this tale is laced with repressed sexuality and psychological ambiguity. James plays his cards close to the vest, leaving readers still arguing today about whether the ghosts are real.

Originally published in 1898 in serial form in *Collier's Weekly*, the best movie made from it was *The Innocents* in 1961 with luminous Deborah Kerr as the young governess.

"[T]he only person in the story who sees the ghosts is the narrator herself. So is it a ghost story, or a study of hysteria? It is, of course, both—and more."

—JOHN BANVILLE, *IRISH TIMES*

War of the Worlds

BY H. G. WELLS

No one would have believed in the last years of the nineteenth century that this world was being watched keenly and closely by intelligences greater than man's and yet as mortal as his own; that as men busied themselves about their various concerns they were scrutinised and studied, perhaps almost as narrowly as a man with a microscope might scrutinise the transient creatures that swarm and multiply in a drop of water.

FIRST PUBLISHED IN magazine form in 1897 when the automobile was still a novelty and commercial air travel was a dream, this classic sci-fi novella was the first ever alien-invasion story. In it, a huge cylinder from Mars lands in England creating a crater. What emerges first looks like "a little grey snake." Not nearly so benign, it's the tentacle of one of the gigantic creatures that emerge, glistening like leather. Men approach, waving a white flag. They are immediately incinerated. Not an auspicious start. Told from the point of view of an anonymous Londoner, what ensues is nothing less than an apocalyptic disaster.

It turns out that Mars is a planet that is in the "last stage of exhaustion," accelerating the evolution of its inhabitants. "The immediate pressure of necessity has brightened their intellects, enlarged their powers, and hardened their hearts." Looking across space, Earth beckoned: their brave new world waiting to be taken.

On October 30, Halloween eve, 1938, Orson Welles read an adaptation of the novel on the radio. Many listeners panicked, believing that a Martian invasion was in progress.

"There is nothing like a whole statewide destruction to make a boy sit up and eat his spinach."

—RAY BRADBURY, FOREWORD TO
THE 2001 (SOURCEBOOKS) EDITION

DRACULA

BY BRAM STOKER

3 May. Bistritz.—Left Munich at 8:35 P.M., on 1st May, arriving at Vienna early next morning; should have arrived at 6:46, but train was an hour late.

WRITTEN AS A pastiche of journal entries, letters, and newspaper articles, this novel sweeps the reader along with young attorney Jonathan Harker, riding by train and carriage through the Carpathian Mountains to Count Dracula's crumbling castle. It's a terrifying trip, deep into the forest. Dogs howl and wolves bay, powerfully foreshadowing what's to come.

Harker is there to give the count legal advice but soon he's a prisoner. He encounters three female vampires and barely escapes with his life. But more than Harker, Count Dracula desires Lucy, the spunky friend of Harker's fiancée Mina, and Mina herself. Soon, Dracula and his army of blood-sucking slaves are threatening to take over London.

Stoker claimed the idea for the novel came to him in a nightmare. Despite less-than-literary-caliber writing, this enduring and gripping tale of horror continues to fascinate readers. First published in 1897 (the same year H. G. Wells published *The War of the Worlds*), it seethes with sexuality. The plethora of modern vampire stories suggests that Jonathan Harker's fear that Dracula would breed "a new and ever-widening circle of semi-demons to batten on the helpless" has been realized.

"Beware. Dracula can be a flypaper trap. First you read it, casually, and then, once you've put it away, you might find yourself, almost against your will, wondering about things in the crevices of the novel, things hinted at, things implied."

—NEIL GAIMAN, INTRODUCTION TO
THE NEW ANNOTATED DRACULA

November

THE LAST HURRAH

BY EDWIN O'CONNOR

It was early in August when Frank Skeffington decided—or rather announced his decision, which actually had been arrived at some months before—to run for re-election as mayor of the city.

FOUR YEARS AFTER populist Democratic mayor Frank Skeffington "is inaugurated for what his opponents fondly hope is the last time," the seventy-two-year-old man of the people announces he'll run for re-election. He sees this as his last chance to keep his beloved city from "reverting to Government by the Pigmies." Ultimately he goes down to defeat and death, his successor a handsome neophyte with little political experience.

This 1956 classic provides a fascinating commentary on the Irish American experience. Much of the story is narrated from the viewpoint of the Mayor's nephew, Adam Caulfield, and takes us through the labyrinthine world of old-time city politics. The last great "big-city politician" of his era, Skeffington's campaign is a "last hurrah" for that era's political machines.

Like legendary Boston Mayor James Michael Curley, Frank Skeffington was one of the Irish political bosses who traded in corruption but understood their constituents. Though O'Connor denied that he based Skeffington on Curley, or the unnamed city on Boston, the similarities speak for themselves. When the *Boston Globe* sent the book to Curley for comment, he returned it with a note that hinted he was considering filing a lawsuit. Later, Curley sued to prevent the motion picture version from opening.

In a survey of Boston literature, Shaun O'Connell calls the whole novel "an extended Irish wake."

"You've written quite a nice book. I like that book. . . . Do you know the part I enjoyed most? The part where I die."

—EDWIN O'CONNOR'S RECOLLECTION OF
WHAT JAMES MICHAEL CURLEY SAID TO HIM

Under the Volcano

BY MALCOLM LOWRY

Two mountain chains traverse the republic roughly from north to south, forming between them a number of valleys and plateaus.

THE LOVE "TRIANGLE" in this 1947 novel—between former British consul Geoffrey Firmin, who has come to Mexico to recuperate; his estranged American wife, Yvonne, who has returned to try to save him; and his half-brother, Hugh Firmin, who is Yvonne's former lover—has a fourth element. Alcohol. The novel contrasts Hugh and Geoffrey. Hugh, a journalist who was once a sailor and a jazz guitarist, wants to be a hero. But his every move is safe and planned out. Geoffrey is who Hugh wishes he was, a man of emotions and action. But Geoffrey is also a consummate narcissist who poisons his own life.

Set amidst political turmoil, the novel takes place over a single day, the Day of the Dead, 1939. Volcanoes loom on the horizon, a backdrop for tragedy and a symbol of the coming World War II. At the end, as Geoffrey falls to his death into a ravine, he hallucinates that he is falling into a volcano, "yet no, it wasn't the volcano, the world itself was bursting, bursting into black spouts of villages catapulted into space, with himself falling through it all, through the inconceivable pandemonium of a million tanks, through the blazing of ten million burning bodies."

Lowry takes a page from Joyce, telling this story as an extended interior monologue and filling it with the minutiae of a day in the life. He was also influenced by the complex psychological lyricism of poet Conrad Aiken, who became Lowry's friend, surrogate father, and even caretaker.

"Lowry succeeded only because he persisted in destroying himself with alcohol; he is consequently a disturbing as well as a tragic writer."
—MARTIN SEYMOUR-SMITH, *WHO'S WHO IN TWENTIETH-CENTURY LITERATURE*

THE PLAGUE

BY ALBERT CAMUS

The unusual events described in this chronicle occurred in 194— at Oran.

AT THE START of what is more parable than novel, rats spew forth from the sewers of the Algerian city of Oran and die in massive numbers. Weeks later, people are coming down with a raging fever and dying, too. The first to notice is wealthy Dr. Rieux. The concierge of his building dies from a fever that Dr. Rieux and his colleague Castel conclude is the plague. They try to raise the alarm with fellow doctors and government officials but their concern is dismissed.

More and more of the townspeople die the same horrific death, and still authorities refuse to admit that an epidemic of bubonic plague is engulfing the city. Until the last possible moment, they pretend that the deaths are something else, something that happens to "others." Only when the city's gates are closed does "the plague become a matter for us all." Ironically, by the time the plague begins to abate, many have become incapable of hope and are unable to throw off their skepticism.

This work was published in 1947. In 1957, Camus was awarded the Nobel Prize in Literature. When doctors identified the first patients with symptoms of AIDS and for years American government leaders remained in a state of denial, many were reminded of this book.

"Camus has left nihilism far behind him and his existentialism can be reasonably called a form of humanism."

—DR. ANDERS OSTERLING, SECRETARY OF THE
SWEDISH ACADEMY OF LITERATURE

THE STRANGE CASE OF DR. JEKYLL AND MR. HYDE

BY ROBERT LOUIS STEVENSON

Mr. Utterson the lawyer was a man of a rugged countenance, that was never lighted by a smile; cold, scanty and embarrassed in discourse; backward in sentiment; lean, long, dusty, dreary, and yet somehow lovable.

FRAMED AS A detective story, this timeless novella, which first appeared in 1886, tells the harrowing tale of Dr. Henry Jekyll, a man who is not what he seems. His friend, attorney Gabriel John Utterson, discovers a mysterious liaison between Dr. Jekyll and the reputedly murderous Edward Hyde.

Ingenious in its structure, the novel tells its story backward, and it isn't until the next-to-last chapter that the reader discovers Jekyll and Hyde are one and the same.

Stevenson told an interviewer that the idea for the novel came to him in a dream: "All I dreamed about Dr. Jekyll was that one man was being pressed into a cabinet, when he swallowed a drug and turned into another being." Stevenson wrote, rewrote, and published this novella in under ten weeks. Its allegorical battle of good and evil within a single human being has inspired legions of mad-scientist characters. The main character appears to have, what we now call, a multiple personality disorder. In fact, "Jekyll and Hyde" has become shorthand for multiple personality. In its day, the story was considered a morality tale.

"The evil of Mr. Hyde, who would rather walk over a small child than stop and go around her, is an evil that proceeds from the human mind."

—STEPHEN KING, INTRODUCTION TO
FRANKENSTEIN, DRACULA, DR. JEKYLL AND MR. HYDE

RETURN OF THE NATIVE

BY THOMAS HARDY

A Saturday afternoon in November was approaching the time of twilight, and the vast tract of unenclosed wild known as Egdon Heath embrowned itself moment by moment.

AT NINETEEN, EUSTACIA Vye is "queen of night," her "pagan eyes, full of nocturnal mysteries," not to mention smoldering passion. She dreams of being swept off to Paris high society by a prince and consumed in "a blaze of love and extinction." Instead, she's stuck in Dorset, on backward, suffocating Egdon Heath. If only she can find a man worthy of her dreams.

At first Eustacia sets her sights on Damon Wildeve, a local innkeeper betrothed to marry sweet, simple Thomasin Yeobright. Eustacia is exultant when Wildeve leaves Thomasin, publicly humiliated at the altar: "And I knew it was because you loved me best, and couldn't do it."

But when he proposes to Eustacia, she rejects him as not good enough and fastens her attentions on Clym Yeobright (Thomasin's cousin), who has returned from Paris where he made his fortune in the diamond trade. They marry, but Clym disappoints Eustacia with his determination to remain on Egdon Heath and become a teacher. The honest and true Diggory Venn, a former suitor of Thomasin, vows that she should marry the man she loves and helps reunite her and Wildeve. The figures in this many-sided love "triangle" are so intertwined in love and hate that they destroy one another.

Published in 1880, critical response to it was overwhelmingly negative. Many reviewers didn't know what to do with the novel's pessimism or its lower-class characters. Only 900 of the initial 1,000 copies printed were sold.

"Throughout Hardy's novels there is a spirit which burns and burns with a passionate flame; anger grows to a white heat and leaps uncontrolled to a fervor of scorn and wrath."

—JOHN D. ANDERSON, *NEW YORK TIMES*

A Separate Peace

BY JOHN KNOWLES

I went back to the Devon School not long ago, and found it looking oddly newer than when I was a student there fifteen years before.

EXPLORE THE DARK side of adolescence in this story of two boys. Less than a year after the 1941 bombing of Pearl Harbor, the war casts a shadow over the lives of alienated, introverted, intellectual Gene Forrester and brash, daredevil athlete Finny. The cruelties of individuals at their prep school are played off against the backdrop of the cruelties of war.

The story has been hailed as a parable about good and evil that explores loyalty and betrayal. Generations of readers have debated whether Gene deliberately causes Finny to fall and injure his leg, crippling him for life and leading indirectly to his death. But by the end, both boys have made their own "separate peace."

Knowles was an editor for *Holiday* magazine when this, his first novel, was published in 1960. Thornton Wilder had encouraged him to write a book based on his vivid memories of his experiences as a student at Phillips Exeter Academy (called "Devon" in the novel). He based the character of Gene on himself, and he told an interviewer that the novel was "based on experiences that I had, but it is not literally true." It became a classic the moment it was published and is often compared to Salinger's *The Catcher in the Rye* and Golding's *Lord of the Flies*.

"*In* A Separate Peace . . . *John Knowles demonstrated a seemingly durable, if slender, talent for delineating the emotional geometry connecting members of certain rarefied worlds (prep school, Yale University, the Riviera) in deft, coolly-refined prose.*"

—MICHIKO KAKUTANI, *NEW YORK TIMES*

A Tale of Love and Darkness

BY AMOS OZ

I was born and bred in a tiny, low-ceilinged ground-floor apartment.

BEAR WITNESS TO the birth of a nation in this moving memoir of childhood. Oz examines his family's life against the backdrop of Israel's emergence as a nation.

Oz was born in 1939. His parents were Eastern European Jews who came to Palestine out of desperation, not religious zeal. Poverty and disappointment embittered their lives. Oz's father's potential to be a renowned scholar was never realized. His beautiful, cultivated mother shared haunting stories of her lost homeland and youth, and was deeply unhappy in her marriage.

Oz tries to come to terms with his mother's suicide, three months before his bar mitzvah, and his subsequent rift with his father. Oz shows what it was like to grow up in an atmosphere of fear and in the shadow of so much loss. He takes us from his birth to his flight from Jerusalem to a kibbutz, dramatizing along the way the moment when an entire neighborhood stands in silence around a single radio, hearing that the UN has voted to create two independent states in Palestine. He mourns both his mother's death and the death of the socialist-Zionist dream of a just society.

This is one of the bestselling literary works in Israeli history. The English translation was published in 2004.

"The Jews had nowhere to go, and this is difficult to convey today. People now ask, Was it good to come here? Was it a mistake? Was Zionism a reasonable project? There was no place else."

—AMOS OZ, *NEW YORKER*

THE ASSISTANT

BY BERNARD MALAMUD

The early November street was dark though night had ended, but the wind, to the grocer's surprise, already clawed.

SET IN THE Great Depression, this novel tells of Jewish grocery store owner Morris Bober's struggle to make a success of his business. His son is dead, his wife Ida a tyrant, and his beautiful daughter Helen is a brilliant, frustrated intellectual. Morris helps out a destitute Italian stranger, Frankie Alpine, by giving him a job as the eponymous assistant.

While Alpine helps run the shabby grocery store more efficiently, he also helps himself, from the till, taking as much as he apparently gives. He falls in love with Helen. Slowly she overcomes her contempt for him, urging upon him the novels of Tolstoy, Flaubert, and Dostoyevsky. Alpine, who already has a profound admiration for St. Francis of Assisi, ends up transformed and playing the role of redeemer.

Malamud described his typical character as "someone who fears his fate, is caught up in it, yet manages to outrun it; he's the subject and object of laughter and pity." Surrounding them all is a maelstrom of ugly events—a brutal holdup, a fire, and rivalries and vendettas.

Published in 1957, this was Malamud's second novel and the one many critics consider his best. The author grew up in the Brooklyn he writes about. Like Morris Bober, Malamud's father ran a small grocery.

"The Jews of . . . The Assistant are not the Jews of New York City or Chicago. They are Malamud's invention, a metaphor of sorts to stand for certain possibilities and promises."

—PHILIP ROTH, *READING MYSELF AND OTHERS*

INVISIBLE CITIES

BY ITALO CALVINO

*Leaving there and proceeding for three days toward the east,
you reach Diomira, a city with sixty silver domes, bronze statues
of all the gods, streets paved with lead, a crystal theater, a cock
that crows each morning on a tower.*

AN IMAGINARY EMPEROR Kublai Khan asks Venetian traveler Marco Polo: What is in my empire? In response, Marco Polo describes one haunting city after the next, each in a nearly perfect story of just one or two pages, each sprung whole from the adventurer's imagination.

The great emperor is enthralled. "Already the Great Khan was leafing through his atlas, over the maps of the cities that menace in nightmares and maledictions: Enoch, Babylon, Yahooland, Butua, Brave New World."

The cities come in groupings of eleven (thin cities, trading cities, continuous cities, hidden cities, and so on). As the travelogue continues, the cities become increasingly desolate. One of the last, Procopia, is so crowded that people hide the place. Penthesilea is described as a limbo of endless outskirts.

Interspersed between the tales is an ongoing conversation between the traveler and the pessimistic emperor. One reviewer called this series of interwoven fables and meditations "a string of tiny narrative pearls." Calvino is widely considered one of the great European writers of the twentieth century. Gore Vidal wrote, "Europe regarded Calvino's death as a calamity for culture." An English translation of this surreal fantasy was published in 1974.

*"Reading Calvino, you're constantly assailed by the notion that he is
writing down what you have always known, except that you've never
thought of it before."*

—SALMAN RUSHDIE

THE THURBER CARNIVAL

BY JAMES THURBER

I suppose the high-water mark of my youth in Columbus, Ohio, was the night the bed fell on my father.

SURREAL AND FUNNY, this collection of essays, short stories, and cartoons from the great humorist was published in 1945. It includes "The Night the Bed Fell," based on a hilarious incident from Thurber's childhood. People knew that story by heart, the way many of us know all the words to "Alice's Restaurant."

Another story tells of the night a ghost got into the house and "caused my mother to throw a shoe through a window of the house next door and ended up with my grandfather shooting a patrolman." Thurber set these stories at a fictional address because there really *was* a ghost and he didn't wish to alarm the current residents.

In another classic, "More Alarms at Night," our hero wakes up and can't remember "Perth Amboy" ("I thought of every other town in the country, as well as words and names and phrases as terra cotta, Walla Walla, bill of lading, vice versa, hoity toity . . ."). "The Secret Life of Walter Mitty" opens with our hero steering an ice breaker through treacherous waters, only to have his wife bring him back to earth with, "You're driving too fast!"

Thurber could be churlish and misanthropic, and his writing is clearly misogynistic, yet his unique brand of humor with dark undertones has remarkable staying power.

"*[Thurber's] thoughts have always been a tangle of baseball scores, Civil War tactical problems, Henry James, personal maladjustment, terrier puppies, literary tide rips, ancient myths and modern apprehensions. Through this jungle stalk the unpredictable ghosts of his relatives in Columbus, Ohio.*"

—E. B. WHITE, QUOTED IN *TIME* MAGAZINE

A FAREWELL TO ARMS

BY ERNEST HEMINGWAY

In the late summer of that year we lived in a house in a village that looked across the river and the plain to the mountains.

NOBEL LAUREATE HEMINGWAY tells a tender tale of love and loss. It's World War I and the doomed lovers are Lieutenant Frederic Henry and nurse Catherine Barkley. He's a wounded American ambulance driver assigned to a unit in Italy. She works at the army hospital in Milan where Frederic is sent for treatment. He goes back to the war, barely escapes with his life, and returns to find Catherine.

Exquisite writing, of course, from an author considered the most influential of his generation.

Like his character, Hemingway was an American Red Cross ambulance driver during the First World War and was severely wounded on the Austrian front. Hemingway based this 1929 novel on the true story of his love affair with Agnes von Kurowsky, a nurse seven years his senior, who cared for him while he was recovering from machine-gun and shrapnel wounds and who broke his heart by refusing to marry him.

Hemingway was only thirty years old when he published this novel which built on the huge success, three years earlier, of *The Sun Also Rises*. An installment of the book published in the June 1929 issue of *Scribner's Magazine* was banned in Boston, part of it deemed "salacious." By 1950, John O'Hara was proclaiming in the *New York Times* that Hemingway was "the most important author living today since the death of Shakespeare."

"Somewhere in Hemingway is the hard mind of a shrewd small-town boy, the kind of boy who knows you have a real cigar only when you are the biggest man in town, because to be just one of the big men in town is tiring, much too tiring, you inspire hatred, and what is worse than hatred, a wave of cross-talk in everyone around you."

—NORMAN MAILER, *ADVERTISEMENTS FOR MYSELF*

ATONEMENT

BY IAN MCEWAN

The play, for which Briony had designed the posters, programmes and tickets, constructed the sales booth out of a folding screen tipped on its side, and lined the collection box in red crepe paper, was written by her in a two-day tempest of composition, causing her to miss a breakfast and a lunch.

ON A SULTRY, midsummer day in 1935 at a bucolic English country house, thirteen-year-old Briony Tallis watches her older sister Cecilia and her lover and fellow Cambridge graduate, Robbie. Robbie is the son of a cleaning woman, his education paid for by the Tallises.

A budding writer, Briony watches the pair from a distance and concocts a monstrous lie that sends Robbie to prison. Later, when Briony serves as a nurse in St. Thomas Hospital during the war and Robbie is released from prison to fight at Dunkirk, she tries to make amends.

This 2001 novel paints a vivid picture of British upper-class society before the war. Its story reaches across six decades, exploring the consequences of the lie for Briony and the Tallis family. It asks whether we can ever atone for what we have done or forgive those who have wronged us.

This unforgettable book from an author one critic called "an expert on human violence—its rules, roots, and reverberations" won the 2002 National Book Critics Circle Award.

"Atonement *is a magnificent novel, shaped and paced with awesome confidence and eloquence; as searching an account of error, shame and reparation as any in modern fiction.*"

—BOYD TONKIN, *INDEPENDENT*

THE GINGER TREE

BY OSWALD WYND

I was sick yesterday on my birthday, after not having been sick crossing the Bay of Biscay and even in the storm off Malta.

AT THE START of this sprawling, epistolary novel spanning forty years and set against a backdrop of Japan, Russia, and China vying for Manchuria, twenty-year-old Scotswoman Mary Mackenzie travels to Peking to wed British military attaché Richard Collingsworth. An independent, lively girl, she soon discovers that her husband is not only stuffy and painfully formal, he's also sexually inhibited.

She bridles under the yoke of her disastrous marriage and struggles to learn the language and the rules of this Eastern culture. In a gloomy household, she gives birth to a daughter. Lonely and unhappy, she drifts into an affair with a Japanese nobleman. She becomes pregnant. The entries in her journal chronicle the pain of the scandal and banishment that follow.

Her husband disowns her, her mother won't answer her letters, and her friends abandon her. She follows her lover to Tokyo where she must live as his concubine. She rallies, succeeding at a Western-style fashion house, but disaster strikes again when she loses her infant son. Still she perseveres.

Wynd was a Scotsman born in Tokyo. He based the unforgettable Mary MacKenzie of this 1978 novel on his own grandmother.

"Mary does not try to change Japan—a mistake too often made by Westerners who believe that the Japanese secretly yearn to be like everyone else. She simply fights to be acknowledged as more than an appendage to society."

—MICHAEL SHAPIRO, *NEW YORK TIMES*

THE WAPSHOT CHRONICLE

BY JOHN CHEEVER

St. Botolphs was an old place, an old river town.

HONORA WAPSHOT IS the novel's formidable, domineering doyenne of this down-at-the-heel, eccentric (to say the least), but once-august New England family. It's through her largesse that her brother Leander commands a large excursion boat.

Honora says she plans to leave her considerable fortune and what is left of her decaying dynasty to Leander's sons, her nephews Moses and Coverly. There's a catch: They must have sons to carry on the Wapshot name.

But Honora is a character subject to whims of the moment, and one never knows exactly what she's really going to do. The fun begins when Honora finds herself trapped in a closet while in the room just beyond, Moses frolics with a liberated, "modern" girl.

Later, Moses saves a damsel from being carried away by a runaway horse, then falls for the ward of a relative and agrees to live on one of the family's crumbling estates. Coverly marries a forlorn but pretty southern girl and his work takes him to an island in the Pacific until he is called back by the premature news of his father's death.

Cheever, who has been called an American Chekhov, said this book was his "posthumous attempt to make peace with my father's ghost." It won the National Book Award in 1958.

"Afflicted with nostalgia and recurrent bouts of memory and desire, his characters stagger uncertainly through a changing world, looking for the old-fashioned virtues of beauty and love but often succumbing instead to drink, divorce and other modern confusions."

—MICHIKO KAKUTANI, *NEW YORK TIMES*

EXCELLENT WOMEN

BY BARBARA PYM

"Ah, you ladies! Always on the spot when there's something happening!" The voice belonged to Mr. Mallett, one of our churchwardens, and its roguish tone made me start guiltily, almost as if I had no right to be discovered outside my own front door.

BRITISH NOVELIST BARBARA Pym is one of those excellent authors whose work is often compared to Jane Austen. Her comedies of manners masquerade under a veneer of gentility.

First published in 1952, this novel tells the story of witty, self-deprecating, contented Brit Mildred Lathbury. She busies herself with friends, church jumble sales, and assorted charitable works on behalf of "distressed gentlewomen." Like her fellow spinsters, she is expected to be smitten by her local clergyman, Julian Malory. When Malory becomes engaged to another, she realizes it's useless to try to convince him of the truth: that she is not heartbroken.

All is well until Helena and Rocky Napier rent the flat below her. Inevitably, Mildred gets drawn into their marital woes. As she quips, "An unmarried woman, just over thirty, who lives alone and has no apparent ties, must expect to find herself involved or interested in other people's business." Mildred's tidy life turns messy when she finds herself attracted to dashing Rocky.

The book, Pym's second novel and considered one of her best, raises the radical possibility that a woman might be better off alone.

"Barbara Pym [is] Jane Austen reincarnated. I understand there's still one last book of hers I haven't read, but I'm in no hurry. I'm saving it. Whom do people turn to when they've finished Barbara Pym?"

—ANNE TYLER, QUOTED IN THE *NEW YORK TIMES*

GILEAD

BY MARILYNNE ROBINSON

*I told you last night that I might be gone sometime, and you said,
Where, and I said, To be with the Good Lord, and you said, Why,
and I said, Because I'm old, and you said, I don't think you're old.*

NEARING THE END of his life, Reverend John Ames writes a
long letter to his six-year-old son whose very existence is an
unexpected blessing. He writes of falling in love with the boy's
mother and shares memories of his father and grandfather. He
traces his son's "begats," writing of his own pacifist father and
rabidly abolitionist grandfather, and rendering a provocative,
sympathetic account of the abolitionist movement and John
Brown.

Jack, a friend's prodigal son, enters Ames's life. Jack has
come back bringing with him a terrible secret and seeking abso-
lution in Gilead, a town that was once a refuge for runaway
slaves. Ames struggles, trying to understand what God would
want him to do.

This thoughtful and beautifully written book set in the
1950s, in the small-town Midwest, Robinson's long-awaited
second novel coming twenty-three years after the award-winning *Housekeeping*, is a lyrical evocation of existential solitude.
A book to be read slowly and savored, it took the Pulitzer and
National Book Critics Circle awards in 2005.

*"In a sense, Robinson is a kind of contemporary George Eliot: socially
engaged, preoccupied with the environment and the moral progress of
man (especially as catalyzed through art) and preoccupied with the
legacy of John Calvin (a misunderstood humanist, by Robinson's
lights)."*

—MEGHAN O'ROURKE, *NEW YORK TIMES*

GO TELL IT ON THE MOUNTAIN

BY JAMES BALDWIN

Everyone had always said that John would be a preacher when he grew up, just like his father.

IN 1953, JAMES Baldwin burst onto the literary scene with this masterpiece of autobiographical fiction. Its protagonist, fourteen-year-old John Grimes, is the stepson of Gabriel Grimes, a fiery Pentecostal preacher in Harlem. Everyone assumes he will follow in his father's footsteps and become a preacher.

The novel spans a single day and reveals John's moral awakening. Baldwin takes the reader through three generations to understand what led up to that moment. The rocking rhythms of the prose echo a church meeting in this unflinching tale of damaged lives.

Baldwin grew up, like John Grimes, in poverty in Harlem in the 1930s, the son of an autocratic preacher who hated his son. Three decades after the book was published, Baldwin reflected: "*Mountain* is the book I had to write if I was ever going to write anything else. I had to deal with what hurt me most. I had to deal, above all, with my father. He was my model. I learned a lot from him. Nobody's ever frightened me since."

"At his peak [James Baldwin] had the beautiful fervor of Camus or Kafka. Like them he revealed to me the core of his soul's savage distress and thus helped me shape and define my own work and its moral contours. This would be the most appropriate gift imaginable to the grandson of a slave owner from a slave's grandson."

—WILLIAM STYRON, *NEW YORK TIMES*

TALES OF THE SOUTH PACIFIC

BY JAMES A. MICHENER

I wish I could tell you about the South Pacific. The way it actually was.

THIS 1948 PULITZER winner contains eighteen chronologically linked stories set in a tropical paradise where war is a war of waiting ("You rotted on New Caledonia waiting for Guadalcanal."). As the narrator says, "I try to tell somebody what the steaming Hebrides were like and the first thing you know I'm telling about the old Tonkinese woman who used to sell human heads."

This was Michener's first book of fiction, written when he was in his mid-thirties and a naval historian assigned to the South Pacific. It takes the reader deep inside a war zone. Entertaining and bitingly satirical, the stories explore courage, boredom, discipline, love, and sex with as much seriousness and effectiveness as a great novel. Of course, one story explores the prejudices of a young nurse who falls in love with a French planter. He has eight mixed-race illegitimate daughters by four different women, none of whom he married.

In the final story, after months of enforced idleness, the troops finally get the action they've been craving. Blue skies darken as they ship out. The reader knows that their likely mission will be to storm the beach at Tarawa where more than 1,000 Americans and 4,000 Japanese died in brutal fighting over a three-day period.

The Rodgers and Hammerstein musical *South Pacific* was based on these stories.

"South Pacific *isn't pro-war or antiwar. But it makes you think about the costs.*"

—FRANK RICH, *NEW YORK TIMES*

THE THINGS THEY CARRIED

BY TIM O'BRIEN

First Lieutenant Jimmy Cross carried letters from a girl named Martha, a junior at Mount Sebastian College in New Jersey.

THIS BRILLIANT COLLECTION of interconnected short stories tells of a fictional Alpha Company of American soldiers. In the title story, Mr. O'Brien as narrator describes the quotidian items—can openers, pocketknives, wristwatches, mosquito repellent, chewing gum, letters, good luck charms, and the like—that soldiers carried into battle along with M-16 assault rifles, M-60 machine guns, and M-79 grenade launchers. He also reveals the less visible, powerful emotions, like grief and terror, love and guilt, that soldiers carry within.

Beyond the horror of the fighting, these stories examine the very nature of courage and fear as men survive in body but not in soul. Medic Rat Kiley triages hundreds of wounded men and sends more home in body bags. Then hallucinations begin. Finally he shoots himself in the foot and gets shipped home. Norman Bowker makes it all the way back to Iowa in one piece, only to later hang himself. Tying the stories together is "the common secret of cowardice."

Published in 1990, this gives new meaning to the war in Vietnam for America and for the soldiers who served there. It received nominations for the Pulitzer Prize and the National Book Critics Circle Award. Reviewers compared it to Stephen Crane's *Red Badge of Courage* and Kurt Vonnegut's *Slaughterhouse-Five*.

"In prose that combines the sharp, unsentimental rhythms of Hemingway with gentler, more lyrical descriptions, Mr. O'Brien gives the reader a shockingly visceral sense of what it felt like to tramp through a booby-trapped jungle, carrying 20 pounds of supplies, 14 pounds of ammunition, along with radios, machine guns, assault rifles and grenades."

—MICHIKO KAKUTANI, *NEW YORK TIMES*

THE ADVENTURES OF HUCKLEBERRY FINN

BY MARK TWAIN

You don't know about me, without you have read a book by the name of "The Adventures of Tom Sawyer," but that ain't no matter.

THIRTEEN-YEAR-OLD HUCK RESISTS all attempts to "sivilize" him. When his violent, drunken father shows up to take over his rearing and nearly kills him, he fakes his own death and sails down the Mississippi. Adrift on the river, he takes refuge on Jackson Island. There he comes upon Jim, Miss Watson's slave from home.

Like Huck, Jim is on the run. Together the pair head for safety in Illinois. Their plans are soon scuttled by a passing steamship that swamps their boat. Separated, reunited, in and out of danger, their adventures take them up and down the Mississippi. Disguised as a girl, Huck returns home and discovers that a group of men are planning to recapture Jim. Huck can't let that happen.

This sequel to *Tom Sawyer* has been controversial since it was first published in 1885. One contemporary reviewer opined: "Mr. Clemens has contributed some humorous literature that is excellent and will hold its place, but his *Huckleberry Finn* appears to be singularly flat, stale and unprofitable." Generations of readers have been baffled as to why Huck doesn't reveal that Jim is legally a freed slave. Modern readers object to the book's stereotyped portrayal of Jim. But few would argue with the novel's virtues: humor, lyricism, and a distinctive casual and, at the time, revolutionary narrative voice.

"In its pioneering of the vernacular first person, its search for authentic American experience among the dispossessed and traditionally voiceless and its use of comedy to bring home grim realities in ways that gravity cannot, Huckleberry Finn *is a bantamweight story with a heavyweight's impact."*

—JONATHAN FRANZEN, *NEW YORK TIMES*

THE ILLUSTRATED MAN

BY RAY BRADBURY

It was a warm afternoon in early September when I first met the Illustrated Man.

WALKING THE HOT, humid back roads of Wisconsin, the narrator meets another wanderer, a former carnival freak whose body is covered with vivid tattoos. At night the "pictures move" and predict the future. This eponymous "illustrated man" provides a framing device for eighteen sci-fi short-story gems, originally published between 1948 and 1951. In the epilogue, the narrator lies by the campfire and glimpses empty space between the pictures on the tattooed man's back. There he sees his own fate.

Many stories in this anthology are unforgettable. In "Marionettes, Inc.," a man unhappy in his marriage decides to replace himself with a robot so he can leave his wife, only to discover that, for quite some time, he's been living with a robot version of her. In "The Veldt," parents who've threatened to take away their children's high-tech nursery simulation of the African veldt end up victims of simulated lions.

Published when many American families were just getting their first TV sets, Bradbury was channeling the public's distrust of the new medium. Later, Rod Serling asked Bradbury to write for *The Twilight Zone*. Bradbury contributed one screenplay based on a short story in one of his other anthologies, *I Sing the Body Electric*.

Coming on the heels of another Bradbury anthology, *The Martian Chronicles*, this book was a critical and commercial success and cemented Bradbury's reputation as one of the finest science fiction writers of our time.

"My first experience of real horror came at the hands of Ray Bradbury."
—STEPHEN KING, *DANSE MACABRE*

Profiles in Courage

BY JOHN F. KENNEDY

These are the stories of the pressures experienced by eight United States Senators and the grace with which they endured them—the risks to their careers, the unpopularity of their courses, the defamation of their characters, and sometimes, sadly only sometimes, the vindication of their reputations and principles.

THIS ANNIVERSARY OF JFK's assassination is a good time to remember this great book, conceived when Kennedy was a freshman senator in 1954. It profiles eight great senators from history and highlights the moment when each stood alone for what he believed in. Kennedy includes John Quincy Adams, the only Federalist to vote for the Louisiana Purchase; Sam Houston, who refused to support the Kansas-Nebraska Act of 1854, which would have allowed residents of the territories to decide the slavery issue for themselves; Thomas Hart Benton, who remained loyal to the Democratic Party despite his opposition to the extension of slavery in the territories; and Edmund G. Ross of Kansas, who saved the Johnson presidency by voting to acquit Andrew Johnson of impeachment. Kennedy shows the price each man paid for choosing to do the right thing. This book reminds us why it's so important that the best and the brightest go into public service.

How many of this book's words Kennedy penned himself is the subject of some controversy. Many believe that Theodore Sorensen did much of the actual writing. In 1957 it was awarded the Pulitzer Prize.

"Courage is the virtue that President Kennedy most admired."
> —ROBERT KENNEDY, IN THE ORIGINAL FOREWORD

"My father taught us all that we are never too old or too young for public service."
> —CAROLYN KENNEDY, IN THE INTRODUCTION
> TO THE 2003 REISSUE

THE GHOST ROAD

BY PAT BARKER

In deck-chairs all along the front the bald pink knees of Bradford businessmen nuzzled the sun.

THIS FINAL VOLUME of a trilogy of World War I novels (including *Regeneration* and *The Eye in the Door*) tells the story of Billy Prior, a British army officer being treated for shell shock in the Great War. Prior is a patient of William Rivers, a character based on a real psychologist who experimented with neurological surgery and electric shock for treating emotionally traumatized soldiers.

The ultimate outsider, Prior is not of the same social class as fellow officers. Though he's engaged to be married, he is bisexual. He returns for a fourth time to the killing fields of France rather than return to Britain where he has no place.

A second narrative tells of Rivers's work before the war, among headhunters in the Pacific. The horrors he encountered there mirror the horrors of the Great War.

This 1995 Booker Prize winner is as much an antiwar novel as an exploration of British society. Barker wrote it so readers would think about the war, "why it happened and the effects it had on society." Barker grew up with a grandfather who bore a bayonet scar on his back from World War I, and whose war stories spoke to the emotional scars the war left in a generation.

"Despite the novel's flaws, one values Pat Barker's nervy willingness to imagine the gory and savage past that so chillingly resembles the bloody, barbaric present."

—FRANCINE PROSE, *WASHINGTON POST*

AMERICAN PASTORAL

BY PHILIP ROTH

The Swede. During the war years, when I was still a grade school boy, this was a magical name in our Newark neighborhood, even to adults just a generation removed from the city's old Prince Street ghetto and not yet so flawlessly Americanized as to be bowled over by the prowess of a high-school athlete.

SET IN THE turbulent '60s and '70s, this 1997 novel goes to the heart of what the parents of youngsters coming of age then stood for, and what their offspring rejected. It tells the story of Seymour "Swede" Levov, an American success story. The strapping blond, blue-eyed high-school sports legend, grandson of immigrant Jews, makes a fortune running his family's glove factory in Newark. He's civic-minded and tolerant and an all-around nice guy. The perfect assimilated Jew, he's married to an Irish Catholic former beauty queen. Their daughter, Meredith, is transformed from the dutiful daughter to all-out radical by the antiwar movement. She comes to hate everything Swede values.

Like a willing Patty Hearst, Meredith participates in the bombing of a store, killing a doctor. Then she goes underground and her father absorbs the shockwaves as in short order his wife parts company with her sanity, his factory goes bankrupt, and Newark falls into anarchy. Swede wonders, "What turned my country into an ash tip echoing to the sound of small-arms fire?"

Roth called this and the two novels that followed it (*I Married a Communist* and *The Human Stain*) his "American Trilogy." *Pastoral* won the 1997 Pulitzer Prize for Fiction.

"The agonized question that ripples through American Pastoral *is 'what happened?' How did the pastoral America of Newark in the '40s and '50s—an Eden only in retrospect—come apart?"*

—A. O. SCOTT, *NEW YORK TIMES*

INFINITE JEST

BY DAVID FOSTER WALLACE

I am seated in an office, surrounded by heads and bodies.

PART PHILOSOPHICAL QUEST, part extended comedy routine, this hefty (1,000-plus pages) and widely praised novel (it brought comparisons to Thomas Pynchon and John Irving) features hundreds of characters and a baroque narrative with more than 400 footnotes.

The *Infinite Jest* of the title is a movie so mesmerizing that anyone who watches it loses all desire to do anything else. Set in a not-too-distant future in which years are corporate-sponsored ("Year of the Depend Adult Undergarment"), the novel tells of the movie's effect on residents of Ennet House, a Boston home for recovering drug addicts and alcoholics, and at nearby Enfield Tennis Academy, founded by mad genius James O. Incandenza and inhabited by athletic and academic prodigies. Among the meandering narratives is the story of the three Incandenza brothers and a band of wheelchair-bound terrorists.

The emphatically nontraditional writing ("metafiction") is exuberant, filled with surprising metaphors and what one reviewer called "amphetaminelike stream-of-consciousness riffs." The title refers to a line from *Hamlet*. As Hamlet stands in a graveyard, he looks at the skull of Yorick, the court jester, and grieves for his friend: "Alas, poor Yorick! I knew him, Horatio: a fellow of infinite jest, of most excellent fancy. . . ."

Hamlet, like Wallace, goes on to consider the fate of us all.

This sprawling 1996 work made Wallace a literary star. Sadly, Wallace committed suicide in 2008 at the age of 46.

"The overall effect is something like a sleek Vonnegut chassis wrapped in layers of post-millennial Zola."

—JAY McINERNEY, *NEW YORK TIMES*

PRIDE AND PREJUDICE

BY JANE AUSTEN

It is a truth universally acknowledged, that a single man in possession of a good fortune, must be in want of a wife.

THIS IS A genteel comedy of manners in which the quick-witted but prejudiced Elizabeth Bennet finally finds her match in the honorable but prideful Mr. Darcy, while Elizabeth's mother bustles about in muddled determination to make "appropriate" matches for her girls. The suspects include the good-natured Mr. Bingley, the dashing Mr. Wickham, and the odious and insufferably dull Mr. Collins, whom Elizabeth rejects at the outset. And of course, there's the smoldering Mr. Fitzwilliam Darcy.

The story begins with the news that Mr. Bingley has leased nearby Netherfield estate. Staying with him is his friend, Mr. Darcy. At a dance, Mr. Bingley shows his attentions to Jane, the eldest Bennet sister, while Mr. Darcy seems bent on insulting Elizabeth. Jane is invited to Netherfield. There, she falls ill and must stay and be nursed back to health. Enter Mr. Wickham with his tales of Mr. Darcy's betrayal. He's revealed to be a cad when he scoops up the silliest Bennet sister, Lydia, and carries her off without benefit of marriage.

Austen wrote this in less than a year when she was just twenty-one years of age. It was published in 1813. "Gentle Jane?" Not hardly.

"One day I happened to pick up a copy of Pride and Prejudice *that I'd been using to weigh down a glue job. I loved it. It was so slow and detailed. In the winter and early spring, I read all of Jane Austen, used up three boxes of English tea and sent away for an 'I'd rather be reading Jane Austen' bumper sticker."*

—ANNE TYLER, QUOTED IN THE *NEW YORK TIMES*

EVA LUNA

BY ISABEL ALLENDE

*My name is Eva, which means "life," according to a book of
names my mother consulted.*

EVA LUNA IS a poor Chilean peasant girl with a gift for storytelling. In this 1988 novel, Allende's third, Eva becomes a
Scheherezade, telling of her own conception and of her mother's
mysterious origins in a Roman Catholic mission in the South
American jungle. Through storytelling she escapes repression.

Eva takes the reader through the houses where her mother
and she worked for eccentric masters, including a European
scientist who embalmed human bodies. She tells "the tales my
mother told me when we were living among the Professor's
idiots, cancer patients, and mummies; a snakebitten Indian
appeared, and a tyrant with hands devoured by leprosy; I rescued an old maid who had been scalped as if by a spinning
machine, a dignitary in a purple plush chair, an Arab with a
generous heart, and the many other men and women whose
lives were in my hands to dispose of at will."

But this is not a true retelling. It is her life set in a land of
magical realism and told as she "would like it to be." Through
these lush, romantic stories, Eva Luna finds the lover of her
dreams.

Niece of the assassinated Chilean president Salvador
Allende, Isabel Allende grew up in Chile where she was a journalist before moving to Venezuela and then to the United States.
The storyteller Eva Luna resembles the author herself. She
didn't publish her first novel, *The House of Spirits*, until 1982
when she was forty years old.

"Writing Eva Luna *was joyful. I felt that she was speaking for me, talking about being a woman, about politics, about writing. It was wonderful to put on her lips things I had wanted to say all my life."*

—ISABEL ALLENDE, *DAILY VARIETY*

THE SUPPER OF THE LAMB: A CULINARY REFLECTION

BY ROBERT FARRAR CAPON

Ingredients. Let me begin without ceremony.
LAMB FOR EIGHT PERSONS FOUR TIMES

APPROPRIATELY, THIS "CULINARY reflection" by an Episcopalian priest and self-professed amateur chef begins with the ingredients for a lamb supper. Much more than a cookbook, its reflections on life and on the virtues of a home-cooked meal and a well-set table range from the culinary to the theological and metaphysical.

There's more than you ever thought possible to say about the Zen of dismantling an onion, and why a dull knife should never be used to carve roasts (better to "see them kicked apart with a pointed shoe"). Among the philosophizing there are recipes, too—for spaetzle and puff paste and hollandaise sauce. It includes a prayer for "soups that spoons will not sink into."

Like Julia Child, Capon is a proponent of cream and wine over calorie-counting, an advocate of simple, excellent-quality ingredients over packaged food. He admits that he likes food and drink, and that his children call him "the walking garbage pail," though prairie oysters and eyeballs give him pause.

Beneath the wit runs a more serious message: Capon chastises us to fulfill our spiritual obligation to stop and think about how we eat, and moreover, to delight in it. This funny, wise, and moving guide to "festal and ferial" (celebratory and everyday) cooking, first published in 1969, has become a cult classic.

"To call The Supper of the Lamb *a cookbook would be like calling* Moby Dick *a whaling manual."*

—FREDERICK BUECHNER, *NEW YORK TIMES*

THE TIME TRAVELER'S WIFE

BY AUDREY NIFFENEGGER

Saturday, October 26, 1991 (Henry is 28; Clare is 20)

Clare: The library is cool and smells like carpet cleaner, although all I can see is marble.

HENRY DETAMBLE IS a time traveler. His wife and the love of his life, Clare Abshire, is not. Afflicted with "Chrono-Impairment," he finds himself catapulted from one random time in his lifetime to another. And so, repeatedly he visits Clare through her childhood and adolescence.

When she is twenty and he's twenty-eight, she finally meets him "for the first time" in his time continuum. He doesn't recognize her but she's already encountered him many times and knows him well. He explains his abilities to her: "I can only do things that work toward what has already happened. I can't, for example, undo the fact that you just took off your shoes."

They marry. Clare suffers many miscarriages and at last gives birth to a daughter who turns out to have her father's genetic gift for time travel.

This astonishing debut novel is a soaring love story with a twelve-hankie ending. The film rights were snapped up by Brad Pitt and Jennifer Aniston in 2003 (before Angelina came into their timelines).

"The Time Traveler's Wife *is an infection that pleasantly invades your system and refuses to let go of the imagination even after you turn the last of its 518 pages and move on to the next book on your shelf.*"

—DAVID ABRAMS, *JANUARY MAGAZINE*

THE BIG SLEEP

BY RAYMOND CHANDLER

It was about eleven o'clock in the morning, mid October, with the sun not shining and a look of hard wet rain in the clearness of the foothills.

A DYING MILLIONAIRE hires Philip Marlowe to deal with his daughters' troubles. The older one, Vivian, has gambling debts. The younger one, Carmen, is a drug addict and is being blackmailed for the return of negatives of photographs that show her posing naked. Their father wants Marlowe to destroy the crooks who are trying to extort money from him.

The work takes Marlowe into Los Angeles's criminal underworld. Though he fixes the gambling debts and reclaims the negatives, he can't free the women from the grip L.A. casino owner Eddie Mars has over them.

This is the book that introduced the world to Marlowe, one of the first hardboiled private dicks. With his "powder-blue suit, with dark blue shirt, tie and display handkerchief, black brogues, black wool socks with dark blue clocks on them," only the attitude resembles Bogey's portrayal on the silver screen.

The hard-drinking Chandler didn't begin to write fiction until he was well into his forties after losing his job as an oil industry executive. He wrote short stories for the pulps, and was fifty-one when this, his first novel, was published. He went on to write six more Marlowe novels and became one of the few genre fiction writers whose works are compared to Fitzgerald and Hemingway.

"Down these mean streets a man must go who is not himself mean, who is neither tarnished nor afraid. The detective in this kind of story must be such a man. He is a hero, he is everything."
—RAYMOND CHANDLER, "THE SIMPLE ART OF MURDER," *ATLANTIC MONTHLY*

December

IN COLD BLOOD

BY TRUMAN CAPOTE

The village of Holcomb stands on the high wheat plains of western Kansas, a lonesome area that other Kansans call "out there."

THE VILLAGE OF Holcomb was the real-life setting for a brutal murder of four members of the Clutter family. Flamboyant author Truman Capote journeyed there to write about the murders, traveling with the more outwardly conventional Harper Lee. When he arrived, killers Perry Smith and Richard Hickock were being held in jail.

Immersing himself in the setting and developing a personal, emotional relationship with both killers, particularly Smith, Capote pushed the bounds of journalism. He took liberties—lying to get his subjects to reveal their stories and imagining the chilling drama of real events in vivid detail—as no journalist had ever done before. He wormed his charming way into the head of Smith who told him: "I really admired Mr. Clutter, right up until the moment I slit his throat."

This true-crime masterpiece, which Capote called a nonfiction novel, was published in 1965 after Smith and Hickock had been hanged for their crimes. Capote witnessed their executions.

In a "self-interview" published in 1980, Capote summed up his life: "I'm an alcoholic. I'm a drug addict. I'm homosexual. I'm a genius. Of course, I could be all four of these dubious things and still be a saint." Capote died four years later at the age of fifty-nine.

"Capote wrote the best sentences of anyone of our generation."
—NORMAN MAILER, *THE SPOOKY ART: SOME THOUGHTS ON WRITING*

KILLSHOT

BY ELMORE LEONARD

The Blackbird told himself he was drinking too much because he lived in this hotel and the Silver Dollar was close by, right downstairs.

THIS 1989 CRIME novel pits a Native American hit man named Armand "the Blackbird" Degas and a psychopathic punk named Richie Nix against real-estate agent Carmen Colson and her ironworker husband, Wayne, who live near the Michigan-Canada border. Degas has just rubbed out a Detroit mobster and is riding around in his payment—a baby-blue Cadillac—when his path crosses that of Nix. The pair, prime wacked-out Leonard characters, pull off a petty extortion scheme, which the Colsons have the misfortune of witnessing.

Fortunately for the Colsons, Nix is as stupid as he is incompetent; unfortunately, the law enforcer who should be providing them refuge, a federal marshal named Ferris ("just like the wheel"), is no straight-shooter. While they're just a pair of average folks (his hobby is deer hunting, hers is handwriting analysis), the Colsons look after themselves remarkably well.

With his trademark smart dialogue and fast action, Leonard has been dubbed the "Dickens of Detroit" and his writing has been compared to the work of Dashiell Hammett, Raymond Chandler, and Ross MacDonald. Leonard, who still writes his manuscripts on unlined yellow legal pads, disagrees: "I was more influenced by Hemingway, Steinbeck, John O'Hara and James Cain."

"I want to adapt Killshot. . . . *There are two parts that would be perfect for me and Harvey Keitel."*

—QUENTIN TARANTINO,
QUENTIN TARANTINO INTERVIEWS

THE 39 STEPS

BY JOHN BUCHAN

I returned from the City about three o'clock on that May afternoon pretty well disgusted with life.

LOOK IN THE rearview mirror of James Bond's Aston Martin and you'll see, fading in the distance, Richard Hannay, the mining engineer/British amateur spy of *The 39 Steps*. In the novel, Hannay meets an American journalist who tells of an international assassination plan. When the journalist is murdered and his body is found in Hannay's flat, Hannay becomes the prime suspect. As Hannay searches for the mysterious "Mr. Memory" and the man with the tip of his little finger missing, he realizes that only he can save the nation.

With this 1915 novel, Buchan invented the modern spy novel. Despite plotting that occasionally defies logic and the taint of anti-Semitism, this remains a classic work with its paranoid vision of German spies nestled in the English countryside. Hitchcock made a memorable version for the screen in 1935.

This was one of more than fifty fiction and nonfiction books, including six other novels featuring Hannay, that Buchan published in his lifetime.

"John Buchan is the father of the modern spy thriller. This is so even though the Hannay books are not, strictly speaking, about spies at all. . . . They are about penetration of the enemy, about lonely escape and wild journeys, about the thin veneer that stands between civilization and barbarism even in the most elegant drawing-room in London."

—ROBIN WINKS, INTRODUCTION TO
THE FOUR ADVENTURES OF RICHARD HANNAY

TINKER, TAILOR, SOLDIER, SPY

BY JOHN LE CARRÉ

The truth is, if old Major Dover hadn't dropped dead at Taunton races Jim would never have come to Thursgood's at all.

GEORGE SMILEY IS the anti–James Bond. The former spy is fat, middle-aged, middle-class, mild-mannered, unhappily married, and a genius at bureaucratic maneuvering. Retired in disgrace after a botched espionage operation, he's lured back to work for one division of MI6 (the "Circus") to discover and destroy a double agent, a mole who has penetrated the top levels of Britain's Secret Service. The nursery rhyme of the title refers to the codewords for the suspects—the four men now running the Service. Smiley can trust no one, so he must operate without the resources of the intelligence network.

There's no imaginary, high-tech wizardry here. John Le Carré (pen name of David John Moore Cornwell) gives a realistic account of how such an investigation is carried out and of the bureaucracy that surrounds it. Le Carré pits his agent's beliefs against his actions, his loyalty to his country against his respect for his enemy. As in the real world, paranoia prevails.

This 1974 work is the first volume in Smiley's "Karla Trilogy," all considered modern masterpieces, and all populated by thoroughly human characters who take their time. This book demonstrates why "character-driven thriller" isn't necessarily an oxymoron.

"The convolutions of conspiracy in [the George Smiley novels] are as elaborate and grandiose as medieval theology—a Byzantine struggle between the forces of light and darkness. The conflict is not simply between them and us, but, on both sides, between ourselves and our governments."

—ANATOLE BROYARD, *NEW YORK TIMES*

THE MURDER OF
ROGER ACKROYD

BY AGATHA CHRISTIE

*Mrs. Ferrars died on the night of the 16th–17th September—
a Thursday. I was sent for at eight o'clock on the morning of
Friday the 17th.*

THE NARRATOR, DR. Sheppard, is called to the home of
wealthy widow Mrs. Ferrars. At first her death looks like suicide, but when her fiancé Roger Ackroyd is also found dead, it
smells more like murder.

Hercule Poirot, the diminutive and oh-so-precise Belgian
detective, investigates. When Poirot tells Dr. Sheppard that his
life's work is "the study of human nature," Sheppard concludes
at first that Poirot is a retired hairdresser. Sheppard becomes
Poirot's helper in the investigation.

Suspects abound—Roger's debt-ridden sister-in-law, his
niece, his stepson, a maid, a butler, and so on. When all are
eliminated, an unprecedented plot twist reveals the true killer.
On publication, there was a great hue and cry about the ending
of this 1926 novel. No doubt Dame Agatha chuckled all the
way to the bank.

Sheppard's spinster sister Caroline, who "can do any amount
of finding out by sitting placidly at home," was the model for
the celebrated Miss Marple of Christie's later novels.

Christie, who wrote more than eighty detective novels in
addition to romances under the pseudonym Mary Westmacott,
was the single most popular novelist of the twentieth century.

*"His constant preening and fractured English notwithstanding, Hercule
Poirot ranks among the greatest detectives of all time. Holmes possessed an unapproachable glamour and Father Brown an even more
subtle mind, but Poirot took on problems of greater variety and
ingenuity."*

—MICHAEL DIRDA, *CLASSICS FOR PLEASURE*

From Here to Eternity

BY JAMES JONES

When he finished packing, he walked out on to the third-floor porch of the barracks brushing the dust from his hands, a very neat and deceptively slim young man in the summer khakis that were still morning fresh.

JAMES JONES BASED this novel, set in Diamond Head in 1941 just before Pearl Harbor, on his own army experiences. Between the wars, soldiers spent their time and energy fighting one another.

The novel tells of two angry soldiers. One is Private Robert E. Lee Prewitt, a brilliant bugler and talented boxer who refuses to bugle or box in contrition for the man he killed in the ring. The other, Milton Anthony Warden, is a frustrated sergeant who begins an affair with Karen, his commanding officer's promiscuous, neglected wife. Against this melodramatic backdrop, Japan attacks Pearl Harbor.

Jones created a novel of startling realism. He ignored the conventions of grammar and syntax to create a loose, sprawling narrative laced with vulgarity, colloquial dialogue, explicitly rendered sex, and the grisly, dehumanizing details of combat. This was the first of a trilogy of World War II novels.

Considered *the* great novel of World War II, this first in a trilogy of novels won the National Book Award in 1952. It is unique both for taking the point of view of the enlisted man and for its bold experimental style.

"The only one of my contemporaries who I felt had more talent than myself was James Jones. . . . What was unique about Jones was that he had come out of nowhere, self-taught, a clunk in his lacks, the only one of us who had the beer-guts of a broken-glass brawl."

—NORMAN MAILER, *ADVERTISEMENTS FOR MYSELF*

EMPIRE OF THE SUN

BY J. G. BALLARD

Wars came early to Shanghai, overtaking each other like the tides that raced up the Yangtze and returned to this gaudy city all the coffins cast adrift from the funeral piers of the Chinese Bund.

J. G. BALLARD'S luminous novelistic memoir takes place in wartime China. An eleven-year-old British boy named Jim, whose father owns a textile mill in Shanghai, witnesses a Japanese sneak attack on British and American warships on the Shanghai waterfront. The attack is timed to coincide with the raid on Pearl Harbor. Many British dependents have long ago fled the threat of Japanese domination.

In the midst of the turmoil that follows, Jim is separated from his parents. Alone, he must survive for months before taking refuge with a couple of not-so-nice Americans. He soon realizes that he'd be better off in a Japanese prison camp.

For three years more, he survives in a prison camp outside the city. He gets away when the camp is evacuated and, from a sports stadium in Shanghai, sees a brilliant flash in the sky—an atomic bomb has destroyed Nagasaki, 500 miles away. This he recognizes as the rebirth of Japan, a new empire of the sun.

This autobiographical work was based on Ballard's boyhood experiences in the Lunghua Civilian Assembly Center near Shanghai from 1942 to 1945. Ballard's prior works were science fiction. Widely praised, this was shortlisted for the Booker Prize.

"He aims to render a vision of the apocalypse, and succeeds so well that it can hurt to dwell upon his images. For Mr. Ballard seems to be against all armies and the ideologies that mobilize troops; he seems also to believe that the horror of his youth ended only when World War III began with a nuclear sunburst over Nagasaki."

—JOHN CALVIN BATCHELOR, *NEW YORK TIMES*

THE COLLECTOR

BY JOHN FOWLES

When she was home from her boarding-school I used to see her almost every day sometimes, because their house was right opposite the Town Hall Annexe.

FREDERICK CLEGG, AN odd, prudish, unattractive man, is one of society's lonely outsiders. He collects butterflies. When he wins a small fortune in the football pools, he gives up his boring job at the Town Hall and buys a secluded country house in Sussex and a van to use in his search for rare specimens. He spiffs up the cellar, turning it into a luxurious prison for his heart's desire, art student Miranda Grey ("Seeing her always made me feel like I was catching a rarity, going up to it very careful, heart-in-mouth as they say").

Clegg stalks Miranda, captures her with the help of chloroform from his killing bottle, and imprisons her like a specimen lepidoptera. A master of self-delusion, Frederick fantasizes that she will fall in love with him. Instead, she falls ill and no outsider or Clegg himself can save her. As he buries her, he's already staked out her successor.

This 1963 debut novel is a masterpiece of claustrophobic obsession. The story is told both from the viewpoints of the collector and the collected (we get to read Miranda's diary).

"If ever there was a book that expresses the banality of evil, The Collector is it. . . . In the long canon of work about obsession, few get closer to what lies beneath, or find so terrifyingly little there."
—IAN MACLEOD IN *HORROR: ANOTHER 100 BEST BOOKS*,
EDITED BY STEPHEN JONES AND KIM NEWMAN

THE FRENCH LIEUTENANT'S WOMAN

BY JOHN FOWLES

An easterly is the most disagreeable wind in Lyme Bay—Lyme Bay being that largest bite from the underside of England's out-stretched southwestern leg—and a person of curiosity could at once have deduced several strong probabilities about the pair who began to walk down the quay at Lyme Regis, the small but ancient eponym of the inbite, one incisively sharp and blustery morning in the late March of 1867.

WORLDS AWAY FROM the creepy narrative of *The Collector*, Fowles explores a different kind of obsession in this enigmatic novel. He found the inspiration for this work in dreams haunted by the recurring image of a mysterious woman standing and looking out to sea. In the novel, the woman is penniless ex-governess Sarah Woodruff, who stands at the end of a break-water at Lyme Regis, Dorset, in 1867. Watching her is Charles Smithson, an amateur geologist and an advocate of Darwin's theories. He wonders if the rumors he's heard are true, that she's a fallen woman awaiting the return of the French sailor who abandoned her. Smithson befriends her and helps her, then sends her away, resisting the pull he feels (he's engaged to another). But distance is no deterrent. Obsessed, he must pursue her.

Though this 1969 novel is written in Victorian style, it uses the modern conceit of the author himself interrupting the story with commentary about various subjects and people, often outside the framework of the book itself. Extensive epigraphs introduce each chapter, and in a radical departure from tradi-tional storytelling, alternative endings are presented.

With this work, Fowles staked out turf as one of the English-speaking world's first postmodern novelists.

"*[The French Lieutenant's Woman] started as a visual image. A woman stands at the end of a deserted quay and stares out to sea. That was all.*"

—JOHN FOWLES

KATE VAIDEN

BY REYNOLDS PRICE

The best thing about my life up to here is, nobody believes it.

KATE VAIDEN IS a character haunted by severed ties. Her maternal grandparents died when her mother was eight. Kate's father fatally shot her mother after seeing her with another man; then he shot himself. Kate deserts her adoptive parents, a devoted aunt and uncle. Just when it seems she's about to start afresh with Gaston, the love of her life, he's called away by the war and dies in a freak accident during training. Later, on her way to Raleigh to marry and start anew, she abandons the lover who has impregnated her. She tells herself, "Leave people before they can plan to leave you."

At seventeen, she abandons her newborn son. Then, in middle age, she has a change of mind and reaches out to him.

This rich Southern gothic tale tells of Kate's first fifty-seven years, up to 1984, set against the backdrop of the Depression, World War II, and the war's aftermath. It's about a woman who yearns for love but can't accept it when it comes within reach.

A *New York Times* reviewer called this "the product of a storyteller working at the full height of his artistic powers." It was chosen as the best work of fiction in 1986 by the National Book Critics Circle.

"The novel is also a version of picaresque in which our 'heroine' reveals herself as a modern-day Moll Flanders, a woman possessed of and by a restlessness of mind and spirit that make her unable to give herself wholly to anyone, or to anything, including her only child."

—GEORGE CORE, *WASHINGTON POST*

FRANKENSTEIN; OR, THE MODERN PROMETHEUS

BY MARY WOLLSTONECRAFT SHELLEY

To Mrs. Saville, England.
St. Petersburgh, Dec. 11th, 17—.

You will rejoice to hear that no disaster has accompanied the commencement of an enterprise which you have regarded with such evil forebodings.

THIS ICONIC NOVEL opens with letters from Captain Robert Walton to his sister, soon after he witnesses the rescue of Dr. Victor Frankenstein who was crossing the ice on a dog sled. On shipboard, Dr. Frankenstein related his story. A scientist, he'd longed to infuse "life into an inanimate body." When he succeeded, he recoiled from the ugliness of the reanimated being that he assembled from body parts obtained from corpses. He rejected his creation a second time and it fled, only to seek him out later to wreak its revenge.

By the end, the reader is not sure who has humanity—the doctor himself and by extension the rest of us, or the monster.

Considered the mother of horror, Shelley was the daughter of radical political thinker William Godwin and feminist Mary Wollstonecraft. She was the wife of poet Percy Bysshe Shelley. She was only twenty-one on New Year's Day in 1818 when this novel was published anonymously. The book was a commercial success. Reviewers who assumed it had been written by a man were much kinder to it than reviewers who knew otherwise.

"Prometheus, bringer of fire, ended chained to a stone, his eyes pecked out by ravens—punishment for stealing what belonged to the gods. Frankenstein comes to a similar end—not in fire but in ice—for his temerity in usurping the power which belongs to God alone: the power to create life."

—STEPHEN KING, IN THE INTRODUCTION TO
FRANKENSTEIN, DRACULA, DR. JEKYLL AND MR. HYDE

PORTRAIT OF A LADY

BY HENRY JAMES

Under certain circumstances there are few hours in life more agreeable than the hour dedicated to the ceremony known as afternoon tea.

THE LADY IN the portrait is Isabel Archer, a young American who departs with her wealthy aunt for a European adventure before the man she loves, Caspar Goodwood, can ask for her hand in marriage. Abroad she receives two proposals of marriage, one of them from an English lord. Proudly committed to her own freedom and independence, she turns down both. One of her suitors induces his father to leave her a considerable fortune.

But no wisdom flows from her newfound financial independence. In England, Isabel meets and unwisely marries American expatriate Gilbert Osmond. He turns out to have a great appreciation for her fortune but little affection for the spirited woman he's married. At the crux of the novel is Isabel's realization of the trap she's fallen into.

Published as a book in 1881, contemporaries felt it "unfinished," as it leaves so many questions unanswered. In its characters, James distills the essence of American versus European, old world versus new, as well as shades of British class differences. Isabel may be based on Isabella Stewart Gardner, the belle of James's era who snubbed Boston's high society and lavished her energy on travel and fashion and art.

"*We got the corset down to 19 inches one day, and I would be in pain and have bruises and stuff on my body when I took it off. But it was a psychological thing, a thing where I wanted to be restricted really, really tight so that the more repressed I was, the more I felt it.*"

—NICOLE KIDMAN, ON PLAYING
ISABEL ARCHER IN THE 1996 FILM

WUTHERING HEIGHTS

BY EMILY BRONTË

1801—I have just returned from a visit to my landlord—the solitary neighbour that I shall be troubled with.

THIS IS A classic tale of obsession and revenge. The thwarted lovers are the moody, broody Mr. Heathcliff and the passionate but repressed Catherine Earnshaw. Heathcliff was a London street urchin, taken in as a boy by Catherine's father and brought up with Catherine and her brother Hindley.

When Mr. Earnshaw dies, Hindley relegates Heathcliff to servant's status. But Catherine still worships Heathcliff. However, Hindley will have none of it. Catherine declares her love for Heathcliff, but chooses to marry Edgar Linton and Heathcliff takes off. A few years later, he returns having made his fortune. Tragedy on tragedy ensues.

This book and Emily Brontë's older sister Charlotte's *Jane Eyre* moved gothic romance squarely into the mainstream. All the fantasy and supernatural events of the book are rooted in the reality of daily life. Its extraordinary passion and violence are set within a placid routine of domesticity. A prim and proper parson's daughter, Emily Brontë died of consumption in 1848, just a year after this, her only book, was published.

"One of the most perfect and marvelous endings in literature—it raises my hair now—is the little boy at the end of Wuthering Heights, *crying that he's afraid to go across the moor because there's a man and a woman walking there."*

—KATHERINE ANNE PORTER, IN *THE WRITER'S CHAPBOOK*, EDITED BY DAVID GEORGE PLOTKIN

The Hitchhiker's Guide to the Galaxy

BY DOUGLAS ADAMS

The house stood on a slight rise just on the edge of the village.

THIS SCI-FI CLASSIC coined the phrases "mostly harmless," "don't panic," and "42" (the answer to life's ultimate question and one that takes the largest computer ever built seven and a half million years to reach). Its discontinuous narrative starts with Arthur Dent throwing himself in front of a bulldozer that's about to destroy his house to make way for a highway (see *Watership Down*).

Dent's best friend, Ford Prefect, a visitor "from a small planet somewhere in the vicinity of Betelgeuse," persuades him that the Earth is about to be obliterated to make way for a galactic freeway. The dynamic duo hastily hitch a ride on a passing starship.

Prefect is actually a roving researcher for a hitchhiker's guide to the galaxy. The fictional guide itself includes such must-haves as a recipe for Pan Galactic Gargle Blasters and a summary of the health risks associated with listening to Vogon poetry.

Adams, who started his writing life working on *Monty Python's Flying Circus*, writes with mirth and whimsy. Started as a BBC radio series, this was published as a novel in 1979. It went on to spawn more radio episodes, albums, a television series, four more novels, a stage play, comics, a movie, and a computer game.

"*I had a copy of a book called* The Hitchhiker's Guide to Europe, *and one night I was lying in a field in Innsbruck—I have to say that I was drunk—and I was staring at the stars. It was one of those beautiful starlit nights, and it occurred to me that at some point somebody should write a hitchhiker's guide to the galaxy as well. I fell asleep and forgot about it for six years.*"

—DOUGLAS ADAMS

TOM JONES

BY HENRY FIELDING

An author ought to consider himself, not as a gentleman who gives a private or eleemosynary treat, but rather as one who keeps a public ordinary, at which all persons are welcome for their money.

THIS BAWDY COMIC novel, first published in 1749, tells of a foundling, abandoned at Squire Allworthy's county estate. The Squire, who has "a good heart, and no family," wakes up one morning to find the baby tucked into bed with him. He and his kind sister Bridget locate the baby's mother, unmarried maidservant Jenny Jones. The boy is named Tom Jones and the Squire takes him in and cares for him.

Tom grows into a vigorous lad and falls in love with Sophia Western, the beauteous and virtuous daughter of the owner of a neighboring estate. But since Tom is a bastard, the union is unthinkable. Sophie's father wants her to marry the odious Master Blifil, but Sophie runs away instead.

By the age of fourteen, Tom has been convicted of robbing an orchard, stealing a duck, and picking Master Blifil's pocket. His unfettered temper and unbridled lust get him thrown off the Allworthy estate, and his bad judgment soon leaves him destitute.

The story continues for eighteen "books" in which Tom steadfastly follows his heart and his beloved Sophie. His travels are far ranging and his luck abysmal. At one point, he rescues an older woman, Mrs. Waters. She seduces him, and after a night together he discovers she's Jenny Jones, the woman he thinks is his mother. Fortunately for Tom, it turns out she's not. Despite Tom's many flaws, he is a far finer human being than the "proper" gentlemen and ladies who posture about him.

"[T]he virtues of Fielding's characters were the vices of a truly good man."

—DR. SAMUEL JOHNSON, QUOTED IN
THE HISTORY OF HENRY FIELDING

THE SECRET GARDEN

BY FRANCES HODGSON BURNETT

When Mary Lennox was sent to Misselthwaite Manor to live with her uncle, everybody said she was the most disagreeable-looking child ever seen. It was true, too.

FRANCES HODGSON BURNETT was the J. K. Rowling of her era. Her books were devoured by children and grownups alike. Among her best, published in 1911, was *The Secret Garden*. Its protagonist, Mary Lennox, is a homely and not particularly pleasant little girl. Her parents die when she's ten years old, and she's sent from India to live with curmudgeonly Uncle Archibald on his vast estate in England. When he notices her at all, he asks her whether she'd like toys or books or dolls. Her reply: "Might I . . . might I have a bit of earth?"

Months pass and Mary makes friends with the maid, Martha, with Ben Weatherstaff, the gardener, and with a wild sprite of a boy who communes with animals, Dickon. At night she hears someone crying.

Left alone much of the time, Mary wanders about the estate and discovers a locked door to a hidden garden that was built for Uncle Archibald's wife who died ten years earlier. A robin shows Mary a long-buried key. With it, she unlocks a secret from the past, brings the long neglected garden back to life, and heals another wounded soul.

"Anyone who has much to do with children knows that a naughty or disagreeable heroine is far more interesting than a good one and it is the tartness of Mary, the really atrocious behavior of Colin, her sickly cousin . . . , and the downrightness of the old gardener, Ben Weatherstaff, that makes this the best of Mrs. Burnett's books."

—RUMER GODDEN

A HEARTBREAKING WORK OF STAGGERING GENIUS

BY DAVE EGGERS

Through the small tall bathroom window the December yard is gray and scratchy, the trees calligraphic.

"THE EVENTS RAN over me like a truck," Dave Eggers told the *New York Times*. Those events were his parents' deaths from cancer within thirty-two days of each other. He felt he had no option but to write this novelistic memoir.

It tells how, just out of college, Eggers became surrogate father to his eight-year-old brother Toph. The pair moved from Chicago to Berkeley, where Eggers became Toph's parent, buddy, and partner in mischief making. The book recounts Eggers's manic struggle later to get a startup Gen-X magazine off the ground.

Shoehorned in the middle is a Q&A that reveals how Eggers's family never fit in to their affluent Chicago suburb: "We were always so oddly white-trashy for our town, with our gruesome problems, and our ugly used cars, our Pintos and Malibus and Camaros, and our '70s wallpaper and plaid couches and acne and state schools."

Every once in a while a book comes along that breaks the perceived boundaries of what constitutes a memoir or novel. This book, with its over-the-top storytelling, lengthy preface, quirky acknowledgments section, pages-long footnotes, self-indulgent rants, and pages of unattributed dialogue, challenged traditional preconceptions. Critics proclaimed it a dazzling, virtuoso performance, and the Pulitzer Prize committee agreed, nominating it in 2001.

"Mr. Eggers is not simply wielding high-tech devices to create a hip, experimental narrative, but that these self-annotating mechanisms are part of his sensibility, that they are defensive survival tactics, like his love of hyperbole, invoked to deal with his chaotic childhood and the horror of losing his parents."

—MICHIKO KAKUTANI, *NEW YORK TIMES*

Heart of Darkness

BY JOSEPH CONRAD

The Nellie, a cruising yawl, swung to her anchor without a flutter of the sails, and was at rest.

THIS 1902 NOVEL tells the story of a sailor named Marlow who voyages to the Congo, into the physical and emotional heart of darkness. A riverboat captain with a Belgian trading company, Marlow treks up the river to meet Kurtz, the enigmatic chief of the Inner Station, one of the company's trading posts. Along the way, Marlow sees how brutally natives are dealt with by the company's managers.

When he finally reaches the Inner Station, he discovers that the ailing Kurtz has created himself as a despot and is running a business trading in ivory. The voyage ends in a revelation of horror.

In the book's epigraph, Marlow tells the reader: "I've seen the devil of violence and the devil of greed and the devil of hot desire. . . . I foresaw that in the blinding sunshine of that land, I would become acquainted with a flabby, pretending weak-eyed devil of a rapacious and pitiless folly."

One of the most widely read authors of the Victorian era, Conrad based this book on his own experiences in the Congo where he witnessed the devastation wrought by colonial rule. This novel, credited by many as the first twentieth-century novel, was his most influential. Decades later, it inspired T. S. Eliot's poem "The Waste Land" and Francis Ford Coppola's film *Apocalypse Now*, in which Marlon Brando played the part of Kurtz, whom Coppola envisioned as a "battle-mad commander."

"Conrad's book is a breathtaking work of smoke and mirrors—or rather, steam and shadows."

—STEPHEN SMITH, *INDEPENDENT*

THE HOUSE ON MANGO STREET

BY SANDRA CISNEROS

We didn't always live on Mango Street. Before that we lived on Loomis on the third floor, and before that we lived on Keeler. Before Keeler it was Paulina, and before that I can't remember.

THE HOUSE IS small, just one bedroom and a bath, but it's "ours and we don't have to pay rent to anybody, or share the yard with the people downstairs, or be careful not to make too much noise, and there isn't a landlord banging on the ceiling with a broom. But even so, it's not the house we thought we'd get," says Esperanza Cordero.

In this series of connected short stories, a Mexican American girl comes of age. Each story is a powerful vignette that centers on a detail of Esperanza's childhood (a greasy cold rice sandwich, for instance). In "My Name" and "No Speak English," Cisneros explores the differences between English, in which the name *Esperanza* means "hope," and Spanish, in which the name is imbued with sadness and longing.

This book won the 1985 American Book Award. Cisneros's tales of growing up Chicana resonated with teachers and with critics who praised the fresh, original voice. When Cisneros talks to groups of school children, she often passes around her elementary-school report card. She wants the Cs and Ds she got to show youngsters that it's okay "to question the educational system and the whole system that is created to keep them from becoming what I became."

"I am a woman and I am a Latina. Those are the things that make my writing distinctive. Those are the things that give my writing power. They are the things that give it sabor, the things that give it picante."

—SANDRA CISNEROS, INTERVIEW BY MARY B. W. TABOR,
NEW YORK TIMES

Waiting for Snow in Havana: Confessions of a Cuban Boy

BY CARLOS EIRE

The world changed while I slept, and much to my surprise, no one had consulted me.

THIS MEMOIR OF boyhood, a story of growing up privileged in Havana in the idyllic 1950s, is a modern *Paradise Lost*. When Castro swept into power, being prosperous became dangerous.

The "world changed" January 1, 1959, the day Batista fled Cuba and Fidel Castro began to take over. Eire was eight years old, and that moment is seared in his memory: "Fidel came down from the mountains . . . Beelzebub, Herod, and the Seven-headed Beast of the Apocalypse rolled into one, a big fat smoldering cigar wedged between his seething lips, hell-bent on imposing his will on everyone."

Now a professor of religion and history at Yale University, Eire and his brother were among 14,000 children shipped off without their parents in an operation called Pedro Pan. They were delivered to Miami where they became "lost boys." After three years in refugee camps and living with their uncle, the boys were reunited with their mother in Chicago. There, life was hard. Eire never saw his father again.

It's a sad irony that this 2003 National Book Award winner is still banned in Cuba.

"Carlos Eire . . . speak[s] for a whole generation of Cuban children whose childhoods were interrupted when they left their country behind, a country that has changed so radically in the last forty plus years. They all struggle daily to keep that Cuba alive, Cuba B.C. (Before Castro), because their present and future depends on their memories of a country that no longer exists."

—HENRY PÉREZ, PhD

CONTINENTAL DRIFT

BY RUSSELL BANKS

It's December 21, 1979, a Friday, in Catamount, New Hampshire.

IN ITS "INVOCATION," this book introduces "an American story of the late 20th century." Its Everyman is Bob Dubois, a thirty-year-old oil-burner repairman who lives with his family in a crummy New Hampshire town. He "hates his life." He moves his family to Florida where he works in his brother Eddie's liquor store, only to find that he's traded the depressing world of small-town New England for far more dangerous terrain in trailer park Florida.

Bob is a man of deep feelings who wants to do right and messes up at every turn. He can't handle his love for a black woman whose father works in the store; he's pushed to violence when fast-talking Eddie insists he carry a gun; and he's out of his depth in the unfamiliar Florida scene of dope dealing and real-estate and immigrant-smuggling schemes.

In a series of alternating chapters, the novel also follows the story of Vanise, a young Haitian woman who risks her life to find her way to Florida.

This 1985 novel tells of an America that promises gold-paved streets and delivers "Disney World and land deals and fast-moving high-interest bank loans, and if you don't get the hell out of the way, they'll knock you down, cut you up with a harrow and plow you under, so they can throw some condos up on top of you or maybe a parking lot or maybe an orange grove."

"In novels like . . . Continental Drift Mr. Banks has deepened Hemingway's investigation of American maleness, lending a voice to working-class fathers who want to be 'good' men but are reduced, by economic brutalities and some essential rage riding on the Y chromosome, to bad ones."

—JONATHAN FRANZEN, *NEW YORK TIMES*

BEL CANTO

BY ANN PATCHETT

When the lights went off the accompanist kissed her.

DIVA ROXANE COSS, a beautiful and internationally revered soprano whose presence makes "Callas look like a spear carrier," is singing at the lavish home of the vice president of an impoverished South American country. The gathering is ostensibly to celebrate the birthday of a powerful Japanese electronics executive. Festivities go horribly awry when a band of terrorists break in and take the partygoers hostage.

But this story doesn't go where it seems to be headed as guests, forced to lie on the floor, begin to chat with one another. Soon the event resembles "a cocktail party in which everyone [is] lying prone." Meanwhile, the country's president whom the terrorists had hoped to capture is safe at home watching his favorite TV soap opera.

Menacing guns, soaring arias, tragedy, and comedy are layered into this fable. Only one guest, "the interpreter," is able to decipher what is happening, and music is the only language understood by terrorists and terrorized alike.

This 2001 bestseller took home the PEN/Faulkner Award and the prestigious Orange Prize for fiction.

"[Bel Canto] delineates the way we manage to sustain hope and all the things we must forget in order to experience joy and reasonably pursue the very human desire to be happy."

—ROBB FORMAN DEW, *WASHINGTON POST*

LITTLE WOMEN

BY LOUISA MAY ALCOTT

"Christmas won't be Christmas without any presents," grumbled Jo, lying on the rug.

THE BOOK OPENS with the four March sisters—Meg, Jo, Amy, and Beth—spending a presentless Christmas ("It's so dreadful to be poor," says Meg). Father March is off fighting in the Civil War. Marmee suggests that the girls play a game they once invented based on John Bunyan's *Pilgrim's Progress*. They dress up like pilgrims and journey from the "City of Destruction" in their cellar, through the rooms of their house, and end up on the top floor where they create a "Celestial City."

The novel follows the girls from youth to young adulthood, through tragedy, friendship, and romance, as each struggles against her own particular weakness. Willful, rebellious Jo, who is brave enough to cut off her hair as a sacrifice for her family and who inspired many girls to become writers, bridles against nineteenth-century expectations that she and her sisters behave like "little women."

The story, in all its sentimental splendor, is based on Alcott's life. She had three sisters. Surely the character of Jo is the author. Alcott's publisher asked her to write the book, and Alcott expressed doubts about it in her journal: "I don't enjoy this sort of thing. Never liked girls or knew many, except my sisters, but our queer plays and experiences may prove interesting, though I doubt it." So much for author's prescience. Published as a single volume in 1880, this and sequels *Little Men* and *Jo's Boys* have captivated generations.

"Little Women gave my generation of women permission to write about our daily lives. . . . Without even meaning to, Alcott exalted the everyday in women's lives and gave it greatness."

—SUSAN CHEEVER, ALCOTT'S BIOGRAPHER

A CHRISTMAS CAROL

BY CHARLES DICKENS

Marley was dead: to begin with.

READ THE ORIGINAL story of Ebenezer Scrooge, a middle-aged "man of business," and how the cold-hearted miser, who mistreated his employees and had no friends or loved ones, was transformed by a glorious overnight of visitations.

First comes the ghost of his former business partner, the recently deceased and now "dead as a door-nail" Jacob Marley. Scrooge is horrified when Marley removes the bandage from his head and his entire lower jaw drops, like an effect in a not-yet-invented horror movie, onto his chest. Then along come Ghosts of Christmases Past and Present, and the terrifyingly silent Ghost of Christmas Yet to Come. One by one, they grab the old geezer by the collar and shake him good. But it's the sight of his own neglected grave that yanks him from self-imposed solitary gloom.

In the end, Scrooge vows to reform and make mankind his business. The miser who got no pleasure from his wealth rejoins humanity and takes pleasure in giving it away.

Dickens wrote this novel in a white heat between October and November, 1843. It was first published in book form a few days prior to Christmas in 1844, and became an immediate sensation. Six thousand copies of it sold in a single week. It's been adapted many times for stage, screen, and even opera. The character of Scrooge most certainly inspired the great Grinch of Dr. Seuss.

"Scrooge may be reformed, but his ghosts are still with us."
—ELIZABETH HAND, ON *A CHRISTMAS CAROL*
BY CHARLES DICKENS, IN *HORROR:
ANOTHER 100 BEST BOOKS*

A Child's Christmas in Wales

BY DYLAN THOMAS

One Christmas was so much like the other, in those years around the sea-town corner now, out of all sound except the distant speaking of the voices I sometimes hear a moment before sleep, that I can never remember whether it snowed for six days and six nights when I was twelve, or whether it snowed for twelve days and twelve nights when I was six.

THERE'S A REASON this short story, written in 1955 for radio, has become a classic. The voice of a small child wonders: Could Christmas really have been so different years and years ago? The narrator answers: "Our snow was not only shaken from whitewash buckets down the sky, it came shawling out of the ground and swam and drifted out of the arms and hands and bodies of the trees; snow grew overnight on the roofs of the houses like a pure and grandfather moss, minutely white-ivied the walls and settled on the postman, opening the gate, like a dumb, numb thunderstorm of white, torn Christmas cards."

The vivid imagery and rolling rhythm of the prose cry out to be read aloud before a roaring fire on Christmas Eve.

Born in Wales in 1914, Dylan Thomas had already begun to make his mark as a poet by the age of eighteen. This poem— based on a piece Thomas wrote for the BBC and an article he penned for *Picture Post* magazine—was published in a 1954 volume of collected works, *Quite Early One Morning*, a year after Thomas's unexpected death at the age of thirty-nine. He is buried in Poet's Corner at Westminster Abbey.

"In a way Thomas is a simple poet; as with Blake, his prophetic revelations are based upon songs of innocence."

—LOUIS MacNEICE, *NEW YORK TIMES*

REBECCA

BY DAPHNE DU MAURIER

Last Night I dreamt I went to Manderley again.

NARRATED AS AN extended flashback by the nameless bride of Maxim de Winter, this novel combines gothic romance, murder, and taut suspense. With shades of *Jane Eyre*, a plucky young woman comes to work for an older man with a dark secret.

Both a Cinderella story and a mystery, *Rebecca* creates uncertainty from the moment that the narrator meets the rich and mysterious Maxim de Winter in Monte Carlo. She is but twenty-one years old and a paid companion of a disagreeable woman who constantly reminds her of her inferior status. Despite Maxim's whirlwind courtship, his bride is unsure of her husband's feelings for her. From the first chapter, when she finds a book of poetry inscribed from Rebecca, de Winter's first wife who mysteriously drowned, the narrator is haunted as Rebecca's spirit holds the house at Manderley and the new bride in its icy grip.

When the new couple returns to England, the narrator's feelings of inferiority are heightened by her new status and the demands of running a great house. The housekeeper, Mrs. Danvers, exhibits a creepy adoration for Rebecca and reminds the narrator at every turn of her own shortcomings, and of how much better Rebecca was at absolutely everything.

The larger-than-life Rebecca returns from the grave when a ship hits a rock in the nearby bay, and the mystery of her death begins to unravel.

"[Daphne du Maurier] could, and did, fall in love with both men and women, and combined in herself those elements of both Rebecca and novel's narrator."

—MICHAEL DIRDA, *CLASSICS FOR PLEASURE*

TROPIC OF CANCER

BY HENRY MILLER

I am living at the Villa Borghese. There is not a crumb of dirt anywhere, nor a chair misplaced. We are all alone here and we are dead.

"THIS IS NOT a book, in the ordinary sense of the word. No, this is a prolonged insult, a gob of spit in the face of Art, a kick in the pants to God, Man, Destiny, Time, Love, Beauty . . . what you will." No, that's not a critic speaking. It's Miller addressing the reader at the outset of this autobiographical fiction.

He goes on to regale the reader with a starving, dissolute, expatriate writer's 300-page rambling monologue recounting his bawdy adventures on Paris's Left Bank where he lived, sponging off friends. Miller moves from one experience to the next with joyous, hedonistic zest, taking American literature's first uninhibited look at sex and sexual promiscuity.

But it's not the sex that makes this a great book—it's the writing, with its pitch-perfect vernacular and conversational style. As critic Anatole Broyard said, "Mr. Miller could write a beautiful sentence."

Published in 1934, this was Miller's first published volume. Censored in America for three decades, it is now considered his masterpiece. In 1986 the original typed 926-page manuscript, completed in Paris in 1932–33, was auctioned at Sotheby's for $165,000. That was the highest price ever paid at auction for a modern manuscript sold in America.

"At last an unprintable book that is fit to read."

—EZRA POUND

A WRINKLE IN TIME

BY MADELEINE L'ENGLE

It was a dark and stormy night.

MEG MURRY IS one of the most memorable little girls in young adult fiction. Smart, prickly, a sour social misfit, she illustrates what it means to "be yourself." She's thirteen years old, with braces and bad hair, and struggling with more than middle-school angst. Her father is missing. The town gossips suggest he's run off with a woman.

Of course, Meg knows her father would never do such a thing. She and her five-year-old brother Charles Wallace, a little genius, search for their missing father. Along the way they befriend three old ladies who've moved into the local haunted house. Mrs. Who, Mrs. Whatsit, and Mrs. Which have come from beyond our galaxy to confirm Mr. Murry's work on tesseracts (folds in the space-time continuum).

Guided by these three intergalactic, not-quite-what-they-seem Auntie Mames, Meg and Charles Wallace and their friend Calvin "tesser" to the "dark planet" Camazotz to save Mr. M. Traveling through time and space, they face their fears, learn about human nature, discover the power of individuality, test their courage, and experience true love.

Adventure. Mystery. Sacrifice. Universal truths. This groundbreaking and thoughtfully charming young adult fantasy has it all. Rejected by twenty-six publishers, this won the Newbery Medal for the best children's book of 1963. Since then, it has been one of the most frequently banned books, accused by some of offering an inaccurate portrayal of God and nurturing a belief in myth and fantasy.

"Of course I'm Meg."

—MADELEINE L'ENGLE

BURY MY HEART AT WOUNDED KNEE

BY DEE BROWN

It began with Christopher Columbus, who gave the people the name Indios.

THIS EXTRAORDINARY NATIONAL bestseller was the first book to tell of the systematic destruction of the American Indian during the nineteenth century. Subtitled "An Indian History of the American West," each chapter tells the tragedy of another tribe, from the Long Walk of the Navahos to the Cheyenne Exodus. Its final scene takes place at Wounded Knee Creek in South Dakota. There, 300 Sioux men, women, and children were killed by the Seventh Cavalry. This is a book to read on this anniversary of the 1890 Massacre at Wounded Knee.

Based on meticulous research, Dee Brown tells of the ruthless mistreatment and eventual displacement of the Indian by whites from 1860 to 1890. When the book was published in 1970, the author was a librarian who wrote at night after his children were in bed. It sold more than 5 million copies, singlehandedly changing how Americans viewed the "heroic" winning of the West and challenging the notion of Manifest Destiny.

Nearly a century after the massacre, in 1973, young Sioux returned to Wounded Knee to protest federal Indian policies. In a seventy-one-day standoff with the police, two Indians were killed.

"Having read Mr. Brown, one has a better understanding of what it is that nags at the American conscience at times (to our everlasting credit) and of that morality which informs and fuses events so far apart in time and space as the massacres at Wounded Knee and My Lai."

—N. SCOTT MOMADAY, *NEW YORK TIMES*

Bright Lights, Big City

BY JAY McINERNEY

You are not the kind of guy who would be at a place like this at this time of the morning.

NARRATED IN THE second person and in the present tense by a nameless hero, a cocaine-addicted, self-absorbed New Yorker, this very funny debut novel defined 1980s Manhattan.

At twenty-four, our hero has met the lovely Amanda and moved from Kansas City to New York so they can be together. She gets modeling jobs and her career is on a stratospheric rise. He gets a job at a prestigious magazine (the *New Yorker*?), but as a lowly fact checker in the Department of Factual Verification. The office is run by a woman with a "mind like a steel mousetrap and a heart like a twelve-minute egg."

He escapes boredom with a pal who works for an ad agency and who leads the way, after work, from one night spot to the next, bent on having "more fun than anyone else in New York City." In short order, our hero's mother dies, his wife leaves him, he loses his job, buys a ferret, tries to kill himself, and takes a limo ride with a cocaine magnate.

Published in 1984, this was McInerney's debut novel. One critic called it the *Catcher in the Rye* of the MBA set.

"[Jay McInerney] has perfect pitch for the inner music of upscale young professionals networking on the fast track. His novel is the Michelob beer commercial re-invented as literature."

—GEORGE F. WILL, *WASHINGTON POST*

THE YEARLING

BY MARJORIE KINNAN RAWLINGS

A column of smoke rose thin and straight from the cabin chimney.

SET ONE APRIL in the late 1800s, this story tells a moving coming-of-age story—a year in the life of twelve-year-old Jody Baxter, a boy growing up poor in rural Florida. He revels in nature ("He was addled with April. He was dizzy with Spring") and feels passionately for the pine land and wild scrub that surround his family's meager farm.

He struggles to explain to his practical, grim, plain-spoken mother how he yearns for a pet: "I jest want something all my own. Something to foller me and be mine. I want something with dependence to it." His kindly father understands.

Jody rescues an orphaned fawn, nurtures and tames it. He names the fawn Flag because his tail looks like a little white flag. The two become inseparable. At a year of age, Flag outgrows his penned-in area and twice tramples the family's tender corn crop. Jody's mother decides that Flag must be killed. Like Huckleberry Finn, Jody takes to the river rather than stay home and endure his beloved friend's murder. When he returns, experience has forever changed him. As his father notes: "You ain't a yearlin' no longer, Jody."

This novel won the 1939 Pulitzer for fiction.

"The thing about The Yearling—*it's great claim to distinction—is that it is able to make so much of so little. The zest of a hunting expedition, the stir of Spring in the forest, a suddenly glimpsed dance of grave, stately cranes—it is out of material as humble as this that the texture of the book is woven."*

—EDITH H. WALTON, *NEW YORK TIMES*

Author Index

Title Index

WHAT *are you*
in the MOOD *for?*

However you feel (or want to feel), let *1001 Books for Every Mood* be your guide. Whether you want to cry or laugh, remember or forget, behave or misbehave—it's all here.

Trade Paperback, $14.95 • 6" x 9" • 400 pages
ISBN 10: 1-59869-585-1 • ISBN 13: 978-1-59869-585-4